Your Sexuality: A Self-Assessment

YOUR
A Self-Assessment
SEXUALITY

ROBERT F. VALOIS

Assistant Professor
Health Promotion & Education
School of Public Health
University of South Carolina

SANDRA K. KAMMERMANN

Health Education Consultant
Valois-Kammermann & Associates
Columbia, South Carolina

THE MCGRAW-HILL COMPANIES, INC.

New York   St. Louis   San Francisco   Auckland   Bogotá   Caracas   Lisbon   London   Madrid
Mexico City   Milan   Montreal   New Delhi   San Juan   Singapore   Sydney   Tokyo   Toronto

McGraw-Hill

A Division of The **McGraw·Hill** Companies

YOUR SEXUALITY *A Self-Assessment*

1 2 3 4 5 6 7 8 9 0 SEM SEM 9 0 9 8 7 6

ISBN 0-07-066853-1

The editors were Katy Redmond and Brian McKean;
the production supervisor was Louise Karam.
The cover was designed by John Hite.
Semline, Inc., was printer and binder.

Library of Congress Cataloging-in-Publication Data is available:
LC Card # 96-79368

http://www.mhcollge.com

CONTENTS

I. SEXUALITY AND GENDER ROLES

II. SEXUAL HEALTH AND SELF-CARE

III. CONTRACEPTION AND ABORTION

IV. PREGNANCY AND CHILDBIRTH

V. COMMUNICATION AND SEXUAL AROUSAL

VI. SEXUAL ATTITUDES, PERCEPTIONS, AND BEHAVIOR

VII. DATING AND RELATIONSHIPS

VIII. LOVE AND INTIMACY

XII. SEXUALITY, ETHICS, AND THE LAW

XIII. SEXUALLY TRANSMITTED DISEASES

XIV. SEXUALITY EDUCATION

APPENDIXES

TO THE INDIVIDUAL USER OR COUPLE

Complete the exercises in this book in any order; however, you should consider the following recommendations:

1. *Take your time responding to each exercise. You should read the purpose* and be sure you *under-stand the directions.* Using a *soft lead pencil,* complete each exercise and score yourself so that you can interpret the results. (You may want to erase your pencil marks so that you can repeat the exercise again at a later date.)

2. Some exercises may not be applicable to your current stage of life. If so, think back to a past relationship or consider a possible future situation. In either case, you will be able to learn more about yourself.

3. Be sure to *"react" to each exercise* by responding to the questions at the end of each exercise.

4. After completing an exercise you are encouraged to read the corresponding pages in a current human sexuality text.

5. *Your Sexuality* is your own personal self-analysis. You are encouraged to share this book with your partner, friends, and family. In this way you can help those individuals who are important to you evaluate their own sexual perspectives. (Needless to say, you will want to use discretion in sharing the more personal portions.) As you complete *Your Sexuality* you will come to the realization that the results of each exercise are not absolute but are only indications of different aspects of your sexuality. No collection of exercises could possibly consider all the variables involved in determining your sexuality. Gaining this awareness is an important step in understanding your own sexuality as well as the broad matrix of human sexual behavior that exists in our society. With an infinite number of variables affecting your sexual lifestyle, sexual responsibility is and always will be yours. The purpose of *Your Sexuality* is to stimulate your active involvement in evaluating your sexual knowledge, attitudes, and behaviors. These lifestyle decisions are yours to make!

TO THE INSTRUCTOR

Your Sexuality has been organized so that it can be used as a supplement to any current sexuality textbook. The exercises in *Your Sexuality* are designed to initiate self-analysis and effective decision making beyond the classroom experience. Because of the personal nature of these exercises and self-disclosing activities, we recommend sensitivity to students' feelings and rights to not disclose.

Although the student might want to rush through the exercises in *Your Sexuality,* we suggest that you encourage a *moderate pace* to ensure complete coverage and understanding of each sexual topic or issue. There may not be time during a semester to use the entire book. In addition, you might consider the following recommendations:

1. If at all possible, assign each exercise a few days before it is to be discussed in class. In this way the student can take as much time as necessary to complete the exercise and to read the corresponding pages in a human sexuality textbook.

2. In class, divide the students into small groups so that they can share their thoughts and feelings in an open forum. Most exercises can trigger discussion leading to a better understanding among group members.

3. Unless an exercise is highly sensitive or personal, you might collect the classroom scores, determine the mean and range, and display the results, enabling students to see where their scores stand in relation to their peers.

4. Maintaining class scores for the exercises you select can be of value to you also. From these you can establish an overview of your students and at the semester's end summarize the class perspectives. Over a period of time, then, this book could help you monitor changes in the knowledge, attitudes, and behavior of your students.

5. If you wish to evaluate changes within a semester, select exercises that are appropriate for pre-and post-testing. Cognitive exercises such as "How Much Do You Know About Male and Female Sexual Functioning?" are excellent for this purpose.

6. Be sure to keep in mind the nature and sensitivity of each exercise before assigning and discussing any of these as in-class projects.

Your Sexuality: A Self-Assessment is a book for life. Its major objective is to stimulate the active involvement of your students in the learning process. As your students complete these exercises they will be taking a positive step toward examining their perspectives regarding a comfortable sexual lifestyle. In the final analysis, though, it is you, the instructor, who will be the ultimate catalyst for whatever happens in the classroom.

TO THE CLASS

Teaching human sexuality is not easy! As a student in class you can often hide behind your book, never ask a question or express your opinion, or even skip class. As a student you have it easy! If the subject matter for a given day happens to be masturbation, homosexuality, anal sex, oral sex, sexually transmitted diseases, or any other topic that you find yourself uncomfortable with, you can use any of the options mentioned above.

There are a few things you can do to make the class more rewarding for yourself.

1. Coming to terms with your sexuality is important. Grappling with the how, what, when, where, and who you are sexually can be valuable in helping you understand the diversity of human sexual attitudes and behaviors in our culture. Asking a student to be comfortable with his or her own sexuality is difficult. Sexuality is a topic of excitement, uncertainty, mystery; there is no reason to ask any individual to be comfortable about it. This does not imply that a person has to be paranoid about a sexual topic. Coming to terms with your own sexuality first can be a valuable step toward personal sexual growth and development.

2. Be able to admit that a topic is uncomfortable and communicate that to the instructor and class members. Talking about an uncomfortable subject can help everyone become more at ease with it.

3. Understand that the instructor is providing you and the class with an open forum for exchanging and evaluating ideas with your peers. He or she is also giving you the chance to approach the subject of sexuality with a high degree of objectivity.

4. The classroom setting can also let you take a problem-solving approach to sexuality, which often aids you, the student, in clarifying your value system.

5. To help you understand the instructor's point of view, ask how he or she became interested in teaching sexuality. Ask which of the course topics are most enjoyable, boring, or difficult to teach. Have your instructor share his or her most memorable experiences as a sexuality educator.

6. Sit down and determine the objectives you expect to achieve as a result of this class. If you can, share your expectations with your classmates. Do your goals match the instructor's? You might find it worth a small amount of time to discuss expectations and objectives.

PREFACE

Your Sexuality: A Self-Assessment, Third Edition, has been prepared for every individual who has the desire to learn about his or her own sexuality in a personal, meaningful way. The approach is *not* to give you vast amounts of sex information, but to help you evaluate sexual attitudes and behaviors that influence your own sexuality. Using this book in conjunction with a current human sexuality text will enable you to obtain factual information and also assist you in developing a clear perspective of human sexuality. This book bridges the gap between the facts and your incorporation of that knowledge into a positive sexual lifestyle for yourself. By responding to each exercise, you will become more aware of how you perceive yourself and others sexually.

The bulk of this book consists of pencil-and-paper exercises that you can complete alone and, if you choose, compare with a partner or friend. Most exercises are prefaced by instructions and a discussion of purpose and followed by directions for scoring and interpreting your results. Questions have also been provided for you to note your reaction to each exercise. These exercises will help you recognize the attitudes and behaviors that affect your sexuality, and develop an awareness that can help you make sound sexual lifestyle decisions. With this emphasis on personal evaluation and decision making, you can take a step toward a broadened perspective of human sexual attitudes, behaviors, and lifestyles.

Although many aspects of your current sexuality might not have a great effect on you now, they may take on great significance ten, twenty, or thirty years from now. Personal sexual difficulties you may possibly encounter through your life span can be avoided by positive and effective self-evaluation.

This book should help you develop a realistic perspective toward your sexuality. Examining your sexual attitudes and behavior will enable you to make the choices that can lead to a positive and compatible sexual lifestyle for you and for those who share their sexuality with you.

ACKNOWLEDGMENTS

Your Sexuality: A Self-Assessment is an eclectic effort extending beyond the talents and contributions of the authors. We offer sincere thanks and appreciation to our colleagues in the College Division of McGraw-Hill, especially Brian McKean, Katy Redmond, and Beth Kaufman. The efforts of the production staff are most appreciated, in addition to those of Reuben Kantor at Quality Electronic Production & Design.

We are also most grateful to our reviewers, including David A. Gershaw, Arizona Western College; Thomas E. Billimek, Sand Antonio College; John T. Long, Mt. San Antonio College; and John W. Engel, University of Hawaii at Manoa.

From the University of South Carolina, School of Public Health, we would like to acknowledge the efforts of Anna Ehrhardt, Greg Thatcher, and Ken Traum.

A sincere appreciation is extended to those instructors and students who have utilized this text in its entirety for their support and constructive suggestions for our third edition.

Our appreciation is also extended to the many contributors to this text. Without their contributions *Your Sexuality: A Self-Assessment* would not be a reality.

Robert Valois

Sandra K. Kammermann

SECTION I

SEXUALITY AND GENDER ROLES

Sexuality is an important aspect of your everyday life. Sexuality is who and what you are. It includes the societal expectations you adopt as well as your reproductive anatomy. Sexuality is at your essence, your being, your existence. Your sexuality itself remains a vital part of your total awareness of the world you live in and of the other human beings who share it with you. Sexuality is an important component of your personality and your self-esteem. The self-assessment exercises in this section can give you insight into your gender role development and your sexual self-identity.

Sexuality and Gender Role exercises include:

1. How Androgynous Are You?
2. Gender Role Development
3. Perspective: Gender Roles and Society
4. Early Sexual Messages: What Did You Learn?
5. Attitude Toward Feminism Scale
6. Sexual Self-Image Checklist
7. Self-Esteem and Sexual Maturity
8. Issues in Human Sexuality: Gender Role Stereotyping

1 | How Androgynous Are You?

DIRECTIONS: Use the scale below to indicate how well each of the following characteristics describes you. Write the number from the scale that is appropriate for each characteristic in the space provided.

1	2	3	4
Usually Not True	Occasionally True	Quite Often True	Almost Always True

_____ 1. aggressive

_____ 2. affectionate

_____ 3. ambitious

_____ 4. compassionate

_____ 5. assertive

_____ 6. gentle

_____ 7. athletic

_____ 8. loving toward children

_____ 9. competitive

_____ 10. loyal

_____ 11. dominant

_____ 12. sensitive to others

_____ 13. forceful

_____ 14. sympathetic

_____ 15. independent

_____ 16. tender

_____ 17. self-reliant

_____ 18. understanding

_____ 19. willing to take a stand

_____ 20. warm

_____ 21. defend own beliefs

_____ 22. yielding

_____ 23. strong personality

_____ 24. cheerful

_____ 25. analytical

_____ 26. shy

_____ 27. have leadership abilities

_____ 28. easily flattered

_____ 29. willing to take risks

_____ 30. feminine

_____ 31. make decisions easily

_____ 32. eager to soothe hurt feelings

____ 33. masculine

____ 34. inefficient

____ 35. acts like a leader

____ 36. childlike

____ 37. individualistic

____ 38. doesn't use harsh language

____ 39. self-sufficient

____ 40. gullible

SCORING: Add up your ratings for all the odd numbered items. This is your **Masculinity Score.** _____

Now add up your ratings for all the even numbered items. This is your **Femininity Score.** _____

Subtract the lower score from the higher score. If the difference is *less than ten* (10), this is an indication that you have a well-rounded personality and to some degree you are an "androgynous" individual. If the difference is *greater than ten*, this is an indication that you tend to exhibit, more often, traditional gender role behavior. The *higher of your two scores* (masculinity and femininity) would indicate the traditional gender role behavior that you exhibit most often.

PURPOSE: The word *androgyny* means "man-woman" and is derived from the Greek roots *andr* = man and *gyne* = woman. Androgyny is a term that is used to describe flexibility in gender role. Androgynous individuals are those who have progressed beyond traditional sex roles. They are people who have integrated aspects of femininity and masculinity into their self-concept in pursuit of a wellness lifestyle. Androgynous individuals have the option of expressing whatever behavior seems appropriate in a given situation instead of limiting their responses to traditional gender roles. Therefore, androgynous women and men could be the aggressive or assertive person on the job and also be tender or nurturing with their lovers and/or children, etc.

It has been suggested by sex researchers that androgynous individuals are able to approach life with more flexibility than strongly gender-roled people. Those who are able to transcend traditional gender ideas may be able to function with more comfort and effectiveness in a broader range of situations. Androgynous individuals are able to select from a broad matrix of feminine and masculine behaviors based not on sex role norms but rather on what gives them the most personal comfort and satisfaction, relative to a given situation. There is also evidence that androgynous individuals, both female and male, have more healthy attitudes toward sexuality than people who are traditionally sex roled.

An androgynous approach to living, loving, and learning can foster an individual sense of well-being and enhance human effectiveness.

REACTIONS: Use the space provided to respond to the following questions.

1. According to your score on this questionnaire, do you more often exhibit masculine or feminine traits? Or does your score fall in the range of androgyny? Explain.

2. In thinking of your own behavior and attitudes, how well do you feel the scoring accurately represents your level of androgyny? Explain.

3. Discuss two characteristics from the list above that you would like to exhibit more often and explain why.

4. Discuss two characteristics from the list above that you would like to exhibit less often and explain why.

2 Gender Role Development

Gender roles are strongly influenced by cultural, environmental, and parental or human factors. Most of us have a set of beliefs regarding behaviors, personality, appearance, etc. that we associate with being male and female. Society continues to encourage gender role socialization. Not only are gender roles imposed on children by society, but children also model behaviors of persons of significance.

PURPOSE: This exercise is designed to help you identify some aspects of gender role development.

DIRECTIONS: Respond to the following questions as best you can.

1. Consider newborn children and infants: How do you picture them being conditioned or socialized into their gender roles?

2. In regard to children aged one to six:
   a. How do little girls differ from little boys in clothing styles, toys, and expected behavior?

   b. How do adults communicate to children, their expectations for certain behaviors?

3. a. What specific behaviors are expected and rewarded in little girls?

   b. What behaviors are discouraged?

4. a. What specific behaviors are expected and rewarded in little boys?

b. What behaviors are discouraged?

5. How do adults respond to those children who do not conform to expected gender roles—for example, the "tomboy-type" girl or the "sissy-type" boy?

6. Do you feel you had a healthy gender role development? Briefly explain why.

7. As a teenager did you change any of your gender role–related behaviors? How did the important people in your life respond to your changes?

3 | Perspective: Gender Roles and Society

Purpose: This inventory will aid you in becoming aware of your attitudes toward stereotypical masculine and feminine roles in society. The views of many people in regard to these traditional roles are changing, but not necessarily together. Therefore, it is important that you understand your own values as well as the values of those with whom you interact.

Directions: Read each statement carefully and respond by using the scale given below. Use the first column of blanks for your own responses. Then use a sheet of paper to cover your responses and have your partner or friend use the second column of blanks to respond to the statements.

Strongly Agree	Agree	Disagree	Strongly Disagree
1	2	3	4

You   Friend

____ ____ 1. Men should feel comfortable receiving flowers from a woman.

____ ____ 2. Women should take the steps necessary to prevent pregnancy, since contraception is the woman's responsibility.

____ ____ 3. The woman's role is to stay home, take care of the children, and support her husband in his work; the man's role is to support the family financially.

____ ____ 4. A man should be open to relocating because of his wife's job, regardless of whose salary is higher.

____ ____ 5. Men should stand when a woman enters the room and should open doors for women.

____ ____ 6. Men and women should share equally in the role of decision maker in the home.

____ ____ 7. Women should pay their half of the expenses on dates.

____ ____ 8. Women should ask men for dates.

____ ____ 9. A woman who pursues a career cannot be a good mother.

____ ____ 10. Men should be free to express their emotions as openly as women.

Strongly Agree 1	Agree 2	Disagree 3	Strongly Disagree 4

You   Friend

____ ____ 11. Women should initiate the sex act.

____ ____ 12. Education is equally important for husband and wife.

____ ____ 13. Only men should be drafted into the army.

____ ____ 14. Society discriminates against women in certain occupations.

____ ____ 15. Society discriminates against men in certain occupations.

____ ____ 16. Parents should allow their sons to play with dolls.

____ ____ 17. A woman should be free to pursue whatever interest or career she would like, providing it does not inconvenience her husband.

____ ____ 18. Girls should be raised feeling proud to say that their vocation is wife and mother.

____ ____ 19. The movement toward desexualization in clothes, jobs, recreation, and education is dangerous.

____ ____ 20. Maternal and nurturing feelings are instinctive only to women.

____ ____ 21. Men are sexual, women are productive.

____ ____ 22. Boys play at love when what they desire is sex, and girls play at sex when they desire love.

____ ____ 23. Married women should feel comfortable keeping their maiden names.

____ ____ 24. Men stand to gain just as much from the women's movement as women do.

____ ____ 25. The ideal couple should go everywhere together.

____ ____ 26. Women should be allowed to serve in combat in the armed forces.

REACTIONS: Use the space provided to respond to the following questions.

1. For which statements were your responses different from those of your partner?

2. After discussing the differences in your responses, decide if these are potential problem areas. Explain why or why not.

3. Discuss whether you feel your beliefs regarding these statements are the same as most people your age.

4 Early Sexual Messages: What Did You Learn?

Compared with other cultures the United States is considered a sexually restrictive society. Our "Victorian hangover" still exerts an influence on us, despite the liberalizing trends that began around the turn of the century. Values and attitudes evolve slowly. A child growing up in our culture today may receive a variety of mixed messages about sex and sexuality.

PURPOSE: These statements will enable you to recall and evaluate the messages you received about sex during your childhood and the teenage years.

DIRECTIONS: Indicate with a YES or NO in the space provided at the right whether each of the statements is a message about sex that you received and whether it was the intended message or not. If it was a message you received, indicate in the second space from WHOM you received that message (i.e., parents, church leaders, friends, cousins, school teachers).

Yes or No Whom

1. Sex is a normal part of life.　　　　　　　＿＿＿＿　＿＿＿＿
2. Sex is only to be shared with the one person you marry.　　＿＿＿＿　＿＿＿＿
3. Sex is a gift from God.　　　　　　　＿＿＿＿　＿＿＿＿
4. Sex is not something I want to discuss.　　＿＿＿＿　＿＿＿＿
5. Your sex life is your own business; we will look the other way.　＿＿＿＿　＿＿＿＿
6. Sex is embarrassing.　　　　　　　＿＿＿＿　＿＿＿＿
7. Sex is dangerous because you can get diseases.　　＿＿＿＿　＿＿＿＿
8. Sex can kill you.　　　　　　　＿＿＿＿　＿＿＿＿
9. Sex is dirty.　　　　　　　＿＿＿＿　＿＿＿＿
10. Only bad girls have sex.　　　　　　＿＿＿＿　＿＿＿＿
11. Boys don't marry the girls they have sex with.　　＿＿＿＿　＿＿＿＿
12. Sex is shameful.　　　　　　　＿＿＿＿　＿＿＿＿
13. You better behave yourself sexually or else.　　＿＿＿＿　＿＿＿＿
14. Alcohol and drugs can lead to sex.　　　＿＿＿＿　＿＿＿＿
15. You better stay out of trouble and don't come home if you are in trouble.　　＿＿＿＿　＿＿＿＿
16. I know you will practice responsible sexual behavior.　　＿＿＿＿　＿＿＿＿

Yes or No Whom

17. Don't use sex the way I did. _____ _____

18. Don't get into trouble the way I did. _____ _____

19. Sex is something you will learn about later. _____ _____

20. Sex is important and you should enjoy it in responsible circumstances. _____ _____

21. Sex can be confusing. _____ _____

22. Sex changes things between people. _____ _____

23. Sex is the only way to show love. _____ _____

24. Sex partners are using each other. _____ _____

25. Sex is a joyous gift. _____ _____

26. You owe your body respect and protection. _____ _____

27. Sex without love is dangerous. _____ _____

28. Abstinence is best until marriage. _____ _____

29. Sex is OK in a long-term relationship even if unmarried. _____ _____

30. Sex is only to make babies. _____ _____

31. Sex will get you pregnant. _____ _____

32. Masturbation is not healthy. _____ _____

33. A girl owes it to her boyfriend to have sex with him. _____ _____

34. Abstinence is OK anytime. _____ _____

35. You can have sex, just use birth control. _____ _____

36. It is the girl's responsibility to use birth control. _____ _____

REACTIONS: Review the statements and from whom you heard each. Then respond to the questions below:

1. From whom did you receive most the messages? Explain what made the messages either positive or negative. Why do you view the messages differently now than when you heard them?

2. From whom did you receive the second most messages? Explain what made the messages either positive or negative? Why do you view the messages differently now than when you heard them?

3. If you were to choose one person or group of persons from whom you would have liked to have received more positive messages, who would it be? What would the messages be?

4. If you raise children, list three or four most important messages about sex and sexuality that you want to teach them?

SOURCE: Sandra K. Kammermann, MS, EdS, and Robert F. Valois, PhD, MPH, Schools of Medicine and Public Health, University of South Carolina. Copyright © 1996 by Valois, Kammermann & Associates. All rights reserved. Used with permission of the authors.

5 | Attitude Toward Feminism Scale

PURPOSE: This scale is designed to provide some indication of your attitudes toward feminism.

DIRECTIONS: Following are statements on a variety of issues. Circle the response that represents how much you agree or disagree. Please respond as you personally feel and use the following letter code for your answers:

SA = Strongly   A = Agree   D = Disagree   SD = Strongly Disagree

					Initial Scoring	Final Scoring
1. It is naturally proper for parents to keep a daughter under closer control than a son.	SA	A	D	SD	_____	_____
2. A man has the right to insist that his wife accept his view as to what can or cannot be afforded.	SA	A	D	SD	_____	_____
3. There should be no distinction made between woman's work and man's work.	SA	A	D	SD	_____	_____
4. Women should not be expected to subordinate their careers to home duties to any greater extent than men.	SA	A	D	SD	_____	_____
5. There are no natural differences between men and women in sensitivity and emotionality.	SA	A	D	SD	_____	_____

					Initial Scoring	Final Scoring
6. A wife should make every effort to minimize irritation and inconvenience to her husband.	SA	A	D	SD	_____	_____
7. A woman should gracefully accept chivalrous attentions from men.	SA	A	D	SD	_____	_____
8. A woman generally needs male protection and guidance.	SA	A	D	SD	_____	_____
9. Married women should resist enslavement by domestic obligations.	SA	A	D	SD	_____	_____
10. The unmarried mother is more immoral and irresponsible than the unmarried father.	SA	A	D	SD	_____	_____
11. Married women should not work if their husbands are able to support them.	SA	A	D	SD	_____	_____
12. A husband has the right to expect that his wife will want to bear children.	SA	A	D	SD	_____	_____
13. Women should freely compete with men in every sphere of economic activity.	SA	A	D	SD	_____	_____
14. There should be a single standard in matters relating to sexual behavior for both men and women.	SA	A	D	SD	_____	_____

		Initial Scoring	Final Scoring

15. The father and mother should have equal authority and responsibility for discipline and guidance of the children.   SA   A   D   SD   _____   _____

16. Regardless of gender, there should be equal pay for equal work.   SA   A   D   SD   _____   _____

17. Only the very exceptional woman is qualified to enter politics.   SA   A   D   SD   _____   _____

18. Women should be given equal opportunities with men for all vocational and professional training.   SA   A   D   SD   _____   _____

19. The husband should be regarded as the legal representative of the family group in all manners of law.   SA   A   D   SD   _____   _____

20. Husbands and wives should share in all household tasks if both are employed an equal number of hours outside the home.   SA   A   D   SD   _____   _____

21. There is no particular reason why a girl standing in a crowded bus should expect a man to offer her his seat.   SA   A   D   SD   _____   _____

					Initial Scoring	Final Scoring

22. Wifely submission is an outmoded virtue.
SA   A   D   SD   _____   _____

23. The leadership of a community should be largely in the hands of men.
SA   A   D   SD   _____   _____

24. Women who seek a career are ignoring a more enriching life of devotion to husband and children.
SA   A   D   SD   _____   _____

25. It is ridiculous for a woman to run a locomotive and for a man to darn socks.
SA   A   D   SD   _____   _____

26. Greater leniency should be adopted toward women convicted of crime than toward male offenders.
SA   A   D   SD   _____   _____

27. Women should take a less active role in courtship than men.
SA   A   D   SD   _____   _____

28. Contemporary social problems are crying out for increased participation in their solution by women.
SA   A   D   SD   _____   _____

29. There is no good reason why women should take the name of their husbands upon marriage.
SA   A   D   SD   _____   _____

			Initial Scoring	Final Scoring

30. Men are naturally more aggressive and achievement-oriented than women.   SA   A   D   SD   _____   _____

31. The modern wife has no more obligation to keep her figure than her husband to keep down his waistline.   SA   A   D   SD   _____   _____

32. It is humiliating for a woman to have to ask her husband for money.   SA   A   D   SD   _____   _____

33. There are many words and phrases which are unfit for a woman's lips.   SA   A   D   SD   _____   _____

34. Legal restrictions in industry should be the same for both genders.   SA   A   D   SD   _____   _____

35. Women are more likely than men to be devious in obtaining their ends.   SA   A   D   SD   _____

36. A woman should not expect to go to the same places or to have quite the same freedom of action as a man.   SA   A   D   SD   _____   _____

37. Women are generally too nervous and high-strung to make good surgeons.   SA   A   D   SD   _____   _____

38. It is insulting to women to have the "obey" clause in the marriage vows.   SA   A   D   SD   _____

	Initial Scoring	Final Scoring

39. It is foolish to regard scrubbing floors as more proper for women than mowing the lawn.   SA   A   D   SD   _____   _____

40. Women should not submit to sexual slavery in marriage.   SA   A   D   SD   _____   _____

41. A woman earning as much as her male date should share equally in the cost of their common recreation.   SA   A   D   SD   _____   _____

42. Women should recognize their intellectual limitations as compared with men.   SA   A   D   SD   _____   _____

SCORING: Score your answers as follows:

SA = +2
A = +1
D = –1
SD = –2

Since half the items were phrased in a profeminist and half in an antifeminist direction, you will need to reverse your scores for the following items: 1, 2, 6, 7, 8, 10, 11, 12, 17, 19, 21, 23, 25, 26, 27, 30, 33, 35, 37, and 42. For these items a:

+2 becomes –2
+1 becomes –1
–1 becomes +1
–2 becomes +2

Now sum your scores for all the items. Scores many range from +84 to –84.

INTERPRETATION: The higher one's score, the higher the agreement with feminist statements. You may be interested in comparing your score, or that of your partner or friend with those obtained by Lott (1973) from undergraduate students at the University of Rhode Island. The sample was composed of 109 men and 133 women in an introductory psychology class, and 47 additional women who were older and participating in a special Continuing Education for Women (CEW) program. Based on information presented by Lott (1973) the following mean scores were calculated:

Men = 13.07, Women = 24.30, and Continuing Education Women = 30.67

More recently, Biaggio, Mohan, and Baldwin (1985) administered Lott's questionnaire to 76 students from a University of Idaho introductory psychology class and 63 community members randomly selected from the local phone directory. Although they did not present the scores of their respondents, they reported they did not find differences between men and women; unlike Lott's students, in Biaggio et al.'s sample, women were not more proliberation than men. Biaggio et al. (1985) stated, "It seems that some of the tenets of feminism have taken hold and earned broader acceptance. These data also point to an intersex convergence of attitudes, with men's and women's attitudes toward liberation and child rearing being less disparate now than during the period of Lott's study."

REACTIONS: Use the space provided to respond to the following questions.

1. Do you feel your score accurately represents your attitudes toward feminism? Why or why not?

2. Explain any aspects of the feminist movement with which you agree. Explain any aspects of the feminist movement with which you disagree.

SOURCE: Biaggio, Mohan, and Baldwin, Sex Roles 12, pp. 47–62 © 1985

3. Would your score on this assessment have been different three years ago? Explain.

SOURCE: "Attitudes Toward Feminism Scale," by Bernice Lott, Ph.D., Department of Psychology, University of Rhode Island. Used with permission.

6 | Sexual Self-Image Checklist

Purpose: In the test that follows you'll be asked to examine a list of adjectives while evaluating yourself sexually. There are no right or wrong responses to this test, but at the end we'll present some guidelines with which you can analyze your score and determine your stage of sexual growth. We've discovered that men and women score quite differently on this checklist, and older men, especially, demonstrate an unusual tendency. We'll tell you about this and other intriguing comparisons after you complete the test.

Instructions: In the test that begins below, you'll be presented with a list of 100 adjectives. You'll be reading through the list twice.

First go down the list and place an X in the column that reads "As I Am Sexually" each time you come to an adjective that describes how you really are.

Now, without paying attention to the marks you made in the first column, read through the list again. This time place an O in the second column which reads "As I Would Like to Be Sexually" by each adjective that describes the way you would like to be.

Keep in mind that for some of the adjectives both columns will be marked, for others only one will be marked, and some will have no marks next to them. Look at the example below:

Controlled	X	__
Satisfied	__	O
Monogamous	X	O
Bored	__	__

The person who responded above was indicating that he felt controlled sexually but didn't necessarily want to be that way. He isn't satisfied but would like to be. He's monogamous and would like to continue to be so. And he's not bored, nor would he want to be.

Remember, read and mark the two columns separately. When you've finished, determine your score.

	(X) As I Am Sexually	(O) As I Would Like to Be Sexually		(X) As I Am Sexually	(O) As I Would Like to Be Sexually
Active	____	____	Demanding	____	____
Adaptable	____	____	Desirable	____	____
Addicted	____	____	Determined	____	____
Affectionate	____	____	Discreet	____	____
Aggressive	____	____	Domineering	____	____
Agreeable	____	____	Eager	____	____
Angry	____	____	Eccentric	____	____
Argumentative	____	____	Elegant	____	____
Assertive	____	____	Emotional	____	____
Athletic	____	____	Entertaining	____	____
Attentive	____	____	Enthusiastic	____	____
Blunt	____	____	Erotic	____	____
Bold	____	____	Faithful	____	____
Boring	____	____	Fickle	____	____
Businesslike	____	____	Flirtatious	____	____
Careful	____	____	Forceful	____	____
Cautious	____	____	Frustrated	____	____
Choosy	____	____	Fussy	____	____
Charming	____	____	Gentle	____	____
Competitive	____	____	Habitual	____	____
Compulsive	____	____	Honest	____	____
Confident	____	____	Humorous	____	____
Conservative	____	____	Imaginative	____	____
Creative	____	____	Impulsive	____	____
Cynical	____	____	Indulgent	____	____
Daring	____	____	Inhibited	____	____

	(X) As I Am Sexually	(O) As I Would Like to Be Sexually		(X) As I Am Sexually	(O) As I Would Like to Be Sexually
Innocent	____	____	Private	____	____
Insecure	____	____	Relaxed	____	____
Jealous	____	____	Responsive	____	____
Judgmental	____	____	Romantic	____	____
Loud	____	____	Rushed	____	____
Mischievous	____	____	Self-conscious	____	____
Modest	____	____	Sensitive	____	____
Moody	____	____	Sensual	____	____
Mysterious	____	____	Sentimental	____	____
Naive	____	____	Sexy	____	____
Naughty	____	____	Show-offish	____	____
Obedient	____	____	Shy	____	____
Obsessed	____	____	Spontaneous	____	____
Open-minded	____	____	Stubborn	____	____
Opinionated	____	____	Tactful	____	____
Opportunistic	____	____	Talkative	____	____
Optimistic	____	____	Teasing	____	____
Out of control	____	____	Temperamental	____	____
Patient	____	____	Timid	____	____
Perfectionistic	____	____	Unselfish	____	____
Persistent	____	____	Vengeful	____	____
Persuasive	____	____	Voyeuristic	____	____
Playful	____	____	Vulnerable	____	____
Possessive	____	____	Wild	____	____

SCORING: To find your score on the Sexual Self-Image Checklist, go back over the list and give yourself one point for each time the columns *do not* match. *If only one column is marked (with either an X or an O), that's not a match and you score one point.* If there's both an X and an O next to an adjective, that's a match and you don't receive a point; if neither column is marked, that's also a match and doesn't score. Once you've determined how many adjectives on your checklist *don't match,* count the total and write it in the box below.

TOTAL SCORE

INTERPRETATION: From Plato, who told us, "Know thyself," to Masters and Johnson, who pioneered the investigation of human sexuality, scientists and philosophers have been urging their fellow man to achieve self-understanding as the path of true fulfillment. In *The Art of Loving,* a treatise on relationship problems, psychiatrist Erich Fromm writes, "Self-love and the love of others go hand-in-hand." Identifying what we consider to be our self, however, isn't an easy task.

Psychologist Carl Rogers innovated a research technique that has become the primary method for such an investigation. His test compares how we see ourselves with how we would like to be. If there's a large discrepancy between how we see ourselves at present (the actual self) and how we would like to be (the ideal self), then we're more likely to have low self-esteem and feel high levels of frustration, stress, and self-doubt. The test you just took is based on Dr. Rogers' work.

Your score on the Sexual Self-Image Checklist represents how integrated your sexual identity is—that is, how your ideal sexual self compares with the way you currently see yourself. Scores indicating a very low level of discrepancy are generally positive, but if you scored low you may not agree. The qualities you wish were different in yourself may be so important to you that you feel discontent with who you are sexually. Very low scorers, too, should be aware of the dangers in being overly complacent sexually. Adjustments are a natural part of sexual growth.

Keep in mind as you interpret your score that understanding yourself a little better is the goal of the Sexual Self-Image Checklist. Use the norms to compare yourself to others, but also use your results to examine who you are sexually—and who you want to be.

NORMS TABLE					
	Very Low	Low	Average	High	Very High
MEN	6 and below	7–10	11–23	24–31	32 and above
WOMEN	11 and below	12–16	17–27	28–39	40 and above

In the Norms Table you'll see that there are significant differences between self-image scoring levels for men and women. (Remember that a low score means a low level of discrepancy between how you see your sexual self and how you would like to be.) The table shows that women tend to be more unhappy with themselves sexually than men are. Could this be a part of a cultural idea that insists women must strive to be prettier, slimmer, sexier, than they are? Is it easier for men, given their traditional role as the sexual aggressor, to be more at ease with who they are because they feel in more control? We believe the results may indicate this cultural bias.

LOW/VERY LOW SCORES: Low scores on the Sexual Self-Image Checklist generally indicate a positive view of who you are sexually. For you, this probably translates into good feelings about yourself, a willingness to take the necessary risks in order to initiate sexual relationships, and the ability to work through the problems that are inevitable in ongoing relationships. For men, a positive sexual self-image is related to a high overall level of sexual satisfaction and to a willingness to move toward commitment in relationships. Women who score in this range generally view themselves as attractive and desirable and report low levels of jealousy in their sexual relationships. A positive self-view, it seems, makes it easier to take sexual risks and to feel able to work out sexual problems should they develop.

A very positive view of yourself sexually can be beneficial as long as you continue to grow and develop. Even a positive self-image has its risks. If you scored well here you must continue to be sensitive to your partner, who may not be as secure as you are. Sometimes, it seems, a high level of confidence in one partner can add to the insecurity of the other, unless effective communication and openness keep the relationship channels clear.

AVERAGE SCORES: Most healthy people have several qualities that they wish were different about themselves, and that's probably true for you if you scored in the average range. As we discussed earlier, the meaning of discrepancies between who you are and who you would like to be can be understood only by you. You may look at your average score and feel that it's okay because you can't really change who you are. Or you may look at your score and find a challenge; you may see a solid base upon which to build a higher level of sexual self-esteem. Our results say that you'll feel better about your sexual life if you choose the latter.

HIGH/VERY HIGH SCORES: If you scored in the high or very high range for your own sex, chances are you feel a low level of control in your sexual relationships. High-discrepancy scorers also report a high level of concern about being rejected sexually, as well as a strong fear of commitment in their sexual relationships.

A large gap between how you see yourself and how you would like to be may suggest that you're going through a major change in your sexual life. You may have decided to take a close look at who you are because of events that made you feel the need for sexual change. Or you may be in the process of developing a new sexual personality. Among our test subjects, older men tended to score in the high or very high range. This could be an indicator of the so-called midlife crisis in men.

If you scored in this range, look back over the list and decide how important each of those discrepancies is in your life. You may feel overwhelmed looking at how far you have to go to become who you want to be, but keep in mind that sexual growth is a lifelong process. Use this information to determine where you want to start. Your sexuality can take a happy leap forward if you'll continue the growth process that you've started by taking this test.

REACTIONS: What was your score for this exercise? How would you interpret your score? Do you agree with the interpretations listed above?

7 | Self-Esteem and Sexual Maturity

Theorists and researchers who study psychosexual development generally agree that self-esteem is a significant variable in sexual maturation.

DIRECTIONS: Complete the scale below by responding to each question. Place an X in the space next to your response.

1. I feel that I'm a person of worth, at least on an equal plane with others.

____ a. Strongly agree

____ b. Agree

____ c. Disagree

____ d. Strongly disagree

2. I feel that I have a number of good qualities.

____ a. Strongly agree

____ b. Agree

____ c. Disagree

____ d. Strongly disagree

3. All in all, I am inclined to feel that I am a failure.

____ a. Strongly agree

____ b. Agree

____ c. Disagree

____ d. Strongly disagree

4. I am able to do things as well as most other people.

____ a. Strongly agree

____ b. Agree

____ c. Disagree

____ d. Strongly disagree

5. I feel I do not have much to be proud of.

_____ a. Strongly agree

_____ b. Agree

_____ c. Disagree

_____ d. Strongly disagree

6. I take a positive attitude toward myself.

_____ a. Strongly agree

_____ b. Agree

_____ c. Disagree

_____ d. Strongly disagree

7. On the whole, I am satisfied with myself.

_____ a. Strongly agree

_____ b. Agree

_____ c. Disagree

_____ d. Strongly disagree

8. I wish I could have more respect for myself.

_____ a. Strongly agree

_____ b. Agree

_____ c. Disagree

_____ d. Strongly disagree

9. I certainly feel useless at times.

_____ a. Strongly agree

_____ b. Agree

_____ c. Disagree

_____ d. Strongly disagree

10. At times I think I am no good at all.

_____ a. Strongly agree

_____ b. Agree

_____ c. Disagree

_____ d. Strongly disagree

SCORING: To score this scale and thereby derive a measure of your self-esteem, follow these directions:

1. The positive responses for questions 1–3 are:

   question 1: a or b

   question 2: a or b

   question 3: c or d

   If at least two of these questions were answered positively, give yourself one point.

2. The positive responses for questions 4 and 5 are:

   question 4: a or b

   question 5: c or d

   If either one or both of these questions were answered positively, give yourself one point.

3. If question 6 was answered a or b, give yourself one point.

4. If question 7 was answered a or b, give yourself one point.

5. If question 8 was answered c or d, give yourself one point.

6. For questions 9 and 10, if either or both of these were answered c or d, give yourself one point.

TOTAL all the points you gave yourself. _____

The range of scores on this self-esteem scale is 0–6. *The higher the score, the more positive your self-esteem.* According to the author of the scale, high self-esteem means that individuals respect themselves, consider themselves worthy, but do not necessarily consider themselves better than others, but definitely do not consider themselves worse. They do not feel themselves to be the ultimate in perfection, but, on the contrary, recognize their limitations and expect to grow and improve. Self-esteem is the most important variable in regard to psychosexual development and maturation. It is the master key that can open the door to the actualization of an individual's human sexuality potential.

REACTIONS: Use the space provided to respond to the following questions.

1. Regardless of your score, at what level is your self-esteem in your own estimation? Explain why you feel it is at the level you stated.

2. Give one example and discuss how your self-esteem or lack of self-esteem has affected your sexuality.

SOURCE: Morris Rosenberg, *Society and the Adolescent Self-Image.* Copyright © 1965 by Princeton University Press; Princeton Paperback, 1968. Self-Esteem Scale, Appendix D, pp. 305–319. Reprinted by permission of Princeton University Press.

8 Issues in Human Sexuality: Gender Role Stereotyping

Is gender role stereotyping bad?

DIRECTIONS: Read each paragraph below carefully, making sure you clearly understand both sides of the issue before you write your reactions.

Some people believe that gender role stereotyping serves a useful purpose and should be maintained. They argue that clearly defined gender roles provide guidance to young people—boys and girls—regarding the training they should acquire. Girls should develop nurturance by baby-sitting, learn how to cook by helping their mothers, and prepare for a career that will also allow them to do their homemaking and mothering chores (for example, teaching). Marriages are breaking up because gender roles are not clearly defined, they contend. A man and a woman enter marriage expecting certain things from each other. If the roles aren't well defined, these expectations are likely to go unmet, resulting in marital dissatisfaction and divorce. Further, schools should teach children to accept traditional gender roles, because the purpose of schooling is to help young people fit into society. Otherwise, schools create citizens who are ill prepared to contribute to a stable society and who will be malcontents.

Others believe gender role stereotyping is too limiting; that is, it prohibits a free choice of lifestyle. Why shouldn't people be free to choose those roles they want rather than having certain ones forced upon them? People cannot be self-actualized unless they are able to choose a career suited to them, can develop a family style consistent with their needs, or develop abilities and characteristics natural to them. These opponents of gender role stereotyping believe schools should develop citizens with inquiring minds who can examine their society and identify ways to improve it. Teaching young people to fit into the society, with no questions asked, rather than help it to evolve, would defeat this purpose.

REACTIONS: What do you think about this issue? Use the space provided to record your feelings.

SOURCE: George B. Dintiman and Jerrold S. Greenberg, *Health Through Discovery,* © 1983, Addison-Wesley Publishing Co., Inc., Reading, MA, p. 283. Reprinted with permission.

SECTION II

SEXUAL HEALTH AND SELF-CARE

Fundamental to the understanding of human sexuality is an accurate knowledge of, and positive attitude about, sexual anatomy and physiology, both female and male. Unfortunately, some of us grow up feeling somewhat ambivalent about our genitalia. The sex organs could be considered the most fascinating parts of your body. They have been displayed in the highest forms of art, idolized as religious symbols, and often mutilated by cultural traditions. People can be sexually active and even become parents without having any real idea of the nature of their sexual response and reproductive systems. A good understanding of your sexual anatomy and physiology can promote good genital health, responsible sexual behavior, and a better understanding of your sexuality. The exercises in this section present an opportunity to expand your awareness of sexual anatomy and physiology in promoting good genital health.

Sexual Health and Self-Care exercises include:

9 How Much Do You Know About Female Sexual Functioning?

PURPOSE: This quiz focuses on frequently misunderstood sexual matters pertaining to women. Before you will be able to comprehend the psychological aspects of sexual functioning you should have a basic knowledge of the anatomy and physiology of the woman's body.

DIRECTIONS: Read each statement or question carefully to determine which response is most accurate. Write the letter of the response you choose in the blank to the left of the question. If you have a friend, relative, roommate, or partner who would like to take this quiz, cover your answers with a sheet of paper and compare them, if desired, when completed.

You   Friend

_____ _____ 1. The most sexually sensitive part of the female body is (are) the:

     a. Inner portion of the vagina

     b. Breasts

     c. Clitoris

     d. Labia

_____ _____ 2. Some vaginas are "too large" and others "too small."

     a. True

     b. False

_____ _____ 3. An orgasm in the female may result in "penis captivus."

     a. True

     b. False

_____ _____ 4. With the greatest number of females, orgasms usually occur after how many minutes of foreplay?

     a. Less than one minute

     b. One to ten minutes

     c. Eleven to twenty minutes

     d. More than twenty minutes

You   Friend

____ ____ 5. With increasing sexual stimulation, as a woman nears orgasm, the clitoris tends to:

        a. Withdraw under the hood

        b. Project further out from under the hood

        c. Secrete lubricating fluids

        d. Stay the same

____ ____ 6. When a woman has several orgasms within a short time, she generally finds that the first orgasm is more satisfying than the later ones.

        a. True

        b. False

____ ____ 7. Mucoid fluid that lubricates the vagina in preparation for intercourse is secreted mainly by the:

        a. Uterus

        b. Bartholin gland

        c. Clitoris

        d. Vaginal walls

____ ____ 8. All human male embryos have female genitalia during the first few months of development.

        a. True

        b. False

____ ____ 9. Which part of the vagina is most sensitive to sexual stimulation?

        a. The lower third

        b. The inner third

        c. The inner two-thirds

        d. The entire vaginal barrel

____ ____ 10. Women's orgasms may vary a great deal in intensity.

        a. True

        b. False

You   Friend

____ ____ 11. The hormone(s) most directly responsible for ovulation is (are):
- a. Progesterone
- b. FSH
- c. LH
- d. FSH and LH

____ ____ 12. Examination of the hymen can prove that a woman is not a virgin.
- a. True
- b. False

____ ____ 13. A retroflexed, or tipped, uterus may interfere with conception.
- a. True
- b. False

____ ____ 14. The best method for determining when ovulation occurs is to count to:
- a. Day fourteen of the menstrual cycle
- b. Fourteen days before the first day of the menstrual flow
- c. The midpoint of the menstrual cycle
- d. Day seventeen of the menstrual cycle

____ ____ 15. A woman must reach orgasm in order to conceive.
- a. True
- b. False

____ ____ 16. Sexual stimulation in what form is needed for vaginal lubrication to take place?
- a. Sight
- b. Sound
- c. Touch
- d. Smell

____ ____ 17. A woman is safe from conception if sexual intercourse occurs during menstruation.
- a. True
- b. False

You   Friend

_____ _____ 18. Menstrual cramps and pain have no physiological cause.

                          a. True

                          b. False

_____ _____ 19. Sperm may live in a woman's body for:

                          a. Twelve to twenty-four hours

                          b. Twenty-four to thirty-six hours

                          c. Forty-eight to seventy-two hours

                          d. Twelve days

_____ _____ 20. The probability that one specific act of intercourse will result in pregnancy is about:

                          a. 6 percent

                          b. 24 percent

                          c. 56 percent

                          d. 84 percent

_____ _____ 21. A small gland on the front wall of the vagina and emptying into the urethra that has been hypothesized to be responsible for ejaculation in some women:

                          a. Clitoris

                          b. Hymen

                          c. Grafenberg spot

                          d. Bartholin gland

_____ _____ 22. A combination of severe physical and psychological symptoms occurring just before menstruation is called:

                          a. Menstrual blues

                          b. Premenstrual syndrome

                          c. Baby blues

                          d. Period

_____ _____ 23. Symptoms associated with Toxic Shock Syndrome (TSS) include all the following except:

                          a. High fever

                          b. Vomiting

                          c. Red rash on trunk

                          d. Diarrhea

You   Friend

____ ____ 24. Females who have large breasts have more female hormones than small breasted females.
    a. True
    b. False

____ ____ 25. As she matures a female's fallopian tubes do not change in size .
    a. True
    b. False

____ ____ 26. A clear or whitish, odorless, nonirritating vaginal discharge is normal for most females.
    a. True
    b. False

____ ____ 27. A physician can tell if a female has had sexual intercourse.
    a. True
    b. False

____ ____ 28. In the United States approximately how many teenagers become pregnant each year?
    a. 500,000
    b. 1 million
    c. 1.5 million
    d. 2 million

____ ____ 29. Women experience nocturnal genital arousal.
    a. True
    b. False

____ ____ 30. Females are born with approximately _____ ova with their ovaries.
    a. 100,000
    b. 200,000
    c. 300,000
    d. 400,000

You   Friend

___ ___ 31. Female roommates may have closely timed menstrual cycles.

  a. True

  b. False

___ ___ 32. Female pubic hair plays no significant role in sexual stimulation.

  a. True

  b. False

___ ___ 33. In 1990, what percentage of American women have had anal intercourse?

  a. 10–20 percent

  b. 30–40 percent

  c. 50–60 percent

  d. 70–80 percent

___ ___ 34. A female can become pregnant even if the male withdraws his penis before he ejaculates.

  a. True

  b. False

___ ___ 35. Unless they are having sexual intercourse, women do not need to have regular gynecological examinations.

  a. True

  b. False

___ ___ 36. Menopause, or "change of life," does not cause most women to lose interest in having sex.

  a. True

  b. False

___ ___ 37. In 1990, what percentage of American women have masturbated either as adolescents or after reaching adulthood?

  a. 5–10 percent

  b. 20–30 percent

  c. 40–50 percent

  d. 60–80 percent

You   Friend

____   ____   38. Most women prefer a male sexual partner with a larger-than-average penis.

a. True

b. False

____   ____   39. Beginning externally and proceeding internally, the structures of the female reproductive system are:

a. ovaries, vagina, uterus, fallopian tubes, ovaries

b. vulva, vagina, uterus, fallopian tubes, ovaries

c. uterus, vagina, fallopian tubes, vulva, ovaries

d. vagina, fallopian tubes, uterus, ovaries, vulva

SCORING: The correct answers are:

1. a. The clitoris has virtually as many nerve endings as the male penis. However, many women find that indirect stimulation of the clitoris is most satisfying due to its sensitivity.

2. b. The vagina is a muscular organ that will adapt to the size of any penis during intercourse.

3. b. Despite observations of penis captivus among lower animals such as dogs, penis captivus can only occur when the penis contains a bone. There is no documentation or anatomical explanation for penis captivus in women since the human male penis has no bone.

4. d. Many women find they need sexual stimulation or foreplay for more than twenty minutes to be able to relax emotionally and/or physically enough to reach orgasm.

5. a. The clitoris tends to withdraw under the folds of the labia minora as sexual excitement increases and the woman approaches orgasm.

6. b. Many women who report multiple orgasms report that subsequent orgasms are more satisfying than the first.

7. d. The vagina is kept moist by secretions from the vaginal walls. These secretions increase with sexual stimulation. The secretions from the Bartholin glands are minimal and seem to secrete only enough fluid to create a genital scent.

8. a. In the first few weeks after conception, although genetically different, all human embryos' external genitalia appear to be female. By the fourth month of development, male hormones have caused differentiation of the external sex structures in the male embryo.

9. a. Only the lower one-third of the vaginal barrel contains adequate nerve endings to be sensitive to stimulation. Therefore, penis size (length) is not a physiological factor in the degree of sexual satisfaction through intercourse.

10. a. Research studies show that orgasms vary a great deal in intensity and duration, even for one woman.

11. d. The follicle-stimulating hormone (FSH) and luteinizing hormone (LH) are both released by the pituitary gland. The FSH stimulates the follicles and several eggs mature. The LH causes the Graafian follicle to rupture, releasing the ovum.

12. b. Absence of the hymen is not proof that a woman is no longer a virgin. The opening in the hymen can be stretched by horseback riding, gymnastics, motorcycle riding, and even use of tampons.

13. b. A tipped, or retroflexed, uterus simply means the uterus lies at a different angle in relation to the vagina. The position of the uterus has no effect on a woman's ability to conceive.

14. b. Even when a woman's menstrual cycle is irregular, it has been found that the menstrual flow begins two weeks after ovulation. Therefore, variation in the length of the cycle is in the number of days before ovulation.

15. b. Ovulation does not occur as part of the sexual response cycle but instead is caused by the release of hormones as part of the menstrual cycle.

16. a, b, c, or d. In as short as ten seconds, any of the senses may provide enough sexual stimulation to cause vaginal lubrication.

17. b. Although ovulation theoretically occurs fourteen days before the menstrual flow, ovulation does not always follow that pattern. Therefore, if a couple want to be certain the woman will not get pregnant, contraceptives should be used even during menstruation.

18. b. The dilation of the cervix to allow passage of blood clots may be one cause of pain during menstruation. In addition, menstrual cramps and pain may be caused by an overproduction of prostaglandin hormones, which causes strong uterine cramps.

19. c. Many sources report that forty-eight to seventy-two hours is the norm. However, sperm have been found alive for five or even up to ten days.

20. a. This is the likelihood of one single act of intercourse resulting in pregnancy. However, the likelihood does exist, so contraceptives should be used.

21. c. The Grafenberg spot, or G-spot, is hypothesized to be located on the top side of the vagina about halfway between the pubic bone and the cervix. The G-spot is stimulated through the vaginal wall. Some research suggests the possibility of a female ejaculation from this gland. Some studies have shown the tissue to be similar to that of the male prostate gland.

22. b. Premenstrual syndrome (PMS) is the hypothesized to be combination of severe physical and psychological symptoms occurring just before menstruation. These mood fluctuations maybe due to changes in hormone levels during the cycle or due to cultural expectations and taboos surrounding menstruation.

23. c. TSS is usually associated with tampon use which encourages abnormal growth of bacteria. The presence of bacteria results in the high fever and vomiting or diarrhea. It is now recommended that women change tampons frequently during the day and that they do not use tampons continuously throughout a menstrual cycle.

24. b. Breast size is not related to hormone levels in females. Heredity, however, does play a role in determining breast size among other factors.

25. b. A female's fallopian tubes become longer and wider as she matures. Each tube elongates to about 4 inches and increases in width to that of a regular strand of spaghetti.

26. a. It is common for females to experience a clear or whitish, nonirritating vaginal discharge. If the discharge is accompanied by itching or discomfort, however, it may be a sign of infection.

27. b. In general, a physician cannot determine if a female has had sexual intercourse by a routine exam. However, finding sperm in the vagina during a microscopic exam or finding signs of a sexually transmitted disease (STD) may indicate some form of sexual contact has occurred.

28. b. Approximately one million teenagers become pregnant each year in America. Evidence is growing that a significant percent of these pregnancies are by older partners.

29. a. Research has discovered that women also experience periodic nocturnal genital arousal similar to the pattern of men during REM sleep.

30. d. 400,000. At birth, the two ovaries contain about 400,000 ova. Unlike a male's continual production of sperm, a female will form no additional ova during her lifetime.

31. a. Research studies have shown that female cohabiters may have closely timed or synchronized menstrual cycles. The theory is that pheromones secreted during the menstrual cycle by one roommate will affect the cycle of the other. In addition, similar patterns of weekly and monthly behavior also play a role in menstrual synchrony.

32. b. Pubic hair functions as an "odor trap" for secretions released by the apocrine glands located in the pubic and armpit areas of the female. Once secretions are released, the hair traps the scent, enabling it to linger and act as an erotic stimulus. In addition, females possess about 75 percent more scent glands than males.

33. b. According to the Kinsey Institute for Sex Research, between 30 and 40 percent of women report having tried anal intercourse at least once. In addition, researchers believe that respondents tend to underreport anal intercourse and this 30 to 40 percent could be a conservative estimate.

34. a. The drops of clear mucoid fluid that appear at the tip of the penis during arousal and prior to ejaculation may contain enough sperm to fertilize an egg. There is no sensation involved in the secretion of this clear mucoid fluid, therefore withdrawal of the penis prior to ejaculation is not an effective form of contraceptive.

35. b. Whether or not they are having sex, all women should have annual gynecological examinations beginning around age 16 to 18—or before that if they are sexually active—and continuing throughout their lives, even after menopause. STDs, cervical cancer, endometriosis, pelvic inflammatory disease, and other disorders must be detected as soon as possible for effective treatment.

36. a. Research studies have suggested that for most women, menopause does not mean an end to interest and involvement in sex. Although some women do experience a lowered sex drive during menopause, hormone-replacement therapy (HRT) can help. Most people over 50, including menopausal women, continue to have a healthy and active sex life.

37. d. 60–80 percent. Masturbation in general, has been considered a forbidden topic among female adolescents and women. Attitudes and behaviors in this regard are changing and reflected in self-report surveys, movies, and magazines.

38. b. Research studies have indicated that women in general do not have a preference regarding penis size. Anecdotal evidence from women indicate that when they are concerned about penis size, it is more often a concern about a partner being too large, not too small.

39. b. Vulva, vagina, uterus, fallopian tubes, and ovaries.

INTERPRETATION: Count your total number of correct responses.

Total Correct = _____

If you had 35–39 correct answers you have an excellent base of knowledge regarding female sexual functioning. A score of 29–30 correct responses represents a good understanding of female sexual functions. If you scored 23–28 correct answers you have a fair understanding of female sexual functioning and you should correct your mistakes on this self-test. A score of below 23 is poor and you should correct your mistakes and read for comprehension the appropriate chapters of a recommended human sexuality text.

REACTIONS: Write your responses to the following questions in the space provided.

1. What were the most interesting 2 or 3 pieces of information about female sexual functioning that you learned from this self-test?

2. How will the information from this self-test help you in the future?

10 How Much Do You Know About Male Sexual Functioning?

P URPOSE: The following exercise is designed to provide some thought, expand your knowledge, and offer a perspective about male sexuality, including anatomy, physiology, and changes through the life cycle. The more practical information you have about male sexuality, the more capable you will be of understanding yourself, if you are male, or your partner. This information can also help you make sound decisions regarding your sexuality.

DIRECTIONS: Read each statement or question carefully and place your response in the space provided to the left of the question. If you have a friend, relative, roommate, or partner who would like to take this quiz, cover your answers with a sheet of paper and compare them, if desired, when completed.

You   Friend

____ ____   1. A man must have an erection in order to ejaculate.
　　　　　　　　　a. True
　　　　　　　　　b. False

____ ____   2. In each average ejaculation, there are approximately how many sperm?
　　　　　　　　　a. 20,000
　　　　　　　　　b. 175,000 to 200,000
　　　　　　　　　c. 30 to 40 million
　　　　　　　　　d. 200 to 500 million

____ ____   3. Today in the United States the average age at which males reach puberty is:
　　　　　　　　　a. 12.4 years
　　　　　　　　　b. 13.4 years
　　　　　　　　　c. 14.5 years
　　　　　　　　　d. 15.4 years

You   Friend

____ ____   4. Is a single sperm enough to fertilize the ovum?

   a. Yes

   b. No

____ ____   5. Does the sperm reach the ovum solely under its own power during implantation?

   a. Yes

   b. No

____ ____   6. When does ejaculation occur?

   a. At the moment of climax

   b. After the climax

   c. Prior to the climax

   d. During resolution

____ ____   7. Prior to ejaculation, a small amount of mucoid fluid from the Cowper's gland is secreted through the urethra. This fluid may contain up to:

   a. 5,000 sperm

   b. 50,000 sperm

   c. 90,000 sperm

   d. 1 million sperm

____ ____   8. Healthy, long-lived sperm cells are prone to produce:

   a. Blondes

   b. Boys

   c. Girls

   d. Twins

____ ____   9. The temperature within the testes is found to be about:

   a. The same as normal body temperature

   b. Two degrees cooler

   c. Four degrees cooler

   d. Two degrees warmer

You Friend

____ ____ 10. A man's penis is the most delicate, sensitive part of his genitalia.
    a. True
    b. False

____ ____ 11. What percentage of the general male population has experienced some form of erectile dysfunction?
    a. 20 percent
    b. 35 percent
    c. 50 percent
    d. 75 percent

____ ____ 12. Do adolescents and younger males have more "erect" erections than older males?
    a. Yes
    b. No

____ ____ 13. Before ejaculation, an average potent male may be able to continue penetration for about:
    a. Three to five minutes
    b. Five to ten minutes
    c. Ten to twenty minutes
    d. Twenty to thirty minutes

____ ____ 14. A man may easily lose an erection during intercourse.
    a. True
    b. False

____ ____ 15. After ejaculation, approximately how long does it take before the average male can achieve another erection?
    a. Ten to fifteen minutes
    b. Twenty minutes to an hour
    c. One to two hours
    d. No time lapse is required

You   Friend

____ ____ 16. Males have fewer erogenous zones than females.
              a. True
              b. False

____ ____ 17. Males are capable of only one type of orgasm.
              a. True
              b. False

____ ____ 18. Males who are in good physical condition have more pleasurable orgasms than those who are not.
              a. True
              b. False

____ ____ 19. Males tend to have fuller, more satisfying orgasms through:
              a. Sex with a partner
              b. Masturbation

____ ____ 20. It is anatomically impossible for a female to "rape" a male.
              a. True
              b. False

____ ____ 21. In 1990, what percentage of married American men have had an extramarital affair (i.e., been sexually unfaithful to their wives)?
              a. 10–20 percent
              b. 30–40 percent
              c. 50–60 percent
              d. 70–80 percent

____ ____ 22. About 25 percent of American men have had a sexual experience with another male during either their teen or adult years.
              a. True
              b. False

____ ____ 23. Men should examine their testicles regularly, just as women self-examine their breasts for lumps.
              a. True
              b. False

You   Friend

_____ _____ 24. Male problems with erections are most often started by a physical problem.
                  a. True
                  b. False

_____ _____ 25. What is the length of the average man's erect penis?
                  a. 2–4 inches
                  b. 5–7 inches
                  c. 8–9 inches
                  d. 10–12 inches

_____ _____ 26. What is the length of the average man's (flaccid) unerect penis?
                  a. 2.5 inches
                  b. 4 inches
                  c. 5.5 inches
                  d. 6 inches

_____ _____ 27. How many calories are there in a teaspoon of semen?
                  a. 5 calories
                  b. 12 calories
                  c. 15 calories
                  d. 35 calories

_____ _____ 28. How many calories are burned during an average act of sexual intercourse?
                  a. 50 calories
                  b. 75 calories
                  c. 100 calories
                  d. 175 calories

_____ _____ 29. Though genetically different, normal male and female fetuses are anatomically identical until which week of gestation?
                  a. 5th
                  b. 6th
                  c. 7th
                  d. 8th

You   Friend

____ ____ 30. The left testicle usually hangs lower than the right in most males.

            a. True

            b. False

____ ____ 31. The seminiferous tubules of the testes, if laid out in a straight line, would extend over a quarter mile in length.

            a. True

            b. False

____ ____ 32. At least _____ million sperm per milliliter of semen are required for fertilization of an ovum to occur.

            a. 20

            b. 40

            c. 60

            d. 80

____ ____ 33. Male infertility is defined as the consistent ejaculation of fewer than 60 million sperm, of which less than _____ percent have motility.

            a. 35

            b. 40

            c. 45

            d. 50

____ ____ 34. Saltpeter (potassium nitrate) will decrease the male sex drive.

            a. True

            b. False

____ ____ 35. Frequent intercourse in middle age may provide protection against arthritis.

            a. True

            b. False

SCORING: The correct answers are:

1. b. A male cannot perform intercourse without an erection; however, manual or oral manipulation of a flaccid penis can lead to ejaculation, in some cases even when the male is impotent.

2. d. More than 99 percent of these sperm will die in the acidic environment of the vagina before they reach the Fallopian tubes, where fertilization takes place.

3. b. This age has been decreasing over the years due to improved nutritional practices, prenatal care, birthing procedures, medical technology, and the increased emphasis on health and well-being.

4. b. One sperm eventually fertilizes the ovum, but the cooperation of thousands is needed. Prior to penetration of an egg, a large number of sperm must release a chemical called hyaluronidase, which weakens the egg's outer protective layer. Then one sperm is able to penetrate.

5. b. Sperm do swim upward toward the ovum; however, they are aided by tiny, hairlike structures called cilia in the Fallopian tubes. Cilia work in a wavelike motion that helps the sperm on their journey.

6. b. At the exact moment of orgasm, semen is released into the ejaculatory duct. From this duct, however, the ejaculate must travel the length of the penis prior to being expelled from the urethra. This process takes place almost immediately and with explosive force in adolescents and younger men. In older men the journey is a little slower, taking two to three seconds to complete.

7. b. This is only a fraction of the number of sperm found in the actual ejaculate (200–500 million). However, this fact alone is enough to make "withdrawal" or "coitus interruptus" a highly ineffective form of birth control. In fact, any form of penis-vagina contact without some type of contraceptive can result in pregnancy.

8. c. Research studies on long-lived sperm have indicated that they tend to produce girls; boys are more often produced by speedy sperm. If a couple should desire a girl, intercourse should be planned two or three days prior to ovulation. If a boy is desired, intercourse on the day of ovulation is best.

9. b. This slight difference in temperature is vital to production and storage of healthy sperm. Males whose testicles have not descended and remain at 98.6°F cannot manufacture live sperm.

10. b. A man's testicles are the most sensitive part of his sexual anatomy. The slightest pressure or a tap or glancing blow to the testes can result in pain. The testes can be involved in lovemaking by being stroked or cupped in the hand or mouth, but should be treated gently. The penis is capable of enduring considerable pressure, the stress of heat and cold, and even very rough handling but not being bent in half while erect (this can damage the spongy bodies that cause an erection). The penis does respond to gentle stimulation; even though most of its nervous structure is concentrated deep within the shaft, a number of nerve fibers run to the surface. The frenulum or V-shaped section found on the underside of the head, or glans, tends to be the most sensitive part of the penis for most males.

11. c. It has been estimated that half of the general male population has experienced occasional episodes of erectile dysfunction, well within the range of normal sexual response. The percentage is not as important as whether the individual or couple see the occurrence as a problem. PRIMARY ERECTILE DYSFUNCTION—a case in which the man has never been able to obtain an erection sufficient enough to have intercourse. SECONDARY ERECTILE DYSFUNCTION—a case in which the man has difficulty getting or maintaining an erection but has been able to have vaginal or anal intercourse at least once. For men seeking therapy, erectile dysfunction is common, and secondary cases are more common than primary ones. Frequently erectile dysfunctions are due to combinations of organic and psychological factors. Fifty percent are estimated to be primarily caused by physiologic factors and another 25 percent have a contributory physiologic basis. Erectile difficulties affect men of all ages from teenagers to the elderly.

12. a. Erections occur by an increased inflow of blood filling the two corpora cavernosa and the corpus spongiosum. As men age, the cardiovascular system gradually loses its efficiency and therefore lessens the blood supply to the penis. Also, the pubococcygeus (PC) muscles in younger males are well toned and hold the penis at a very high angle, almost parallel to the body. In older males, these muscles gradually lose their tone and tend to hold the penis about halfway or a little more than halfway parallel to the body.

13. b. A variety of factors influence the ability to delay ejaculation. Men under thirty are prone to climax more quickly than older partners. Most young men ejaculate more rapidly than usual after extended foreplay, when lovemaking follows a period of abstinence, or with a new partner.

14. a. Regardless of the intensity of stimulation, a man can lose an erection if distracted by a negative reaction from a partner, a ringing phone, or even a sudden awareness that a room is too hot or cold. A single factor or variety of factors can cause a momentary drop in excitement, causing the loss of an erection.

15. b. This refractory period can range from minutes to days, depending on a variety of factors such as age, frequency of previous sexual activity, degree of emotional closeness, and sexual desire for a partner. Recovery time tends to be shorter for men in their teens and twenties and tends to increase with age or when a relationship has continued for some time after the initial passions have leveled off.

16. b. Some people will say they have dozens of erogenous zones and others will say they only have one or two. There seems to be more variation within males and females than between them.

17. b. Many men will report that they have experienced orgasms in varying degrees of intensity. Minor climaxes, or miniorgasms without ejaculation, can occur both before and after a very strong orgasm. Homosexual or gay men who engage in anal intercourse also report the experience of "rectal" or "prostate" orgasms similar to those experienced by females during intercourse.

18. a. Males tend to experience orgasm more in the overall body muscles than females. These feelings are more intense when the muscles are in good tone.

19. b. Although solitary sex is not preferred, research studies indicate that the climaxes men achieved through masturbation were more dependable and physically satisfying than those with a partner. The ability to control stimulation directly and the use of fantasy are contributing factors.

20. b. Males can be aroused to an erection against their conscious will, then be able to perform for the female (this is rare, but possible).

21. b. 30-40 percent. Based upon a comprehensive review of published research over the last 40 years, the Kinsey Institute estimates that 37 percent of married men have had at least one extramarital affair.

22. a. According to the Kinsey Institute for Sex Research, at least 25 percent of all American men have had a sexual experience with another male as teenagers or adults. Kinsey researchers also feel that 25 percent is a conservative estimate and the data suggest that 1 out of 3 is an accurate estimate. Therefore, having had a same sex experience is not unusual for about one-third of American men, even for those whose sexual orientation is heterosexual through their lives.

23. a. Most common between the ages of 20 and 34, testicular cancer is found in about four out of every 100,000 white males each year and at lower rates in men of color. Early detection of lumps or changes is important for successful treatment; therefore it is imperative that men of all ages, beginning at puberty, check their testicles every month, just as women should self-examine their breasts.

24. b. Until recently many experts believed that erection problems were primarily psychological, not physical. Researchers now believe that most erection difficulties begin with a physical factor, including diabetes and drug or alcohol or a wide range of medications.

25. b. This is the second-most-asked-about topic by men according to the Kinsey Institute. Research by leading sexologists indicates that the average erect penis measures five to seven inches in length.

26. b. According to the Kinsey Institute and other leading sexologists, the average unerect penis is four inches.

27. a. So, weight loss or weight gain should not be a problem with semen loss or gain (via oral sex).

28. c. 100 calories.

29. d. Though genetically different, normal male and female fetuses are anatomically identical until the 8th week of gestation. By the 12th week all internal and external sexual organs are fully formed.

30. a. The left testicle usually hangs lower than the right, although the reverse may be true of left-handed men.

31. a. The seminiferous tubules which produce sperm in the testes, are tightly coiled microscopic channels, that if laid out in a straight line, would extend approximately 500 meters or over a quarter mile in length.

32. a. It required at least 20 million sperm per milliliter of semen for fertilization of an ovum to occur. Although only one sperm will fertilize an egg, it needs the assistance of hundreds of its fellow sperm to secrete hyaluronidase, an enzyme that breaks down the tough protective shell of the ovum.

33. b. Male infertility is defined as the consistent ejaculation of fewer than 60 million sperm, of which less than 40 percent have motility.

34. b. There is no scientific evidence to support the long-held belief that saltpeter (potassium nitrate) will decrease the male sex drive or cause impotence.

35. a. According to leading sex researchers and medical experts, frequent sexual intercourse in middle age may provide protection against the degenerative effects of arthritis. Sexual intercourse stimulates the adrenal glands to produce cortisone, which helps alleviate symptoms of arthritis.

INTERPRETATION: Count your total number of correct responses.

Total Correct = _____

If you had 30–35 correct answers you have an excellent base of knowledge regarding male sexual functioning. A score of 25–29 correct responses represents a good understanding of male sexual functions. If you scored 20–24 correctly you have a fair understanding of male sexual functioning and you should correct your mistakes on this self-test. A score of below 20 is poor and you should correct your mistakes and read for comprehension the appropriate chapters of a recommended human sexuality text.

REACTIONS: Write your responses to the following questions in the space provided.

1. What were the most interesting 2 or 3 pieces of information about male sexual functioning that you learned from this self-test?

2. How will the information from this self-test help you in the future?

11 | The Male Perspective: Lovemaking and Cramps

Purpose: Men who make love with women have to come to terms, in some way, shape, or form, with the reality of women's menstruation and often their menstrual cramps. An understanding of cramps and the factors involved in menstruation can help avoid misunderstandings and build intimacy.

Directions: Read the following suggestions carefully and determine for yourself if you would consider or practice any of the following in your relationships. You might want to share this exercise with your partner and discuss these suggestions upon completion.

Suggestions:

1. You might first ask a partner if she gets cramps, and if so, have her describe to you how they feel. Pain should not be the only consideration. Edema (the bloated feeling caused by water retention) may not actually hurt but can be fairly uncomfortable and irritating. Some women with pronounced menstrual edema report the feeling similar to a flu. Breasts can swell and feel sore, and the entire body may feel like it's encased in a layer of water, sloshing around every time one moves.

2. As a man you can do several things to help your partner deal with dysmenorrhea (the pain associated with menstruation). For example, you could massage your partner's lower back. The abdominal region can be gently massaged. You can also help by preparing a warm drink such as an herb tea or warm apple cider for your partner during her menstrual period.

3. Try to discuss how your partner feels about having sexual intercourse premenstrually or during her period. Keep in mind that some women prefer to avoid coitus. The pain or edema can interfere with the undivided attention that lovemaking deserves; on the other hand some women say lovemaking right before the onstart of menstruation, or during it, can help alleviate cramps. During orgasm, the uterus contracts and the cervix opens. This process helps speed menstrual flow and tends to reduce the duration of cramping in some women. However, men should keep in mind that this experience is reported by a minority of women.

4. Breast tenderness is also associated with menstruation. Men should inquire about breast tenderness and keep this in mind during sensual explorations.

5. Different cultures and religions offer a variety of perspectives on sexual intercourse during a woman's menstrual period. As a result, many people, both men and women, hold very strong feelings about coitus during menstruation. Discuss, and listen carefully to your partner's feelings with regard to sexual intercourse during her period. It is best not to dismiss any feelings on this topic as being silly or archaic.

6. There are several things to keep in mind for couples who do make love during a woman's period. Menstruation can change a woman's natural vaginal lubrication. Some men find menstruational fluid irritating to their penises. A condom could be used if this is a problem for you and your partner. Having sexual intercourse with a tampon in place is not recommended. A woman could use a diaphragm or cervical cap in this situation even if a barrier method is not your primary or preferred form of contraception. Remember that contraception is needed for coitus during menstruation, since no absolute safe period exists.

7. For couples who prefer not to have genital intercourse during a woman's period, there are other satisfying ways to make love. There are a number of touching and communicating exercises that enhance sexual pleasure. The menstrual period can be an excellent opportunity for sensate focus. This nondemand pleasuring shared by sexual partners is an excellent vehicle for mutually enhancing sexual potentials.

8. Communication is the key. Talk openly and honestly about the issues menstruation raises in your relationship, and how you would both feel most comfortable dealing with them.

REACTIONS: In what way have these suggestions broadened your perspective on lovemaking during menstruation? Explain.

SOURCE: Adapted from Michael Castleman, "Men, Lovemaking and Cramps," *Medical Self-Care,* Spring 1981, p. 21.

12 | Breast Cancer: Rating Your Risk

PURPOSE: This test is meant to compute a woman's approximate risk of breast cancer. If you are a male, find a female friend or relative to take the inventory, and discuss the results with her.

MALE PERSPECTIVE: Men should be familiar with the possible health concerns of women. A man's role in breast cancer detection should be to encourage women he knows (family and friends) to practice the breast self-exam monthly. By practicing this self-exam, the woman is aware of any changes that may take place in the breast tissue. As a woman's sexual partner, men are sometimes able to detect changes in breast tissue also. When this occurs, you will be able to encourage your partner to seek appropriate medical attention as soon as possible.

DIRECTIONS: The risk test shown below involves three steps. First, answer each question by filling in the number in parentheses under the description that best fits you. Determine your total. Check your total on the risk scale to see where you fall.

Your Risk

AGE GROUP

20–34	35–49	50+
(5)	(50)	(100)

_____

RACE GROUP

Oriental	Black	Caucasian
(5)	(20)	(25)

_____

FAMILY HISTORY

None	Mother, sister, aunt, or grand-mother with breast cancer	Mother and sister with breast cancer	Mother and sister or 2 sisters with cancer in both breasts before 50
	(50)	(100)	(150)

_____

Your Risk

YOUR HISTORY

No breast cancer   Previous breast cancer
(20)   (100)   _____

MATERNITY

First baby before 30   No child or first baby 30 or after
(5)   (25)   _____

YOUR TOTAL   _____

RISK SCALE: Mark your score on the line below with an "X".

Low 0   100   200   300 High

SCORING: Women 225 and higher on the scale should practice monthly breast self-examination (BSE) and have physical examination of the breast every six months, with annual breast X-ray (mammography).

Women between 100 and 220 on the scale should practice BSE and have physical examination of the breast as part of an annual checkup. Periodic breast x-ray should be included as the doctor may advise.

Women below 100 on the scale should practice BSE and have physical examination of the breast as part of an annual checkup.

Any changes in your breast should receive prompt, expert medical attention no matter where your risk score falls on the scale.

REACTIONS: Use the space provided to respond to the following questions.

1. In which of the above categories lies your score?

2. This questionnaire highlights the factors that increase a woman's risk of developing breast cancer. The risk factors that are listed are not factors that you can control. For instance, when completing the Family Health History, did you know the cause of death for your ancestors?

If you are uncertain, talk with your family to find that information. Family history is important to know in determining cancer risk. Remember you can control cancer most effectively through early diagnosis and treatment. Therefore, women should practice the breast self-exam monthly and watch for symptoms as listed in the Cancer Detection Questionnaire.

SOURCE: American Cancer Society, Illinois Division.

13 | Breast Self-Examination

Purpose: Studies have shown that women who examine their breasts once a month greatly increase their chances of detecting a cancerous growth early enough to effect a cure. If a malignant lump is discovered while it is still localized, the chances of complete recovery are much greater than if the cancer has spread into other organs. Be aware that not all changes in breast tissue indicate that you have cancer or that you should be alarmed. However, the ones mentioned in this exercise should be discussed with your physician.

MALE PERSPECTIVE: Men should be familiar with the possible health concerns of women. A man's role in breast cancer detection should be to encourage women he knows (family and friends) to practice the breast self-exam monthly. By practicing this self-exam, the woman is aware of any changes that may take place in the breast tissue. As a woman's sexual partner, men are sometimes able to detect changes in breast tissue also. When this occurs you will be able to encourage your partner to seek appropriate medical attention as soon as possible. It should be mentioned that although it is not as common, breast cancer can occur in men.

POINTS TO PONDER:

1. Seven out of eight women will not have breast cancer during their lives.
2. Breast cancer is the major cancer killer of women, and its main target is women over thirty-five. Risk increases with age.
3. All women are at higher risk if they have a personal history of breast cancer or if there is a history of breast cancer in their family.
4. Not all lumps are cancerous; the only sure way to know is through a biopsy.
5. Changes such as swelling, puckering, dimpling, red irritation, and changes in the nipples are other signs that should be reported to the physician.
6. About 95 percent of breast cancers are discovered by women themselves, often through the practice of BSE (breast self-examination).
7. Every woman should practice the BSE once a month; the best time is right after her period. After menopause, any set day, such as the first of the month, is a good time to do BSE.

HOW TO DO A BREAST SELF-EXAMINATION

Use the following method of palpation for examination of the breasts: Palpate (touch) by using the middle three fingers, keeping the thumb extended, and always feel with the flat sensitive surfaces of your fingers. Do not use your fingertips, which are much less sensitive. Long fingernails also hamper the examination. Do not compress the breast tissue between thumb and fingers, as this may cause you to feel a lump that does not exist. Palpate the breasts using one of three patterns, pressing gently but firmly to immobilize the skin and roll it over the underlying tissue. By immobilizing the skin, you can feel the bones, tendons, etc. under the fat tissue.

Steps

1. Start the examination in the shower, as wet, soapy skin makes it easier to feel lumps. Keep one hand overhead and examine the breast on that side with the opposite hand. If breasts are large or pendulous, support breast with one hand and examine with the opposite hand.

2. Lying in bed, place a pillow under one shoulder to flatten and elevate the breast. Examine each breast by using the opposite hand. Do this first with the arm under the head and second with your arm at your side.

   a. Make small rotary motions with the flat pads (not tips) of the three middle fingers.

   b. Palpate the breast to feel every part of the breast tissue. Choose the method easiest for you. The diagrams show the three patterns preferred by women and their doctors: the circular, clock or oval pattern, the vertical strip, and the wedge. Feel for knots, lumps, thickening, indentations, or swellings. Be sure to examine the entire area, including lymph nodes from your collarbone to just below your breasts, and from armpits to breastbone.

3. Next stand in front of a large mirror with arms relaxed at your sides. Visually examine the breasts for swelling, dimpling, bulges, retractions, skin irritations, sores, or changes in moles. Also look for changes in nipple color, texture, or orientation. Repeat this procedure with your arms clasped behind your head.

   a. Repeat the above procedure while contracting chest muscles; first clasp hands in front of forehead, squeezing palms together; then place palms flat on side of hips pressing downward. This highlights bulges and indentations which may signal growth of tumors.

   b. Bend forward from the hips, resting your hands on your knees. Use the mirror to examine breasts for normal irregularities and abnormal variances, as both are most pronounced in this position.

   c. Squeeze the nipples to check for secretions and discharge.

WHY: If you find any suspicious lump or thickening or if any other findings strike you as unusual, do not wait. Do not be alarmed, but do visit your doctor and let him or her make the diagnosis. Remember: Early discovery and treatment of cancer greatly increase the chance of cure. Talk with your doctor or health care provider. As partners, you will want to share information and you will want to request advice on where to go to have a mammogram and how often you need to have the exams done.

Patterns for Palpation

You may find these guidelines of the American Cancer Society helpful.

IF YOU ARE LESS THAN 40 YEARS OLD, THE AMERICAN CANCER SOCIETY RECOMMENDS THAT YOU:

- Examine your breast monthly.
- Have a breast exam by your doctor at least every 3 years.
- Have a baseline mammogram between the ages of 35 to 39.

IF YOU ARE BETWEEN 40 AND 49 YEARS OLD:

- Examine your breasts monthly.
- Have a breast exam by your doctor every year.
- Have a mammogram every 1 to 2 years.

NOTE: These recommendations are intended for women who have no breast symptoms.

REACTIONS: Use the space provided to respond to these questions.

1. Have you learned anything new about early detection of breast cancer from this exercise? Explain.

2. Women: On a scale of 1 to 100 (with 100 being the highest level of confidence), how confident are you in being able to perform the breast self-exam effectively on a monthly basis? (Please made an "X" on the scale.)

1————————25————————50————————75————————100

Explain your rating.

SOURCE: American Cancer Society, Inc.

14 | Testicle Self-Examination

PURPOSE: It is important to become acquainted with your body in a normal state, so that you can detect changes especially later on in life. Be aware that not all changes indicate that you have cancer or that you should be alarmed. However, the ones mentioned in this exercise should be discussed with your physician.

PARTNER PERSPECTIVE: It is important for a male's sexual partner to be familiar with changes in his body, and testicular cancer should be a definite concern. However, a partner's role in detection should be limited to encouraging the partner to perform this exam. Assisting your partner in this process could cause him to become sexually aroused. Even the slightest arousal could cause a tightening of the scrotal skin, making this exam more difficult to perform.

CONSIDERATIONS FOR TESTICULAR CANCER AND TSE (A SELF-EXAM)

1. Cancer of the testes is one of the most common cancers in men 15 to 34 years of age. The most vulnerable age group for testicular cancer is between the early twenties and late thirties; however, it also occurs in men as old as forty and as young as fifteen. Testicular cancer accounts for 3 percent of all cancer deaths in the 15–34 age group.

2. If discovered in the early stages, testicular cancer can be treated promptly and effectively.

3. Recent studies indicate that, due to a lack of early symptoms and pain, a majority of men who had discovered a testicular lump or an enlarged testis did not realize the significance of their finding. These men also waited as long as five months before consulting a physician.

4. Men who have an undescended or partially descended testicle are at a much higher risk of developing testicular cancer than others. However, it is a simple procedure to correct the undescended testicle condition. See your physician if this applies to you.

5. Not all lumps are cancerous. Most are not, and the only way to know for sure is through a biopsy.

6. The first sign of testicular cancer is usually a slight enlargement of one of the testes and a change in its consistency. Pain may be absent, but often there is a dull ache in the lower abdomen and groin, together with a sensation of dragging and heaviness.

7. Cancer of the testicles can spread quite rapidly, making early detection and treatment essential.

8. Testicular cancer, if treated early enough, is one of the most curable cancers; if not, it is one of the most deadly.

9. Health professionals agree that the number of deaths from testicular cancer could be greatly reduced if every male in the vulnerable age group (twenties through thirties) would have regular medical checkups, including an examination of the testes, check his testes himself on a monthly basis, and report any unusual findings to his physician.

HOW TO DO A TESTICULAR SELF-EXAMINATION (TSE)

The American Cancer Society recommends the following procedure:

WHEN: Men should do a TSE every month; the best time for the exam is after a warm bath or shower, when the scrotal sac is relaxed. Becoming sexually aroused causes tightening of the scrotal skin, making the exam more difficult. The time involved is usually about two to three minutes. Try to set aside one day every month for your exam, such as payday.

HOW VISUALLY: Allow for good lighting. Examine yourself using a mirror. No man has a symmetrical body. It is very common for one testicle to be sightly larger and hang lower than the other in the scrotum.

ANATOMY INVOLVED: The testicle is the egg mass within the scrotum. It should be smooth and feel like the fleshy part of your hand just lower than your thumb. You should be able to move it freely within the scrotum; it should not be attached to the walls. Along the back of the testis (the side that normally faces your back) is the epididymis. This is a spongy-feeling structure that may have a slightly irregular consistency. Attached to the epididymis is the vas deferens. This is within the blood vessels that supply the testes.

HOW TO PROCEED MANUALLY: A man should examine each testis gently with both hands. Place the index and middle fingers below one testis and the thumbs on top—and then gently roll the testis between the fingers and thumbs to discover any lumps, thickening, or change in consistency. Most lumps are about the size of a pea, having a circular or an irregular shape. They are usually hard and found on the sides or front of the testis. If your entire testicle becomes enlarged, or hard like concrete, have it checked out. Be sure to repeat this process on both testes. Men should also learn to recognize the feel of the epididymis, so it won't be confused with a lump. Palpate the epididymis attached to the lower rear portion of the testes. Feel for a circular lump; if a lump exists, it may be painful. Now look at yourself in the mirror and check again for any abnormal enlargement.

WHY: Again, a lump might be, but isn't necessarily, the symptom of testicular cancer. But if you notice *any abnormality* during your monthly TSE, play it safe and report it to your physician immediately. Early discovery and treatment greatly increase the chance of cure.

REACTIONS: Use the space provided to respond to the following questions.

1. Do you know anyone in your extended family who has had testicular cancer? If yes, describe their age at diagnosis and the circumstances.

2. On a scale of 1 to 100 (with 100 being the highest score), how confident are you that you will correctly perform the TSE each month? (Place an "X" on the scale.)

1————————25————————50————————75————————100

Explain your score.

3. If you are a male, how comfortable do you feel performing the TSE? Explain. If you are female how comfortable are you suggesting that those men who are close to you perform the TSE? Explain.

SOURCE: American Cancer Society, Inc.

15 | All About "Kegels"

INTRODUCTION: Both genders have a group of pelvic floor muscles known as the "PC," or pubococcygenus, muscle. This muscle group has the potential to provide sensations of pleasure and release when contracted rhythmically during orgasm. Women and men are beginning to learn about the sexual benefits of having a strong PC muscle, which is similar to other body muscles in that it can be strengthened by exercise.

Men who exercise the "PC" muscle may have stronger and more pleasurable orgasms. Being able to contract and relax these muscles at will has enabled some men to delay ejaculation. Some men may find they need to relax the PC muscle when near orgasm in order to delay ejaculation, while others find just the opposite is true. Experimentation is needed to determine if either method works for you.

Women who exercise the PC muscle may find themselves experiencing stronger orgasms. Some women who perhaps were previously unable to have orgasms have become orgasmic after strengthening this muscle group. The contracting and relaxing of the muscle can be used by the woman to arouse herself during love play. When used during intercourse, her partner will be able to feel the contractions and may be stimulated by them.

The PC muscle also functions as a support for internal organs. The urinary and anal openings in both sexes are surrounded by this muscle group. The vagina is also supported by the PC muscle; therefore, women with weakened PC muscles may have poorly supported pelvic organs. One possible result is the spilling of urine unexpectedly. Exercises to strengthen the PC muscle may alleviate and even cure many cases of mild to moderate stress incontinence. Sometimes a poorly supported uterus, bladder, or rectum will be displaced downward and begin to drop out of position. The uterus, if traumatized or atrophied, is the most likely to prolapse. These problems, if they occur, usually become evident later in life.

Learning to use the PC muscle is not difficult once it has been identified. The following is a set of exercises originally developed by Dr. Arnold Kegel to help women with problems controlling urination. They are designed to strengthen and give voluntary control of the pubococcygenus muscle.

WHY LEARN TO DO KEGEL EXERCISES?

Learning Kegel Exercises:

Can help you to be more aware of sensations in your genital area.

Can increase circulation in the genital area.

May help increase sexual arousal started by other kind(s) of stimulation.

Can be helpful after childbirth to restore muscle tone in the vagina.

May give you voluntary control of the PC muscle.

IDENTIFYING THE PC MUSCLE

Sit on the toilet. Spread your legs apart. See if you can stop the flow of urine without moving your legs. That's your PC muscle, the one that turns the flow on and off. If you don't find it the first time, don't give up; try again the next time you have to urinate.

The Exercises:

1. *Slow Kegels:*

   Tighten the PC muscle as you did to stop the urine. Hold it for a slow count of three. Relax it.

2. *Quick Kegels:*

   Tighten and relax the PC muscle as rapidly as you can.

3. *Pull in—Push out:*

   Pull up the entire pelvic floor as though trying to suck water into your vagina. Then push out or bear down as if trying to push imaginary water out. (This exercise will use a number of abdominal muscles as well as the PC muscle.)

HOW OFTEN

At first do ten of each of these exercises (one set) five times every day. Each week increase the number of times you do each exercise by five (15, 20, 25, etc.). Keep doing five "sets" each day.

You can do these exercises any time during daily activities which don't require a lot of moving around: driving your car, watching television, each time you answer the phone, doing dishes, sitting in school at your desk, or lying in bed.

When you start you will probably notice that the muscle doesn't want to stay "contracted" during "slow" Kegels and that you don't do "quick" Kegels very fast or evenly. Keep at it. In a week or two you will probably notice that you can control it quite well.

Sometimes the muscle will start to feel a little tired. Not surprising. You probably haven't used it very much before. Take a few seconds, rest, and start again.

A good way to check on how you are doing is to insert one or two lubricated fingers into your vagina and feel the muscle contract through the vaginal wall.

Remember to keep breathing naturally and evenly while you are doing your Kegels.

REACTIONS: Use the space provided to respond to the following questions.

1. What have you learned about how Kegel exercises may effect a person's sexuality?

2. On a scale of 1 to 100 (with 100 being the highest level of confidence), how confident are you that you will correctly perform the Kegel exercises on a regular basis? (Place an "X" on the scale.)

1———————25———————50———————75———————100

Explain your rating.

SOURCE: Adapted from "All About Kegels," *Planned Parenthood Sexual Counseling Series*, 1977, by Planned Parenthood of Central and Northern Arizona. Reprinted with permission.

16 The Vulvar Self-Exam

The vulva, the external portion of the female genital area, can be the site of a variety of diseases. Many of these diseases are relatively minor, causing only discomfort and inconvenience. Others, such as cancer, though rare, can have more serious consequences if not treated early.

PURPOSE: This self-exam will provide information as to how to examine the genital area on a regular basis. This will help identify possible problems at an early stage, when treatment is more successful. Women should practice this self-exam on a regular basis. Men should be aware of the exam and encourage the women they know to conduct the self-exam.

THE VULVAR SELF-EXAM

Because so many diseases that can affect the vulva have similar symptoms, it is important to be aware of any unusual changes in the vulvar area. One of the best ways to do this is to examine the vulvar area. This is especially important if you have ever had any disease that affects the vulva.

Performing this exam will help you to be alert to any changes that could signal an infection or other problem. Any symptoms such as itching or discomfort should also be reported to your doctor. If a problem does occur, your chances of catching it at an early stage—when treatment is most successful—are best if you have examined yourself regularly.

Steps to the Exam

1. Wash your hands carefully before you begin. Lie or sit up in a good, strong light with a hand mirror—a magnifying mirror may work best. It may help to prop up your back with pillows, or you can squat or kneel. The important thing is to find a comfortable position in which you can clearly see the vulvar area, perineum, and anus.

2. Gently separate the outer lips of the vulva. Look for any redness, swelling, dark or light spots, blisters, bumps, or unusual signs.

3. Next, separate the inner lips and look carefully at the area between them, as well as the entrance to the vagina.

4. Gently pull back the hood of the clitoris and examine the area under the hood and the tip of the clitoris.

5. Be sure also to inspect the area around the urethra, the perineum, the anus, the outside of the labia majora, and the mons veneris.

Types of Vulvar Disease

To find the cause of a particular vulvar disease, your doctor will ask questions about any symptoms you are having, and a number of tests may be performed. One of the most common and important of these tests is a *biopsy,* which is the removal of a small piece of tissue for examination under a microscope. Some possible types of disease are:

Contact dermatitis

Vestibulitis

Vulvodynia

Vulvar dystrophies

Paget disease of the vulva

Vulvar intraepithelial neoplasia

Invasive cancer

Melanoma

Genital warts

Herpes

Systemic diseases

Contact Dermatitis

Contact dermatitis is caused by chemical irritation of the skin of the vulva. This irritation may be caused by a variety of sources, such as:

Perfumed or dyed toilet tissue or underwear

Soaps, particularly those with strong deodorants

Talcum powder

Feminine hygiene sprays

Deodorant pads

Spermicidal foams, creams, and jellies

Rubber products such as those used in condoms

Poison ivy or similar plants

Insect bites or stings

Other irritants such as nail polish or nail polish remover that do not normally have contact with the vulva

The chief symptoms of contact dermatitis are redness and itching. A doctor may diagnose it after examining the vulvar area and asking about the substances that come in contact with the vulva.

Treatment usually consists of getting rid of the source of the irritation and, if the dermatitis is severe, applying a steroid cream, such as hydrocortisone cream, three times daily. You might also be told to apply cool compresses to relieve the itching.

To avoid getting contact dermatitis again, a woman is advised to stay away from whatever substance caused it in the first place, as well as those listed above. If panty hose are worn, they should have a cotton crotch, and white cotton underpants should be worn. It may also be helpful to rinse out underwear after it has been washed with detergent. Finally, hands should always be washed before touching the genital area to prevent the transfer of irritating substances.

Finally . . .

Vulvar diseases cover a wide range of disorders. Without proper treatment, some can develop into serious conditions. It's important to take note of an unusual changes in the genital area. The vulvar self-exam, performed on a regular basis, can help alert a woman to problems, especially if there is a history of vulvar disease or discomfort.

Because so many diseases of the vulva have similar symptoms, a woman should report any changes in the genital area to the doctor. See the doctor for regular checkups, and do not hesitate to make an appointment between routine visits if there are any of the symptoms discussed in this self-exam.

REACTIONS: Use the space provided to respond to the following questions.

1. Women: On a scale of 1 to 100 (with 100 being the highest level), how confident are you in being able to perform the vulvar self-exam effectively on a monthly basis?
   (Please make an "X" on the scale.)

   1————————25————————50————————75————————-100
   Explain your rating.

2. Men: What is your part in preventing the diseases of the vulva for your partner? Explain.

SOURCE: Adapted from American College of Obstetricians and Gynecologists, "Diseases of the Vulva," ACOG Patient Education Pamphlet #88 © 1990, Washington, DC 20024-2188.

17 How Much Do You Know About UTIs and Candidiasis?

PURPOSE: Research indicates that in general, women find it necessary to use the medical care system more often than men. Urinary tract infections (UTIs) and vaginal yeast infections are just two of the reasons women need to visit a health care professional. This quiz discusses symptoms, causes, treatment, and some possible preventive measures.

DIRECTIONS: Read each of the following statements and write either TRUE or FALSE in the space provided.

1. UTIs are more common in women than men. _____

2. UTIs may cause a frequent need to urinate. _____

3. Some cases of UTIs may include blood in the urine. _____

4. With UTIs there may be upper abdominal pain. _____

5. A conclusive diagnosis of UTI is made by x-ray. _____

6. The cause of a UTI is usually not known. _____

7. Not much can be done by women to prevent UTIs. _____

8. Yeast infections are caused by the Candida albicans fungus. _____

9. Yeast infections develop when the fungus is introduced to the vagina through sexual activity. _____

10. Vinegar and water douches, anti-itching creams and feminine hygiene sprays are useful in treating yeast infections. _____

11. A woman who suspects she has a yeast infection should purchase an over-the-counter medication and use it rather than making a visit to a health care professional for diagnosis. _____

12. A symptom of vaginal yeast infections is a white clumpy discharge. _____

13. Treatment of vaginal yeast infections is usually by oral medication. _____

14. The use of birth control pills, antibiotics, or a diet high in carbohydrates are factors in the development of yeast infections. _____

SCORING:

1. TRUE. UTIs are more common in women than men. Some women have more than one infection during their lifetime.

2. TRUE. An intense and frequent need to urinate are symptoms of a UTI.

3. TRUE. Blood or pus in the urine is a frequent symptom of UTI.

4. FALSE. There may be lower pelvic pain with UTIs.

5. FALSE. Diagnosis of UTI is usually made by laboratory analysis of a urine sample.

6. FALSE. Bacteria from the rectum or vagina or infectious agents from a partner's sexual organs is usually the cause of UTIs. An improperly fitting diaphragm can prevent a woman from totally voiding and cause a bladder infection. Repeatedly delaying urination and stretching the bladder muscle also results in losing the ability to void the bladder completely.

7. FALSE. There are a few precautions women can take to prevent UTIs. For example, careful wiping from front to back after both urination and bowel movements can help prevent bacteria from getting close to the urethra. Wash the genitals and rectal area each day. Urinate as soon as the urge to urinate is felt. Both partners should wash their hands before sexual contact. Women should use sterile lubricating jelly when vaginal lubrication is not enough. It may also be helpful to drink plenty of fluids high in vitamin C, but not those fluids irritating to the bladder like coffee, tea, and alcohol. Keep the vaginal area dry. Wear 100% cotton underwear.

8. TRUE. Yeast infections, moniliasis, and candidiasis are all names for infections caused by the fungus Candida albicans.

9. FALSE. The fungus causing yeast infections is normally present in the vagina of women. It is also normally present in the mouth and large intestines of both men and women. This fungus causes problems only when conditions change in the vagina to allow an abundance of organisms to flourish.

10. FALSE. Vinegar and water douches, anti-itching creams and feminine hygiene sprays do not cure a yeast infection—they only mask the symptoms.

11. FALSE. If a women is confident the infection is a yeast infection, then over-the-counter medications may be purchased and used. Indications that it is truly a yeast infection may include use of oral antibiotics and recurring yeast infections that have been confirmed by a physician. On the other hand, women who have any doubt as to the type of infection should see their health care practitioner. Many of the different types of vaginal infections have some similar symptoms. Indications that should lead a woman to a medical examination for confirmation are pregnancy, multiple sex partners, high fever, pain in lower abdomen, back, or either shoulder, or a vaginal discharge that smells bad.

12. TRUE. A woman may notice that she has a white discharge that looks similar to cottage cheese. A yellow/green discharge that smells "fishy" may indicate something other than a yeast infection.

13. FALSE. Treatment usually consists of vaginal cream or suppositories used over a period of seven days. Symptoms may disappear in a few days, but treatment should continue. Some of these vaginal creams or suppositories can now be purchased over the counter.

14. TRUE. Some factors known to lead to this condition are the use of oral antibiotics, use of birth control pills, diabetes, pregnancy, and high carbohydrate diet. Other factors include immunosuppressant drugs, exposure to occupational and environmental chemicals, and various kinds of hormonal changes.

REACTIONS: Use the space provided to respond to the following questions.

1. What are the preventive measures for UTIs? Candidiasis?

2. By what information provided in this exercise were you surprised? If you were surprised, explain why.

18 Female Menopause

P URPOSE: Misconceptions exist in our society regarding menopause, or "the change of life," and hysterectomies. This knowledge quiz may answer questions you might have. The hysterectomy is the most common major gynecological procedure and is sometimes performed unnecessarily. As more people gain a better understanding of the process of menopause we may begin to see more positive attitudes regarding this process.

DIRECTIONS: Read each statement or question carefully. Then respond by writing TRUE or FALSE in the space provided at the right.

1. The average age for menopause in the United States is between forty-five and fifty-five. _____

2. Estrogen replacement therapy is recommended for most women after menopause. _____

3. The psychological block to sexual activity after a hysterectomy is often a result of "old wives' tales." _____

4. When menopause takes place, ovulation and menstruation may not necessarily stop at the same time. _____

5. There is a standard set of menopausal symptoms that are universal to all women experiencing the change of life. _____

6. The majority of women have severe menopausal symptoms. _____

7. Many women have reservations about hysterectomies because they feel their female sexuality will be negatively affected. _____

8. When fibroid tumors of the uterus develop, a hysterectomy is necessary. _____

9. Hysterectomy is the only solution for chronic vaginal bleeding. _____

10. Hot flashes during menopause or after a hysterectomy are psychologically caused. _____

11. A woman in the midst of menopause can expect her sex drive to change dramatically. _____

12. If a woman's physician suggests she have a hysterectomy she should seek a second opinion. _____

13. Osteoporosis and heart disease are hereditary — nothing can be done to minimize their effects on the body. _____

14. Women who have had their ovaries and/or uterus surgically removed are exempt from menopausal symptoms. _____

SCORING:

1. TRUE. Menopause is a natural process of declining ovarian function culminating in the end of menstruation, usually between the ages of forty-five and fifty-five.

2. FALSE. Current research suggests that menopausal women should carefully weigh the pros and cons of estrogen replacement therapy (ERT). ERT can have many positive benefits in relieving menopause symptoms and providing protection against osteoporosis. However, there is an increase in risk of endometrial cancer with the use of ERT. In addition, women who have uterine cancer or estrogen dependent breast cancer are not considered candidates for estrogen replacement therapy.

3. TRUE. Many "old wives' tales" or myths surround the entire process of menstruation and menopause. Many of these myths are related to the psychosocial effects of aging in American culture and may cause a disinterest in or psychological block to sexual activity.

4. TRUE. The end of the menstrual cycle does not necessarily signal the end of ovarian release of egg cells. Therefore, many physicians do not consider menopause complete until a woman has gone one or two years without a period.

5. FALSE. Some symptoms are shared by many women, but women are all individuals and symptoms may vary in nature and degree.

6. FALSE. Only about 10 percent of women have severe menopausal symptoms of any kind.

7. TRUE. Some women feel their sexuality will be negatively affected by a hysterectomy, yet there is no physical reason why this should occur. If a lack of sexual desire or feeling of loss of femininity occurs, it is more likely to be a result of "old wives' tales," cultural conditioning, or psychological blocks.

8. FALSE. According to the American College of Obstetricians and Gynecologists, a hysterectomy may be performed when the uterus grows beyond the size of a twelve-week pregnancy from a fibroid tumor. A myomectomy is a procedure in which the tumors are removed but the uterus remains intact. This may accomplish the aim of a hysterectomy, yet leave the woman fertile.

9. FALSE. Chronic vaginal bleeding may be treated by a D&C; therefore, this is one option to consider before having a hysterectomy. A "D&C" is performed by opening the cervix (dilation) and scraping the uterine wall (curettage) with a sterile loop-shaped instrument.

10. FALSE. Hot flashes are believed to be caused by decreasing blood estrogen levels. These reduced blood estrogen levels may affect the hypothalamus, causing the blood vessels to dilate. Blood rushes to the expanded vessels close to the skin surface and causes a sudden sensation of heat for possibly a few seconds or minutes.

11. FALSE. Only if she thinks so. Remember, the brain is the most important sex organ.

12. TRUE. Studies have shown that many hysterectomies are being done unnecessarily. Therefore, any woman who is informed she should have a hysterectomy should seek a second opinion. There may be an alternate form of therapy.

13. FALSE. Regular exercise and adequate calcium consumption minimize the loss of bone mass causing osteoporosis. Regular exercise and a reduced fat diet may help counteract hereditary tendencies toward heart disease.

14. FALSE. Removal of the ovaries from premenopausal women causes an immediate "surgical menopause" that is often more severe than natural. Removal of the uterus only can cause onset of symptoms earlier than if the uterus were intact.

INTERPRETATION: Count your total number of correct responses.

Total Correct = _____

If you had **11 or more** correct responses you have a good knowledge base regarding menopause and hysterectomies. A score of **7–10** correct responses would indicate a fair working knowledge of these topics, but you should seek additional information before making any decisions regarding either issue. A score of **4 or fewer** correct responses represents a poor level of knowledge about menopause and hysterectomies. You definitely need to seek further information regarding these issues prior to making any related decisions.

REACTIONS: Use the space provided to respond to the following questions.

1. What have you learned about female menopause?

2. If you are a female would you choose to use ERT? If you are male, would you want your wife to use ERT?

3. Have you learned anything new about hysterectomies? Explain.

4. Which of these statements and their correct responses surprised you? Explain.

19 | Senior Sexuality

PURPOSE: During the younger years of life the idea of altered sexual expression seems quite unimportant. However, during those later years, most individuals begin to notice some changes occurring in their sexual response. The confusion and frustration that many aging people feel is a result of the notion that old age is a sexless time of life. This exercise is designed to help you understand and eventually accept the nature of these sexual changes.

DIRECTIONS: Read each statement carefully and respond in the space provided by writing either TRUE or FALSE.

1. Most women lose their urge for sex after menopause. _____

2. Men go through a significant hormonal "change of life." _____

3. It is not healthy for persons to engage in sexual intercourse after the age of sixty-five. _____

4. Most people are unable to have a climax after age sixty-five. _____

5. People who have had a heart attack should not engage in sexual activity. _____

6. Good nutrition and good health provide the foundation for good sexual function. _____

7. Sex is a natural, healthy function for people, regardless of their age. _____

8. All men who have prostate surgery will be unable to have sexual intercourse. _____

9. Many women will notice some dryness in their vagina after the menopause, but this can be medically treated. _____

10. In the later years, it may take longer to get an erection, and more touching and stroking of the penis will be helpful. _____

11. If a man cannot get a good erection, he cannot ejaculate. _____

12. After age 50, men are more likely than women to masturbate. _____

13. Many people in their later years find that various aphrodisiacs prove effective. _____

14. People in their later years need touching and cuddling, whether they are having sexual intercourse or not. _____

15. As a man ages, he may notice that it takes longer to achieve an erection and ejaculate again once he has already ejaculated. _____

16. Hypertension poses little threat to sexual activity. _____

17. The physical aging of their mates is a turnoff for most couples.   _____

18. Fear of another heart attack can lead to impotence in a heart patient.   _____

19. Prolonged sexual abstinence can increase "drying up" and shrinkage of a postmenopausal woman's vagina.   _____

20. Women inevitably lose their sexual appetites after a hysterectomy.   _____

21. Sexual intercourse is the aerobic equivalent of walking three blocks or climbing two-and-a-half flights of stairs.   _____

22. A routine sex life between longtime sexual partners becomes less stimulating as time goes by.   _____

SCORING:

1. FALSE. Women who lose their urge for sex after menopause do so for more psychological than physical reasons. A woman's erotic and orgasmic capacities continue after menopause, and many women feel increased freedom with regard to their sexuality because the fear of pregnancy is eliminated.

2. FALSE. As men age, their hormone production decreases sightly, yet there is no definite marking of a time when men go through a change of life. If a definite change of life does occur, it is probably related more to psychological than physical factors.

3. FALSE Most people are able to engage in sexual intercourse after the age of sixty-five. If they do not engage in sexual intercourse after sixty-five, it is because they have chosen not to, they have no suitable partner, or perhaps they take medication that affects sexual function.

4. FALSE. The climax may not be as intensive after age sixty-five, yet a person is able to have a pleasurable orgasm.

5. FALSE. In most cases persons who have had a heart attack are able to return to their normal sexual activity in approximately six weeks. Cardiac rehabilitation programs use the guideline if the person can walk 200 feet and can walk up two flights of stairs without feeling any abnormal heart beats or dizziness, he or she can return to normal sexual activity.

6. TRUE. Good nutrition promotes good health. When older people are in poor health, they may not be interested in sexual activity. Maintenance of a good physical activity program through the years may enhance sexual activity in addition to contributing to one's general health.

7. TRUE. Sex is a natural healthy function for adults of any age. However, an older person may develop physical problems or take medication that alters his or her sexual function.

8. FALSE. Prostate surgery may result in sterility, but the sexual ability does not diminish.

9. TRUE. As estrogen production in the woman's body decreases, there is some dryness and thinning of the vaginal wall. This can be treated with estrogen supplements (which are controversial), or estrogen creams or lubricants may be used to aid in intercourse.

10. TRUE. As a man ages it may take longer to get an erection. The direct stimulation by touching and stroking of the man's penis may be helpful.

11. FALSE. A man can ejaculate even with a flaccid penis. As a man ages, the penis may not become as erect, yet the man may still ejaculate.

12. FALSE. Women are just as likely to masturbate as men, in particular, for women for whom there are fewer male partners available. Self-arousal can provide sexual pleasure and may lead to orgasm, relieving tension that may build up in the absence of intercourse. It may also help to maintain physical responsiveness when intercourse is not possible, by maintaining the shape of the vagina in women and the production of semen in men.

13. FALSE. The best and only true aphrodisiacs are those psychological factors that influence an individual's attitude toward sexual behavior.

14. TRUE. Touching and cuddling, any human contact, is needed at any age. People in their later years who are not as interested in sexual intercourse may find that touching and cuddling are more important than sexual intercourse or orgasm.

15. TRUE. A normal process of aging seems to increase the refractory period for a man. In other words, it may take longer for a man to get another erection once he has ejaculated in a lovemaking situation.

16. TRUE. Hypertension does not in itself usually interfere with a person's sexual life. Sexual activity may elevate blood pressure slightly and accelerate heartbeat, but not enough to spark a heart attack. When hypertension does interfere with sexual functioning, the problem is more likely the hypertension medication than the disease itself.

17. FALSE. In a loving relationship, the lover's body at any age often has a beauty that is timeless. Sexual activity is based at least in part upon one's attractiveness to another person. Who a person is will be more than enough to "turn on" someone deeply cared for. The expression of sexual feelings is a communication between people, not just two bodies.

18. TRUE. Fear and anxiety about having another heart attack can keep a person from enjoying sexual activity. But subsequent attacks due to sexual intercourse virtually never occur. The common procedure after a heart attack is to limit all physical exertion, allowing the damaged heart muscle time to heal. That resting period should gradually give way to increased physical activity under a physician's supervision. When a heart attack does occur, the cause is almost always the "psychic" stress of having sex with a new partner, sometimes a new partner and sometimes in unfamiliar surroundings or circumstances.

19. TRUE. For postmenopausal women, stopping sexual activity for a few months can result in some shrinking, narrowing, and rigidity of the vagina. Estrogen reduction thins the walls and reduces lubrication, resulting in possible painful intercourse. Patience is advised. The vagina may stretch back to normal with use or assisted by oral or vaginal estrogen preparations (combines with progesterone). A water-soluble lubricant such as K-Y Jelly can alleviate some of the discomfort.

20. FALSE. Removal of uterus and/or ovaries does not guarantee loss of sexual appetite. Some women report an increase in sexual desire and pleasure especially if they were experiencing pain from enlarged uterine or ovarian tumors. Some women do report adverse physical and emotional reactions such as depression, feelings of loss, or aging in general can reduce desire. One reason could be the sudden drop of hormone levels following hysterectomy. If total (uterus and ovaries), estrogen-replacement therapy (ERT) is sometimes recommended by a physician, which can alleviate hot flashes and vaginal dryness, but will not effect diminished libido.

21. TRUE. Sexual activity is an excellent form of light exercise. Virtually all body systems are involved in sexual performance, although for most people it is too limited to substitute for continued adequate aerobic exercise. Sexual activity, nevertheless, is a component to sexual physical health, which, in turn, contributes to total health.

22. FALSE. The mystery in sex may lessen over a lifetime, but the pleasure derived from the experience need not lessen. Having a routine allows a person the satisfaction of anticipating the event as well as the actual enjoyment when it does take place. What some people consider "boredom" with their partners often masks other problems, such as anger or apathy. At any age, it is possible to add some variety to lovemaking. The important thing is to enjoy the relationship itself, and enjoyment of sex will follow.

REACTIONS: Respond to the following questions in the space provided.

1. What myth(s) about senior sexuality did you believe prior to taking this quiz?

2. Were you surprised by any of these items? Which one(s)? Explain.

SECTION III | CONTRACEPTION AND ABORTION

Research, technology, and education have made significant advances in contraception. There are a variety of reasons for an individual's use of contraceptives. Many of today's women want to space pregnancies at least two years apart knowing the enhanced effectiveness that this brings to their health and that of their babies. Family size for most couples is usually limited to two children. Unmarried persons, as well as couples who risk genetic birth defects, typically wish to avoid pregnancy. Future fertility, spontaneity, more self-actualization for women, and a host of other variables play a role in the contraception decision process. The self-assessment inventories in this section can give you some insight into the decision-making process and the factors that shape your contraception and abortion attitudes and behaviors.

Contraception and Abortion exercises include:

20 Choosing Contraception: Risks versus Benefits

Purpose: Ideally a couple should choose a method of contraception together, and several factors should be considered. However, the couple must first have accurate information about how the various methods work. The following eleven questions are concerns that any couple making a choice about contraception should consider. Use the space after each question to write your response. At the very least these same questions should be carefully considered by women who are sexually active.

1. What method of contraception would we like to use?
   (List one)_____

2. Why would this method be best for our situation?

3. How does this contraceptive prevent pregnancy?

4. For what reasons does this contraceptive sometimes not prevent a pregnancy? What is the actual failure rate?

5. What are the benefits of this method for us compared to some other method?

6. What are the risks involved with use of this method (side effects, future fertility, medical contraindications)?

7. How well does this method fit our pattern of sexual activity?

8. Do the benefits of this method outweigh the risks? Why or why not?

9. Is there a risk of being exposed to HIV (the AIDS virus) or other sexually transmitted disease? If so, will this method decrease the risk of exposure?

10. What is the cost of this method? Can we/I afford it?

11. Will we both feel comfortable with this method and use it consistently?

EVALUATION: Most individuals will have some concerns regarding every method of birth control. However, if you have more than a few concerns or responded "NO" to question number 11, then you may wish to go back to question 1 and consider another form of contraception.

APPLICATION: Read each case study carefully. Imagine yourself in the place of the people involved. Answer each of the questions listed above as you decide which method of contraception is the best for the people involved in the situation described.

CASE STUDY 1

George and Lucille are both young professional people who are dating each other frequently and also dating others. They are both highly involved in establishing themselves professionally, and their careers are the main focus of their attention. Their relationship has slowly evolved to a point where sexual intercourse sometimes occurs. However, both have stated they have no desire to have children for many years, if ever. Lucille, at twenty-nine, is constantly on the go and tends to be somewhat forgetful and unreliable where her personal life is concerned. In addition, she has had a history of very irregular menstrual cycles since menarche. George, at twenty-eight, is a very successful salesman, yet he often acts on impulse without much forethought. After discussing possible methods of contraception, Lucille and George have agreed on the method best for their situation.

REACTIONS: Now write your responses to the eleven questions, considering George and Lucille's situation.

CASE STUDY 2

Sally and Sam are both college students who are primarily dating each other and occasionally dating others. They are not ready for a marriage commitment as they feel they are too young. Sally is nineteen and Sam is twenty. They have developed a sexual relationship that includes intercourse, though not every week. Because Sally has had a mild case of acne, she does not have a good self-concept. As a result she tends to be easily persuaded to have intercourse, thinking that she does not want to lose Sam. Sam is not very concerned about contraception since he fails to realize fully what Sally's becoming pregnant could mean. They did briefly talk about contraception and agree on the best method for their situation.

REACTIONS: Now write your response to the eleven questions, considering Sally and Sam's situation.

CASE STUDY 3

Marie and Philip are a married couple in their midtwenties with one three-year-old child. They married and had their child one year later. Philip, a sheet metal worker, was raised in a large Roman Catholic family, so he places personal value on a large family. Marie was also raised in a Roman Catholic family but she would prefer to have only two or three children. She is concerned about the cost of raising a larger family since Philip wants her to stay home with their child. Marie works only part-time evenings as a nurse's aide. Marie has high blood pressure and has tried several times, unsuccessfully, to quit smoking.

REACTIONS: Now write your response to the eleven questions, considering Marie and Philip's situation.

22 | Birth Control Pill: Fact or Myth?

PURPOSE. Do you know all there is to know about birth control pills? Since the pills are one of the more effective birth control methods, they are often the method of choice by young sexually active couples. Use these questions to test your knowledge.

DIRECTIONS. Indicate whether each statement is true or false by writing a "T" or "F" in the blank to the right. There is one column for you to write your responses and another column in which your partner can respond.

	Partner	You
1. The actual effectiveness rate for the pill is 97 percent, yet it is even more effective for women who remember to take it every day.	____	____
2. Except for abstinence or sterilization, the pill is the contraceptive method with the lowest failure rate.	____	____
3. The risk of stroke, blood clots, and heart attack associated with the pill occurs in women age 35 or more who smoke.	____	____
4. Women who take the pill have more regular menstrual cycles with fewer cramps.	____	____
5. Amenorrhea occurs with some women who take birth control pills.	____	____
6. Birth control pills prevent pregnancy by suppressing ovulation.	____	____
7. Women who use the pill are at increased risk of getting pelvic inflammatory disease and are at risk for more severe forms of PID.	____	____
8. Birth control pills become effective in preventing pregnancy after the first day of use.	____	____
9. Women may gain a few pounds when taking the birth control pill.	____	____
10. Some antibiotics and pain medications can decrease the effectiveness of the pill.	____	____
11. Diarrhea and vomiting can decrease the effectiveness of the pill.	____	____
12. Birth control pills may have some protective effect against cancer of the ovaries.	____	____
13. Women using the pill do not need a second or backup birth control method.	____	____

Partner   You

14. Headaches are a side effect some women experience while taking the birth control pill.   _____   _____

15. Oral contraceptives provide protection against STDs including HIV.   _____   _____

16. Early pill warning signs include severe abdominal pain, severe headache, and severe leg pain.   _____   _____

17. Birth control pills have no medical use other than to prevent pregnancy.   _____   _____

18. Birth control pills may be used throughout the reproductive years by most women.   _____   _____

SCORING. The statements above do not begin to cover all the issues related to birth control pills. For further information consult your health care provider. The answers to these questions are as follows:

1. TRUE. The percent of women experiencing an accidental pregnancy within the first year of use is 3 percent; however this drops to 0.1 to 0.5 percent with perfect use.

2. TRUE. When comparing actual and perfect-use percentages of forms of birth control, the birth control pill has the highest overall effectiveness rate. However, sterilization and abstinence both have higher effectiveness rates.

3. TRUE. Cigarette smoking is the most important risk factor for vascular disease in women. Women over the age 35 who smoke are at risk for increased risk of heart attack, stroke, and blood clotting problems. Women of any age who take the pill should be advised not to smoke.

4. TRUE. Pills tend to decrease menstrual cramps and pain. Some women consider this the most desirable effect of the pill.

5. TRUE. In most cases the menstrual bleeding continues to take place; however, as the strength of pills has fallen over the years, missed periods have become more common. The cyclic build up of the uterine lining is almost always less in women using pills than in women experiencing natural cycles.

6. TRUE. Since most prescribed birth control pills are a combination of estrogen and progesterone the hormones effect the body in several ways. Ovulation is inhibited partly by suppression of FSH and LH. The pituitary gland does not release hormones to stimulate the ovary.

7. FALSE. The pill seems to have a protective effect against pelvic inflammatory disease, a major cause of female infertility. Moreover, pill users are less likely to develop severe forms of PID than are users of the other contraceptives. This may occur in part because a woman's cervical mucus becomes scanty, discouraging the ascent of sperm from the vagina into the uterine cavity and into the fallopian tubes. Bacteria attached to the sperm enter the upper genital track through the ascent of the sperm.

8. FALSE. Birth control pills become effective in preventing pregnancy after one full cycle of use. During the first cycle, a back-up method of birth control should be used to ensure protection against pregnancy.

9. TRUE. Weight gain during pill use can be related to fluid retention due to the hormones in the oral contraceptive and usually occurs in the month or so after initiating pills. Weight gain due to increased subcutaneous fat is noted after several months on the pills. Rarely do the pills cause a weight gain of 10 to 20 pounds or more and nearly as many women gain weight as lose weight while taking the pill.

10. TRUE. Hormonal contraceptives affect many organ systems and the metabolism of birth control pills is altered by a number of drugs a woman may be taking. Be sure to discuss with your health care provider the possible interactions of any drugs with your birth control pills. Use a backup contraceptive during times you are taking such medications. Even taking doses of vitamin C may alter the effectiveness of the pill.

11. TRUE. If you have diarrhea or vomiting, a backup method of birth control should be used until the next period. Start using the backup method the first day either the vomiting or diarrhea occurs.

12. TRUE. Pills make women less likely to develop three types of cancer: ovarian, endometrial, and choriocarcinoma.

13. FALSE. Every woman should have a backup method of birth control for use at any of the following times: during the first pack of pills, when she runs out of pills, forgets to swallow pills, experiences a serious warning sign and discontinues pill use, wants protection from STDs, or has repeated episodes of spotting.

14. TRUE. Migraine headaches are a side effect some women experience while taking the birth control pill. If this occurs, the pill use should be discontinued.

15. FALSE. Oral contraceptives do not provide protection against HIV and other STDs. For this reason, use of condoms on a regular basis in addition to the birth control pill is recommended until a woman becomes committed to a long-term, mutually faithful relationship.

16. TRUE. Early pill warning signs include severe abdominal pain, severe headache, severe leg pain, eye problems, speech problems, chest pain, shortness of breath, and cough. Should any of the symptoms appear, a woman should see her health care provider.

17. FALSE. The birth control pill has many beneficial effects in addition to that of pregnancy prevention. Some women use birth control pills exclusively for their beneficial effects on menstrual pain that has been resistant to therapy with prostaglandin inhibitors. Pills suppress androgens and are a standard part of therapy for hirsutism. Some women notice a reduction in premenstrual symptoms such as anxiety, depression, headaches, and fluid retention.

18. TRUE. The combined oral contraceptive pill is a safe and effective method of birth control for most women throughout their reproductive years as long as they do not have a specific reason to avoid the pills. Age is not a reason to avoid the use of pills.

INTERPRETATION: Count your total number of correct responses.

Total Correct = _____

If you had 13 or more correct responses you have a good knowledge base regarding the birth control pill. A score of 7–12 correct responses would indicate a fair working knowledge of the pill, but you should seek additional information before relying on this method of birth control. A score of 6 or fewer correct responses represents a poor level of oral contraceptive knowledge and you definitely need to seek further information regarding the birth control pill before choosing this method.

REACTIONS: Write your responses to the following questions in the space provided.

1. What did you learn about birth control pills? Explain briefly.

2. What other questions do you have about the use of birth control pills?

23 Condom Sense: Test Your IQ

PURPOSE: Condoms continue to provide good protection against a number of STDs and unwanted pregnancy. This quiz will help you determine what you know and don't know about condoms.

DIRECTIONS: Read each question carefully and place your answer in the space provided. Have a friend or partner take this test in the second column. Compare your answers and discuss your reactions.

Friend You

____ ____ 1. Condoms that are prelubricated provide sufficient lubrication, even when lovemaking lasts a long time.
   a. True
   b. False

____ ____ 2. A new type of condom made of polyurethane has been found to be more comfortable than latex.
   a. True
   b. False

____ ____ 3. It is okay for a male to keep a condom in his wallet, as long as the condom hasn't exceeded the expiration date.
   a. True
   b. False

____ ____ 4. It's safe for a male to wait until he's lost his erection before withdrawing, as long as he holds the condom near the base of the penis to prevent spills.
   a. True
   b. False

Friend You

____ ____ 5. With condoms, one size fits all.
       a. True
       b. False

____ ____ 6. How effective is latex condom use for preventing the spread of HIV through sexual intercourse?
       a. Highly effective
       b. Somewhat effective
       c. Not at all effective
       d. Not sure

____ ____ 7. The female condom is:
       a. Just like the male condom only larger
       b. A polyurethane sheath with rings at both ends
       c. Like a diaphragm only wider and longer
       d. Similar to the cervical cap, yet longer and wider

____ ____ 8. The female condom is made from the same materials as male condoms.
       a. True
       b. False

____ ____ 9. Condom development and use is somewhat recent, beginning at the outset of World War I.
       a. True
       b. False

____ ____ 10. The pores in natural membrane condoms are larger than the virus that causes HIV infection.
       a. True
       b. False

Friend You

____ ____ 11. Condoms are 100 percent effective in preventing STDs.
                a. True
                b. False

____ ____ 12. In general, as the number of sexual partners increases, condom use also increases.
                a. True
                b. False

____ ____ 13. Despite the widespread understanding that HIV infection is transmitted sexually, most sexually active Americans at risk for acquiring HIV infection have intercourse without using condoms.
                a. True
                b. False

____ ____ 14. Sexual communication between partners and enjoyment of intercourse with condoms seem to be the only significant correlates of condom use.
                a. True
                b. False

____ ____ 15. As a medical device, latex condoms are rigorously tested to ensure that they meet federal and industry quality assurance standards.
                a. True
                b. False

____ ____ 16. When condoms fail, it is usually due to condom quality.
                a. True
                b. False

Friend   You

____ ____ 17. Condoms containing the spermicide nonoxynol-9 provide additional protection against STDs and vaginal infections.

    a. Always

    b. Sometimes

    c. Never

____ ____ 18. A dab of lubricant on the tip of the penis or inside the condom greatly increases the sensation for the male.

    a. True

    b. False

____ ____ 19. A pharmacist may request evidence that persons are over eighteen years of age before selling them condoms.

    a. True

    b. False

____ ____ 20. Condoms enable many men to "last longer" before they ejaculate during sexual intercourse.

    a. True

    b. False

____ ____ 21. Women now purchase 40 percent of condoms sold.

    a. True

    b. False

____ ____ 22. What should you do if a condom breaks after your partner has ejaculated?

    a. I don't know

    b. Write in your answer _____

    _____

    _____

SCORING: The statements above do not begin to cover all the important aspects of condom use and the prevention of STDs and unwanted pregnancy. For further information consult your physician or the U.S. Centers for Disease Control and Prevention in Atlanta, Georgia. The answers to questions 1–18 are as follows:

1. b. FALSE. The prelubricant added to condoms may only last for several minutes. A women's natural vaginal lubrication and the duration of sexual intercourse will determine if additional lubrication is needed. Always have access to a recommended lubricant and always use a water-based lubricant for anal sex. **Insufficient lubrication is a major cause of condoms breaking.** You should always have a water-based lubricant such as K-Y Jelly handy. Remember: A water-soluble lubricant is not necessarily water-based; the label should say the product is safe for use on latex.

2. a. TRUE. A new type of condom made of polyurethane is thinner, stronger, and more heat-sensitive, as well as being more comfortable than latex.

3. b. FALSE. It's okay to keep a condom in a wallet, but experts suggest for no longer than 30 days. After about a month, the condom should be discarded regardless of the expiration date. A man's body heat may cause the latex to deteriorate.

4. b. FALSE. Soon after ejaculation the erection begins to lose its size and firmness. Don't savor the moment until your partner loses his erection. The penis should be withdrawn promptly after ejaculation, while holding the condom at the base to prevent spillage.

5. b. FALSE. Condom sizes vary by brand and style. Condoms can stretch, but comfort and fit are important factors. Because many condom failures are due to condoms being too big or too small, males are encouraged to try different types to find the ones that fit them best prior to a lovemaking situation with a partner. Women should not hesitate to carry a variety of condoms. It is better to use a condom of wrong size than none at all.

6. a. HIGHLY EFFECTIVE. Studies of sexually active persons show that correct and consistent use of latex condoms is highly effective in preventing HIV infection and other STDs including gonorrhea, chlamydia, genital ulcers, pelvic inflammatory disease, hepatitis B virus (HBV), and herpes simplex virus infection.

7. b. The female condom has a flexible plastic ring at the closed end of a polyurethane sheath which fits loosely against the cervix, similar to how a diaphragm would fit. Another ring at the base of the sheath encircles the labial area. Although the female condom fits the contours of the vagina, the penis moves freely inside the sheath. The female condom covers some of the vulva and may provide more protection from some STDs than would traditional condoms. Some users report awkward sounds made by the female condom during sexual intercourse.

8. b. FALSE. At the present time female condoms are made of latex and polyurethane. There are no sheep membrane female condoms currently available.

9. b. FALSE. Condoms have a long history. A penile sheath was used in Japan during the early 1500s and in 1564 an Italian anatomist, Fallopius, described a penile sheath made of linen. Mass production of inexpensive condoms began after the development of vulcanized rubber in the 1840s. Condoms are one of the most popular contraceptive methods used in the United States and, next to the pill, the most commonly used by college-aged adults.

10. a. TRUE. The pores in natural membrane condoms are large enough to permit HIV and some other sexually transmitted diseases to pass through. Latex and polyurethane are better protection against all STDs.

11. b. FALSE. Condoms are not 100 percent effective in preventing STDs and pregnancy. A high degree of individual compliance is required for condoms to be effective. Inconsistent and incorrect use of condoms provides an unacceptably low rate of protection.

12. b. FALSE. Unfortunately, studies on sexually active adolescents and adults have found that those with multiple partners are less likely than those with one partner to use condoms consistently. The burden of negotiating condom use with many partners has been suggested as the major barrier. In addition, decisions regarding condom use may be complicated by strategies for pregnancy prevention. In Philadelphia and Baltimore, women who had undergone surgical sterilization were less likely than nonsterilized women to report condom use. It is possible that if a woman is protected against pregnancy (via another method), the motivation of the woman or the man to use a condom may be reduced.

13. a. TRUE. Americans for the most part are not heeding the message. For example, in San Francisco, only 6 percent of heterosexual males with multiple sex partners reported always using condoms; a much higher proportion (48 percent) of gay and bisexual men reported always using a condom. In another study, only about 20 percent of sexually active American women reported that their male partners used condoms. Even among these couples, condom use was inconsistent; only one in five who reported condom use said that they were used at last intercourse.

14. a. TRUE. Research studies have suggested that among heterosexual men and women and among gay and bisexual men in San Francisco, sexual communication between partners and enjoyment of intercourse with condoms were the only statistically significant correlates of condom use. In another study black and Hispanic women were less likely to report condom use by their partners than were white women; national data suggest that there are no significant differences in reports of condom use by partners of black women, non-Hispanic white women, and Hispanic women once social and demographic variables are accounted for. This suggests that poverty and culture are important determinants of condom use.

15. a. TRUE. Every condom manufactured in the United States is tested by manufacturers electronically for defects, including holes or areas of thinning, before it is packaged. The FDA randomly tests condoms produced domestically or imported into the United States to ensure that they meet quality assurance requirements. The standard test used by the FDA is the water-leak test, in which the condom is filled with 300 ml of water,

stretching it to as much as four times its original size. If FDA finds that more than 4 per 1000 condoms leak, the lot is not allowed to be sold.

16. b. FALSE. Most condom breakage is due to incorrect usage rather than poor condom quality. Common reasons for breakage include teeth or fingernail tears; using oil-based lubricants; using old condoms; exposure to heat; reusing condoms; unrolling the condom before putting it on, or leaving air in the tip. There is no indication that condom breakage rates are different for anal or vaginal intercourse.

17. b. SOMETIMES. Nonoxynol-9 can be added protection as a spermicide and can kill the HIV. However, it can also lead to vaginal irritation (especially among frequent users) which can open pathways for HIV and other STDs. The U.S. Centers for Disease Control and Prevention no longer recommends the use of nonoxynol-9.

18. a. TRUE. Most men report that they prefer the sensation of lubricated condoms to that of dry condoms and report that adding a dab of water-based lubricant before rolling on the condom increases the sensation even more.

19. b. FALSE. A Supreme Court decision in 1977 affirms the right of anyone, regardless of age, to purchase condoms.

20. a. TRUE. The fact that a condom may delay ejaculation is an important advantage for young men who are bothered by very quick ejaculation following penetration.

21. a. TRUE. Women buy almost half of the condoms purchased in the United States today. Increasingly, condom manufacturers are targeting women in their marketing strategies.

22. If a condom breaks or slips off during intercourse, contraceptive foam, cream, or jelly should be inserted into the vagina or rectum **immediately.** Infected persons need to avoid reinfection as it increases viral load and can hasten progression to disease. For females, calculate where you are in your menstrual cycle, and if you are at high risk of pregnancy, call your physician immediately to discuss the pros and cons of the morning-after pill. Also, consult a physician if you believe you or your partner are at risk of catching a sexually transmitted disease

INTERPRETATION: Count your total number of correct responses.

Total Correct = _____

If you had **13 or more** correct responses you have "good condom sense" regarding condoms and their effectiveness. A score of **7–12** correct responses would indicate a fair working knowledge of the pill; however you should correct your mistakes on this self-test and seek additional information on condoms. A score of **6 or less** represents a "condom casualty" or a poor level of condom knowledge, the need to correct your mistakes on this self-test, and the need for additional information before using condoms effectively.

REACTIONS: Write your response to the following questions in the space provided.

1. What was the most important piece of information you learned about condoms? Briefly explain.

2. What else did you learn about condoms that you did not know prior to taking this self-test? Briefly explain.

24 Which Contraceptive Method Is Best for You?

PURPOSE: This exercise attempts to match lifestyles with birth control methods. Whenever you are sexually active, it can assist you and your partner in selecting a method of birth control that you will both feel comfortable using. Both partners in the relationship need to respond to the appropriate statements and then read and discuss the scoring at the end.

DIRECTIONS FOR WOMEN: Circle YES or NO for each statement as it applies to you and your current situation.

1. You and your partner have a set routine for sex.	Yes No
2. You prefer a method of birth control with no bother.	Yes No
3. You have a good memory.	Yes No
4. You have heavy, crampy periods.	Yes No
5. You are a risk taker.	Yes No
6. You have sexual intercourse frequently.	Yes No
7. You need a birth control method right away.	Yes No
8. You are comfortable with your own sexuality.	Yes No
9. You dislike doctors and pelvic exams.	Yes No
10. You are concerned about sexually transmitted diseases.	Yes No
11. You are forgetful.	Yes No
12. You have a cooperative partner.	Yes No
13. You have patience and a sense of humor.	Yes No
14. You have sexual intercourse infrequently.	Yes No
15. You have a lot of privacy.	Yes No
16. You are a nursing mother.	Yes No
17. You feel strongly against the use of unnatural forms of birth control.	Yes No
18. It is very important you do not become pregnant now.	Yes No
19. You have more than one sexual partner.	Yes No

SCORING FOR WOMEN: If you answered YES to the numbers listed below, the birth control method listed on the right may be the best choice for you at this time:

1, 3, 4, 6, and 18	Birth control pills
1, 2, 5, 6, 11, and 18	IUD or Depo-Provera injections
3, 7, 8, 9, 12 ,13 ,14, and 19	Contraceptive spermicide
7, 9, 10, 12, 14, and 16	Male condom with female spermicide
8, 12, 13, 14, 15, and 16	Diaphragm or cervical cap with jelly
3, 8, 12, 13, 14, and 17	Natural family planning methods
9, 10, 12, 13, and 18	Abstinence
7, 8, 10, and 19	Female condom

DIRECTIONS FOR MEN: Circle YES or NO for each statement as it applies to you and your current situation.

1. You and your partner have a set routine for sex.	Yes	No
2. You prefer a method of birth control with no bother.	Yes	No
3. You are a risk taker.	Yes	No
4. You have sexual intercourse frequently.	Yes	No
5. You need a birth control method right away.	Yes	No
6. You are comfortable with your own sexuality.	Yes	No
7. You are concerned about sexually transmitted diseases.	Yes	No
8. You have a cooperative partner.	Yes	No
9. You have premature ejaculation.	Yes	No
10. You have patience and a sense of humor.	Yes	No
11. You have sexual intercourse infrequently.	Yes	No
12. You have a lot of privacy.	Yes	No
13. You have strong personal beliefs against unnatural forms of birth control.	Yes	No
14. It is very important your partner does not become pregnant now.	Yes	No
15. You have more than one sexual partner.	Yes	No

SCORING FOR MEN: If you answered YES to the numbers listed on the left, then the birth control method listed on the right may be the best one for you at this time:

1, 2, 3, 4, 8, and 14	Birth control pill
1, 2, 3, 4, 8, and 14	IUD or Depo-Provera injections
5, 8, 10, 11, and 12	Contraceptive spermicide
1, 5, 6, 7, 8, 9, 10, 11, and 15	Male condoms
6, 8, 10, 11, and 12	Diaphragm or cervical cap with jelly
6, 8, 10, 11, and 13	Natural family planning methods
6, 7, 8, 10, and 14	Abstinence
1, 5, 7, 8, 10, 11, and 15	Female condom

SCORING AS PARTNERS: When you have both completed the questions, discuss your individual responses and scores. If your responses indicate there is more than one method of birth control for you, remember you are likely to use various methods of birth control at different times in your life. Also, do not hesitate to try a combination of methods to increase effectiveness (for example, condoms plus foam, diaphragms or cervical caps plus condoms, IUD plus condoms).

If your responses do not suggest any of these birth control methods, consider abstinence. This is still the only method 100 percent effective and a very real alternative. While this score is NOT ABSOLUTE, it should assist you and your partner in consulting with your physician or other health care provider to make the best choice.

APPLICATION: Which form of birth control do you feel would be the best choice for you and your partner at the present time? (Abstinence is an acceptable choice.)

Is that the same as what the questionnaire indicated? If not, are there additional factors that you need to consider? If so what are they?

25 | Contraception in Carolina?

Various life situations call for considerable thought and decision-making skills. Some life experiences are casual and some are of extreme importance to effective living. Every decision we make is based upon a complex matrix of beliefs, attitudes, values, and intentions.

PURPOSE: Your reactions to the events and people in the following story will reveal some aspects of your beliefs, attitudes, and values in comparison with those of a friend or partner.

Susan came from a small town in South Carolina where her widowed father was an evangelical Christian minister. He raised her very strictly, and it was only with great reluctance that he allowed her to come to the University of South Carolina in Columbia to pursue her college education. He feared that the big city would corrupt her morals. As she boarded the bus, he warned her, "If I ever find out that you've been fooling around with boys or using drugs or alcohol, I'll cut you off from all financial support and never let you enter our home again."

Susan had always obeyed her father and intended to do so while at college. She did stay away from drugs and alcohol, but in October she began dating Larry, a fellow student in her religion class. By December they were sleeping together. Upon her return to school from the holiday vacation, she discovered that she was pregnant. Since neither her father nor the private church-affiliated schools she attended had ever mentioned birth control, she had not taken the proper precautions.

Larry did not want to get married and Susan knew that when her father came to take her home in May, the pregnancy would be obvious. Panic-stricken, she decided to have an abortion. She went to one of the agencies that advertised help for unwanted pregnancies in the University Student Newspaper. At the agency she learned that an abortion would cost her $500. Knowing that she could not earn this sum of money in time, she asked Larry for a loan. "I'm sorry, but I don't have that kind of money," he replied. "Besides, you should have been more careful."

She then asked her best friend Allison for the money. "I don't approve of abortions," she replied. "I can't lend you the money to destroy life."

In desperation, Susan approached a woman on the custodial staff who was rumored to be an ex-prostitute. "Sure, I've got a concoction that will make you miscarry—no charge," said the woman.

After taking the mixture, Susan did miscarry; unfortunately in the process she hemorrhaged severely and died.

DIRECTIONS: Rank each of these people according to their responsibility for Susan's death. Identify the least responsible as No. 6 to the most responsible as being No. 1.

YOU	YOUR PARTNER/FRIEND
____ Susan	____ Susan
____ Her father	____ Her father
____ Larry	____ Larry
____ Agency head	____ Agency head
____ Allison	____ Allison
____ Woman custodian	____ Woman custodian

REACTIONS: After completing the rankings of the people in the story, use the space below to briefly explain why YOU ranked each of the characters in their respective positions.

Most Responsible   1. _____   Why did you rank this person first?

2. _____   Why did you rank this person second?

3. _____   Why did you rank this person third?

4. _____   Why did you rank this person fourth?

5. _____ Why did you rank this person fifth?

Least Responsible 6. _____ Why did you rank this person sixth?

Now take some time to compare your results with your friend or partner. Discuss the similarities and differences among your reactions to the different people in the story.

26 | Abortion Attitude Scale

Directions: Below are thirty statements about induced abortion. In the space beside each statement, place the letter that represents your feeling:

A = I Strongly Agree with the statement.

B = I Tend to Agree with the statement but have some reservations.

C = I am Undecided with the statement.

D = I Tend to Disagree with the statement but have some reservations.

E = I Strongly Disagree with the statement.

_____ 1. Abortion penalizes the unborn for the mother's mistake.

_____ 2. Abortion places human life at a very low point on the scale of values.

_____ 3. A woman's desire to have an abortion should be considered sufficient reason to do so.

_____ 4. I approve of the legalization of abortions so that a woman can obtain one with proper medical attention.

_____ 5. Abortion ought to be prohibited because it is an unnatural act.

_____ 6. Having an abortion is not something that one should be ashamed of.

_____ 7. Abortion is a threat to society.

_____ 8. Abortion is the destruction of one life to serve the convenience of another.

_____ 9. A woman should have no regrets if she eliminates the burden of an unwanted child with an abortion.

_____ 10. The unborn [fetus] should be legally protected against abortion since the fetus cannot protect itself.

_____ 11. Abortion should be an alternative when there is contraceptive failure.

_____ 12. Abortions should be allowed since the unborn is only a potential human being and not an actual human being.

_____ 13. Any person who has an abortion is probably selfish and unconcerned about others.

_____ 14. Abortion should be available as a method of improving community socioeconomic conditions.

_____ 15. Many more people would favor abortion if they knew more about it.

_____ 16. A woman should have an illegitimate child rather than an abortion.

_____ 17. Liberalization of abortion laws should be viewed as a positive step.

_____ 18. Abortion should be illegal, for the Fourteenth Amendment to the Constitution holds that no state shall "deprive any person of life, liberty or property without due process of law."

_____ 19. The unborn should never be aborted no matter how detrimental the possible effects on the family.

_____ 20. The social evils involved in forcing a pregnant woman to have a child are worse than any evils in destroying the unborn.

_____ 21. Decency forbids having an abortion.

_____ 22. A pregnancy that is not wanted and not planned for should not be considered a pregnancy but merely a condition for which there is a medical cure—abortion.

_____ 23. Abortion is the equivalent of murder.

_____ 24. Easily accessible abortions will probably cause people to become unconcerned and careless with their contraceptive practices.

_____ 25. Abortion ought to be considered a legitimate health measure.

_____ 26. The unborn ought to have the same rights as the potential mother.

_____ 27. Any outlawing of abortion is oppressive to women.

_____ 28. Abortion should be accepted as a method of population control.

_____ 29. Abortion violates the fundamental right to life.

_____ 30. If a woman feels that a child might ruin her life, she should have an abortion.

SCORING: To score this exercise, use the following point values for items 3, 4, 6, 9, 11, 12, 14, 15, 17, 20, 22, 25, 27, 28, and 30 only:

A = 5   B = 4   C = 3   D = 2   E = 1

For items 1, 2, 5, 7, 8, 10, 13, 16, 18, 19, 21, 23, 24, 26, and 29, use the following scale:

A = 1   B = 2   C = 3   D = 4   E = 5

Now sum your points; the score should fall between 30 and 150. A score of 30 represents an unfavorable attitude toward abortion, a score of 90 represents a neutral attitude, and a score of 150 represents a favorable attitude toward the freedom to choose abortion.

REACTIONS: Use the space provided to respond to the following questions.

1. Do you feel your score coincides with your attitudes toward abortion? Why or why not?

2. How did this attitude scale assist you in evaluating your position on this issue?

SOURCE: Stanley Snergroff, "Abortion Attitude Scale." *Family Life* Publications. Saluda, NC. Reprinted by permission.

27 | Abortion Situations: You Be the Judge

PURPOSE: This scale is designed to help you examine your degree of favorability toward abortion by responding to the situations listed below.

DIRECTIONS: Read each statement carefully and circle your response to each situation according to the key below.

SF = Strongly Favorable	F = Favorable	U = Undecided	O = Opposed	SO = Strongly Opposed

1. The woman becomes pregnant as a result of rape by a stranger. SF F U O SO

2. The woman becomes pregnant as a result of rape by a date partner. SF F U O SO

3. The woman becomes pregnant as a result of incest. SF F U O SO

4. A 13-year-old becomes pregnant due to sexual abuse by a family member. SF F U O SO

5. Pregnant woman is an unmarried 13-year-old. SF F U O SO

6. Pregnant woman is an unmarried 19-year-old. SF F U O SO

7. Pregnant woman is an unmarried 25-year-old. SF F U O SO

8. Pregnancy would be dangerous to the woman's physical health. SF F U O SO

9. Pregnancy would be harmful to the woman's mental health. SF F U O SO

10. Woman feels that she cannot economically afford the baby. SF F U O SO

11. Woman feels that she cannot afford another baby. SF F U O SO

12. Woman simply does not want a baby at the present time. SF F U O SO

13. Woman simply does not want another baby at the present time. SF F U O SO

14. Woman wants an abortion; her partner disapproves. SF F U O SO

15. Woman wants an abortion; her husband disapproves. SF F U O SO

16. Woman had German measles, and fears the baby may have been harmed. SF F U O SO

17. Woman learns that the baby has a strong possibility of having Down's syndrome. SF F U O SO

18. Woman learns that the baby has a strong possibility of having neural tube defects. SF F U O SO

19. Woman learns that the baby has a strong possibility of having chromosomal defects. SF F U O SO

20. Woman learns that the baby probably has fetal alcohol syndrome. SF F U O SO

21. Woman is a regular crack cocaine user. SF F U O SO

22. Woman is HIV positive. SF F U O SO

23. Pregnant woman is 35 years old and has smoked heavily since her teen years. SF F U O SO

24. Government funds should be used for abortions for woman who can't afford them. SF F U O SO

25. The father's signature should be required before an abortion can be done. SF F U O SO

26. No circumstance ever justifies abortion. SF F U O SO

Scoring: Use the key below to score your responses. Calculate your total score and place it in the space provided.

For items 1–24:
Strongly Favorable = 5
Favorable = 4
Undecided = 3
Opposed = 2
Strongly Opposed = 1

For items 25 and 26:
Strongly Favorable = 1
Favorable = 2
Undecided = 3
Opposed = 4
Strongly Opposed = 5

Total Score: _____

Interpretation: The range of scores on this scale is 26-130. If you scored between **26 and 60**, this indicates a low favorability toward abortion. A score of **61-95** represents a moderate level of favorability toward abortion and if you scored between **96-130** you would have a high level of favorability toward abortion and can justify abortions for most situations.

REACTIONS: Use the space provided to respond to the following questions.

1. Do you feel that your score is an accurate indication of your level of favorability toward abortion? Why or why not.

2. Are there any particular situations in this exercise that are of particular concern to you? Explain why.

28 | Shared Responsibility: Perceptions on Abortion

PURPOSE: This exercise is designed to help you examine your perceptions in regard to shared responsibility and abortion.

DIRECTIONS: Read each statement carefully and mark your responses in the space provided to the left of each situation according to the key below.

KEY:

CI = **Completely Involved** — Male should be informed of pregnancy and abortion should take place only with his complete agreement.

GI = **Greatly Involved** — Male should be informed of pregnancy and should support emotionally and financially the female's decision for abortion even if he disagrees.

MI = **Moderately Involved** — Male should be informed of pregnancy and support the decision for abortion financially even if he disagrees.

SI = **Slightly Involved** — Male should be informed of pregnancy but should not support decision for abortion financially unless he decides.

NI = **No Involvement** — Male should not be informed and the female should take full responsibility for the abortion decision.

_____ 1. Jack and Diane are high school seniors and have been exclusively dating for about two years. Both plan to go to different colleges next year. Diane is 8 weeks pregnant and she decides to have an abortion. To what degree to you feel Jack should be involved in this process?

_____ 2. Marie and Michael are college seniors engaged to be married in May soon after graduation. In March, Marie's pregnancy test is positive (she's 6 weeks pregnant). To what degree do you feel that Michael should be involved?

_____ 3. Lisa and Elvis have been married for three years and have two children. Lisa has recently learned she is pregnant. At the same time Lisa learns she has breast cancer. To stop the cancer, Lisa needs treatment right away. Lisa decides to choose an abortion rather than leave her cancer untreated. To what extent should Elvis be involved in this process?

_____ 4. Luke and Laura have been married for one year when she gets pregnant. They have been struggling financially and neither one can seem to keep a full-time job. Laura makes the decision to have an abortion. To what extent should Luke be involved?

_____ 5. Rachel and Zack are both first-year graduate students and have been dating exclusively for about a year. They have no real plans for marriage, but the subject has been discussed. She is 4 weeks pregnant and decides to have an abortion. To what extent should Zack be involved in this process?

_____ 6. Mark and Mary are high school graduates and have been dating steadily for about two and one-half years. Mary becomes pregnant. Mark wants to get married. Susan wants to have an abortion. To what extent should Mark be involved?

_____ 7. Latrice and William are in the process of a divorce. They were married for three years and now Latrice is pregnant. She decides to have an abortion. To what extent should William be involved?

_____ 8. Three months ago after a somewhat casual date with Roger, Jeanine's pregnancy test is positive. Jeanine and Roger have not "dated" again, yet they see each other socially on campus and at parties. Jeanine decides to have an abortion. To what extent should Roger be involved in this situation?

_____ 9. Doug and Denise have been dating about a year. Doug's behavior has been erratic at times and Denise suspects a drug or alcohol problem but is not sure. Doug has been reliable most of the time and treated Denise with respect when they are together. Denise becomes pregnant and decides to get an abortion. To what degree should Doug be involved in this situation?

_____ 10. Patti and Dale have started dating again after breaking off their engagement about six months ago. Patti is pregnant and decides to have an abortion. To what extent should Dale be involved?

SCORING: Use the key below to score your responses to each situation. Calculate your total score and place it in the space provided.

For items 1–10:　　　　CI—Completely Involved = 5

　　　　　　　　　　　GI—Greatly Involved　　 = 4

　　　　　　　　　　　MI—Moderately Involved = 3

　　　　　　　　　　　SI—Slightly Involved　　 = 2

　　　　　　　　　　　NI—No Involvement　　　= 1

Total Score = _____

INTERPRETATION: The range of scores on this exercise is 10–50. If you scored between **10 and 23** you have a negative attitude toward involvement of the male partner in abortion decision making. A score of **24–37** would suggest that you have a moderate attitude toward male involvement and a score of **38–50** would suggest that you have a positive attitude toward the male partner's involvement in the abortion decision-making process.

REACTIONS: Use the space provided to respond to the following questions.

1. Do you feel that your score accurately reflects your attitude toward the male partner's involvement in the abortion decision-making process? Why or why not?

2. Are there any particular situations in this exercise that are of particular concern to you? Explain why?

29 | Issues in Human Sexuality: Paying for Abortions

S hould the government pay for abortions?

DIRECTIONS: Read each paragraph below carefully, making sure you clearly understand both sides of the issue before you write your reactions.

Those who believe life begins at conception consider abortion murder. The government, they argue, should not be party to murder. In 1977 the efforts of the antiabortion forces resulted in passage of legislation that permits the states to deny payment to physicians or hospitals from Medicaid funds for abortion services. Though the individual states can still use state funds to pay for abortion services, and many do, passage of this legislation has provided encouragement for those advocating a ban on all abortions. These "Pro-Life" people are lobbying for a constitutional amendment outlawing abortion.

Another group of opponents of federally funded abortions views abortion as genocide. Dr. Mildred Jefferson, an African-American surgeon from Boston and a past president of the national Right to Life organization, believes that a federally funded abortion program is aimed at eliminating the poor, black population in the United States. She contends that "abortion is accomplishing what 200 years of slavery and 300 years of lynching didn't" and points out that 30 percent of all Medicaid-funded abortions were performed on black women.

Proponents of federally funded abortion argue that although wealthy women will have the money and be able to find a physician for abortions, poor women will not. Without government assistance poor women are likely to obtain inferior abortion services or even attempt to abort themselves. The dangers of quack abortionists and self-induced abortion were demonstrated vividly in the years prior to legalization of abortions. Many women suffered serious complications or even died. The "Pro-Choice" groups argue further that women throughout history have terminated unwanted pregnancies and will continue to do so. Poor women need government assistance to obtain safe, reputable care.

REACTIONS: Imagine you are a Supreme Court judge and must rule on the issue. Justify and explain your ruling.

SOURCE: George B. Dintiman and Jerrold S. Greenberg, *Health Through Discovery.* © 1983, Addison-Wesley Publishing Company, Inc., Reading, MA, p. 332. Reprinted with permission.

SECTION IV

PREGNANCY AND CHILDBIRTH

One of the most important decisions you will make in your lifetime is whether or not to impregnate or become pregnant. Pregnancy and childbirth are unique experiences for both the woman and her partner, especially if he is involved throughout the entire process. A variety of considerations with regard to preparation for pregnancy, birthplace, and birthing alternatives are now available. Pregnancy and childbirth are changing in contemporary American society. The future aspects of reproduction also play a role in the society of today and tomorrow. The exercises in this section are designed to provoke some thought and provide some insight into pregnancy and childbirth.

Pregnancy and Childbirth exercises include:

30. Pregnancy and Fertility: Test Your Knowledge
31. Childbirth: Test Your Knowledge
32. Infertility Treatment Options
33. Reproduction: Future Aspects

30 | Pregnancy and Fertility: Test Your Knowledge

PURPOSE: Human gestation is a process consisting of a series of events that take place with awe-inspiring precision in the vast majority of pregnancies. The fertilization process that occurs before pregnancy is equally as inspiring and precise. But how does it all come about? We know where we come from, but how do we get here?

DIRECTIONS: Read each statement or question carefully to determine your correct response. Write the letter of the correct response or responses in the blank to the left of the question. For some items there may be more than one correct response.

_____ 1. Fertilization of the ovum usually takes place in the:
   a. Fallopian tube
   b. Ovary
   c. Cervix
   d. Uterus

_____ 2. After being released from the ovary, the ovum is capable of being fertilized for about:
   a. Twelve hours
   b. Twelve to twenty-four hours
   c. Thirty-six to seventy-two hours
   d. One week

_____ 3. How long is it before the fertilized egg attaches to the wall of the uterus?
   a. One day
   b. Three days
   c. Five days
   d. Seven days

____ 4. Most spontaneous abortions occur due to:

   a. Psychological trauma

   b. Physiological trauma

   c. Prematurity of the fetus

   d. The conceptus being defective

____ 5. Pregnancy tests involve a check for the presence of what hormone in the blood or in the urine?

   a. Estrogen

   b. Progesterone

   c. Corpus luteum

   d. Chorionic gonadotropin

____ 6. Two functions of the placenta are:

   a. Transferring nutrients from mother to fetus and eliminating wastes from the fetus

   b. Secreting amniotic fluid and protecting the fetus

   c. Storing nutrients and oxygen for the fetus

   d. Protecting the fetus and initiating parturition

____ 7. The placenta also:

   a. Screens out substances that may be harmful to the fetus

   b. Secretes hormones that help to maintain the pregnancy

   c. Regulates the fetal heartbeat

   d. Protects the fetus

____ 8. The placenta is formed by the:

   a. Fertilized egg

   b. Uterus

   c. Ovum

   d. Fallopian tube

____ 9. The condition known as ectopic pregnancy occurs when a fertilized ovum adheres to the:

   a. Cervix

   b. Ovary

   c. Fallopian tube

   d. Vagina

_____ 10. How many arteries and veins does the umbilical cord contain?

    a. One artery and one vein

    b. Two arteries and one vein

    c. Two arteries and two veins

    d. Hundreds of small arteries and veins

_____ 11. The fetus floats in amniotic fluid to:

    a. Aid in muscle development

    b. Absorb oxygen from the fluid

    c. Cushion it from jolts

    d. Absorb nutrients from the fluid

_____ 12. Amniocentesis is used primarily for:

    a. Detecting birth defects such as sickle-cell trait and Down's syndrome

    b. Detecting sex-linked diseases such as muscular dystrophy

    c. Determining the sex of the child

    d. Checking the developmental stage of the child

_____ 13. What happens to the amnion before birth?

    a. It is expelled from the uterus intact at birth.

    b. It breaks, releasing the fluid before the baby is born.

    c. It degenerates slowly in the last few weeks of pregnancy.

    d. It is absorbed by the uterus in the last few weeks of pregnancy.

_____ 14. The baby's sex is determined by the:

    a. Wishes of the parents

    b. Ovum

    c. Sperm

    d. Fallopian tubes

_____ 15. The heart and brain of the embryo begin to develop during the:

    a. First week after fertilization

    b. First week after implantation

    c. Third week after fertilization

    d. First month after fertilization

____ 16. All the major organs systems are present in the fetus by the end of the:

    a. Third month

    b. Fifth month

    c. Sixth month

    d. Seventh month

____ 17. A husband and wife, both under the age of thirty, have been trying to achieve pregnancy for six months. Assuming their physical exams are normal, what coital frequency would be advisable?

    a. Daily

    b. Whenever desired

    c. Abstaining until the predicted time of ovulation

    d. Alternate days (three to four times per week)

____ 18. Which of the following coital positions will increase the possibility of pregnancy the most?

    a. Male superior

    b. Female superior

    c. Side to side

    d. Position does not matter

____ 19. Coital timing for increasing the possibility of pregnancy must take into account:

    a. Sperm viability and depletion

    b. Cervical mucus receptivity

    c. Day of ovulation and ovum life span

    d. All of the above

____ 20. When evaluation for fertility takes place, the problems of infertility:

    a. Can usually be traced to the woman

    b. Can usually be traced to the man

    c. Can usually be traced to the couple together

    d. Can usually be traced to one of the partners

____ 21. Fetal movement is usually first experienced in the _____ trimester.
   a. First
   b. Second
   c. Third
   d. Birth

____ 22. Drugs used by a mother that may affect the fetus include:
   a. Alcohol
   b. Antibiotics
   c. Steroids
   d. All of the above

____ 23. Which of the following problems is **least likely** to cause female fertility problems?
   a. A Cervical mucus plug that contains antibodies against men's sperm
   b. Scar tissue in the fallopian tubes
   c. Toxemia
   d. Endometriosis

____ 24. Which of the following would be **least likely** to cause male fertility?
   a. The presence of a varicocele
   b. Undescended testes
   c. Sexually transmitted diseases
   d. Contracting mumps during adulthood

____ 25. Which of the following problems would be **least likely** to cause female fertility problems?
   a. Being under emotional stress
   b. Smoking cigarettes
   c. Severe vitamin deficiencies
   d. Being overweight

____ 26. Most causes of male infertility are related to abnormalities in sperm _____ and number.
   a. Motility
   b. Size
   c. Shape
   d. Viscosity

____ 27. The _____ measures the rise in LH in urine prior to ovulation.

    a. Mucus method test

    b. Ovulation-predictor test

    c. Rhythm method

    d. Body-temperature method

____ 28. Sensitive blood tests for HCG can detect pregnancy _____ after conception.

    a. Twenty-four hours

    b. Five days

    c. Ten days

    d. Three weeks

____ 29. By the end of the _____, the gender of the fetus can be distinguished.

    a. First trimester

    b. Second trimester

    c. Third trimester

    d. First month

____ 30. Chorionic villus sampling may be beneficial for women with a:

    a. Previous child with Down's syndrome

    b. History of drug and alcohol abuse

    c. Mental disorder

    d. Severe vitamin deficiency

SCORING:

1.   a. The egg is fertilized in the Fallopian tube, then descends into the uterus.

2.   b. Although the ovum has to be fertilized within twelve to twenty-four hours, the sperm may live for several days, increasing the chance of fertilization.

3.   d. The fertilized egg takes about three days to travel down the Fallopian tube to the uterus and then another three or four days for the fertilized egg to attach itself to the uterine wall.

4.   d. Studies indicate most spontaneous abortions occur because the conceptus was defective. It is estimated that 10 percent of all pregnancies end in spontaneous abortion. Since very early spontaneous abortions may not be detected, the true incidence may be closer to 20 percent or more.

5. d. Chorionic gonadotropin is a hormone produced by the developing ovum that is present in the blood and urine of a pregnant woman.

6. a. The placenta is composed of tiny blood vessels for the exchange of substances between the blood of the fetus and the mother. Nutrients and oxygen transfuse from the mother's blood to the fetus, and fetal wastes pass into the mother's bloodstream.

7. b. Estrogen, progesterone, and other hormones are secreted by the placenta.

8. a. When the fertilized egg begins dividing, one portion of the sphere of cells eventually forms the placenta.

9. c. The condition known as ectopic pregnancy occurs when a fertilized ovum adheres to the Fallopian tube or another site outside the uterus. The most common site is the Fallopian tube; therefore it is often called a tubal pregnancy. Without surgical treatment an ectopic pregnancy may ultimately rupture the Fallopian tube.

10. b. Oxygen and nutrients in the vein are carried to the fetus, while the two arteries remove waste products, which include carbon dioxide.

11. a.,c. Amniotic fluid cushions the fetus from jolts; it also maintains a constant temperature in the uterus and allows the fetus to move about, thus aiding in muscle development.

12. a.,b. Amniocentesis is a prenatal diagnostic technique used primarily to detect genetic and chromosomal defects as well as some biochemical disorders. The fluid withdrawn contains cells and other material shed by the fetus.

13. b. During labor the sac ruptures or is broken and amniotic fluid gushes or seeps from the vagina.

14. c. All ova carry the X-chromosome, which is the female chromosome. The sperm cell will carry either an X-chromosome or a Y-chromosome. If an XX combination results from fertilization, the child will be a girl. If an XY combination results, the child will be a boy.

15. c. The first systems to develop in the embryo are the central nervous system and cardiovascular system, at about the third week.

16. b. Though all major organ systems are present, it is somewhat uncommon for a fetus of this age to survive if born prematurely. The organs are not yet fully developed.

17. d. This choice is a coital pattern that takes into account: (1) that relative oligospermia does not develop; (2) that there must be adequate frequency of intercourse; and (3) that couples must not be put under pressure to "perform" on certain days of the cycle.

18. a. With intercourse in this position, when ejaculation occurs, semen will be deposited and remain deep in the vagina. The woman would also want to lie on her back for about thirty minutes following intercourse to allow time for the sperm to pass through the cervical canal.

19. d. The assessment of all these variables is necessary since many couples who experience difficulty in conceiving are normal. Postcoital tests are usually done about two weeks before the next expected period to check for a possible immune reaction of the woman's system to the man's sperm.

20. d. When evaluation for fertility takes place: 40 percent of the problems are related to the woman, 40 percent of the problems are related to the man, and 12 percent of the problems are a result of the couple together; and in 8 percent of the cases no problem is found.

21. b. Fetal movement or "quickening" is usually first experienced in the second trimester, usually around the fourteenth week of pregnancy.

22. d. The pregnant woman must keep in mind that when she takes a drug, it may circulate through the fetus. Drugs that pregnant women should be cautious in using include some antibiotics, alcohol, tobacco, antihistamines, and marijuana. Pregnant women should always check with their provider during pregnancy before using any drugs.

23. c. Toxemia is least likely to cause female fertility problems. Common causes of female infertility include a cervical mucous plug with antibodies against men's sperm, scar tissue in Fallopian tubes as a result of pelvic inflammatory disease from STDs, and endometriosis.

24. b. Undescended teste(s) is not likely to cause male infertility because it is usually corrected before puberty. Contracting mumps as a teen or adult, sexually transmitted diseases, environmental toxins, a varicocele or infections of the vas deferens are possible causes of male infertility.

25. d. Being overweight is not a factor in female infertility. However, failure to ovulate at regular intervals is quite common. This may be caused by a variety of factors including emotional stress, smoking cigarettes, severe vitamin deficiencies, genetic factors, age, and hormone imbalances.

26. a. Most causes of male infertility are related to abnormalities in sperm motility and number. Motility is how vigorously the sperm propel themselves. Motility and number of sperm can be affected by infectious diseases of the reproductive tract.

27. a. The ovulation-predictor test is used to measure the rise in LH in urine prior to ovulation. These tests can be purchased over the counter and used to time intercourse to increase the likelihood of conception. However, if a couple continues to have difficulty conceiving, they should seek assistance of a fertility specialist.

28. c. Sensitive blood tests for HCG can detect pregnancy as early as 10 days after conception. At-home pregnancy urine tests can detect pregnancy very shortly after a missed period, yet those tests are not always accurate.

29. b. By the end of the second trimester, gender of the fetus can be distinguished. External body parts including fingernails, eyebrows, and eyelashes are clearly formed. Future development consists of growth in size and refinement of the features that already exist.

30. a. Chorionic villus sampling (CVS) is a technique for detection of birth defects. CVS may be of benefit when the mother is over 35 years, a parent has a chromosomal defect, or a previous child has Down's syndrome or defects of the spine.

For further information, refer to any current human sexuality text or other reliable source of information.

REACTIONS: Use the space provided to respond to the following questions.

1. For how many questions were your responses correct?

2. For how many questions were your responses incorrect?

3. What amazes you the most about pregnancy?

31 Childbirth: Test Your Knowledge

PURPOSE: This quiz is designed to test your knowledge about the basics of the childbirth process.

DIRECTIONS: Read each statement or question carefully and then determine the best response. Place your response in the space provided to the left of the question.

_____ 1. During the first stage of labor:

  a. Braxton-Hicks contractions occur.

  b. The baby's head "crowns."

  c. An episiotomy is usually performed.

  d. Effacement and dilatation are completed.

_____ 2. The second stage of labor is characterized by:

  a. Delivery of the placenta

  b. Rupture of the amniotic sac

  c. The beginning of cervical dilation

  d. The passage of the infant through the birth canal

_____ 3. The method most commonly used to determine the expected date of birth is:

  a. Subtract 3 months from the first day of the last menstrual period, then add 7 days and finally add 1 year.

  b. Nine months from the date of conception.

  c. Nine months from the first day of the last menstrual cycle.

  d. Count 1 year from the first day of last menstrual cycle and subtract 3 months.

_____ 4. The third stage of childbirth is characterized by:

  a. Delivery of the placenta

  b. Rupture of the amniotic sac

  c. The beginning of cervical dilation

  d. The passage of the infant through the birth canal

____ 5. Colostrum refers to:

    a. The fluid that causes edema

    b. Stretch marks on the abdomen of a pregnant woman

    c. A precursor of mother's milk

    d. The increased blood supply during pregnancy that can cause varicose veins

____ 6. Medication given during childbirth can affect:

    a. The rate of labor

    b. Newborn sucking behavior

    c. Fetal heart rate

    d. All of the above

____ 7. The LeBoyer method of childbirth focuses primarily on:

    a. Education of the parents about the birth process

    b. Assistance from a labor coach

    c. The use of medical advancements during labor and delivery

    d. Reducing the trauma of birth for the infant

____ 8. Which of the following statements is false?

    a. A miscarriage usually means that later pregnancies will be unsuccessful.

    b. The majority of miscarriages occur in the first three months of pregnancy.

    c. Less than 20 percent of pregnancies end in known miscarriage.

    d. Early miscarriages often appear as heavier than usual menstrual flow.

____ 9. Most hospitals now:

    a. Provide water-birthing experiences

    b. Insist on the use of medication at delivery

    c. Offer birthing-room experiences

    d. Will send medical personnel to private homes to facilitate home births on request

____ 10. Which of the following conditions is **not** related to delivery risk?

    a. Toxemia

    b. Placenta previa

    c. Multiple births

    d. Fetal alcohol syndrome

____ 11. Which of the following is not a reason for performing a cesarean section?

    a. To schedule a delivery on a specific day

    b. Fetal distress during labor

    c. Feet or bottom of the baby presenting first

    d. Large fetal head

____ 12. After childbirth, intercourse can usually resume after the _____ has stopped and episiotomy incisions or vaginal tears have healed.

    a. Postpartum discharge

    b. Lochia

    c. Colostrum

    d. Placental secretions

____ 13. Natural childbirth:

    a. Is not really natural if it occurs in a hospital

    b. Excludes the presence of physicians but allows the presence of nurse-midwives

    c. Is always the safest method of delivery

    d. Is designed to help break the woman's fear-tension-pain reaction chain

____ 14. The Lamaze method of birth stresses:

    a. The use of anesthetics during delivery

    b. The alleviation of pain through certain breathing techniques

    c. Birth without violence for the new born child

    d. A squatting position of the mother during delivery

____ 15. The period of time from fertilization to childbirth is the:

    a. Gestation period

    b. Postpartum period

    c. Refractory period

    d. Proliferative period

SCORING:

1. d. During the first stage of labor, effacement and dilation are complete. This includes the transition phase of labor during which the cervix dilates to 10 centimeters.

2. d. The second stage of labor is characterized by the passage of the infant through the birth canal. This stage begins when the cervix is fully dilated and the baby begins to move into the birth canal.

3. a. The most commonly used method of estimating the birthdate is to subtract 3 months from the first day of the last menstrual period, then add 7 days and finally, add 1 year.

4. a. Childbirth is not complete until the placenta is expelled during the third stage of labor.

5. c. Colostrum is a precursor of mother's milk. For the first several days after delivery, a thin amber or yellow fluid is secreted and is believed to give the baby a temporary immunity to infectious diseases.

6. d. Drugs given during childbirth to alleviate pain can slow the labor process as well as the fetal heart rate. Research also indicates that babies born under anesthesia have poor sucking ability.

7. d. The LeBoyer method of childbirth focuses primarily on reducing the trauma of birth for the infant. The delivery room into which the infant is born is quiet and dimly lit. After emerging from the mother, the baby is placed on the mother's abdomen so she can stroke and bond with the child. The umbilical cord is cut after it stops throbbing. The baby is immersed in water that is the approximate temperature of the amniotic sac. Placing the babies on their back is avoided because it is believed the spine should not be stressed.

8. a. One miscarriage rarely means that later pregnancies will be unsuccessful. About 14 to 19 percent of pregnancies end in miscarriage with the majority occurring within the first trimester before a woman even knows she is pregnant.

9. c. Most hospitals now provide birthing rooms with a homelike atmosphere. The birthing room provides families with the opportunity for an emotionally supportive homelike birth with the medical backup of the hospital.

10. d. Fetal alcohol syndrome is not related to a childbirth delivery risk. A few of the major factors that are related to a high risk delivery are toxemia, placenta previa, multiple births, and blood incompatibility between mother and baby.

11. d. To ensure a delivery on a set date is not a valid reason for performing a cesarean section. Cesarean surgery may be recommended in a variety of situations including maternal illness, indications of fetal distress, birth complications like feet or buttocks presented first, and a baby's head that is too large for a vaginal delivery.

12. b. Intercourse can usually resume in about 3 or 4 weeks after the lochia has stopped and episiotomy incisions or vaginal tears have healed. Lochia is a reddish uterine discharge. One of the most important considerations is when intercourse is physically comfortable for the woman.

13. d. Natural childbirth is designed to help break the woman's fear-tension-pain reaction chain. To reduce anxiety and alleviate fears women and their partners are educated about the birth process. In addition, relaxation and breathing techniques are taught.

14. b. The Lamaze method of birth stresses the alleviation of pain through certain breathing techniques. It also emphasizes learning to voluntarily relax abdominal and perineal muscles. This method is now commonly included in prepared childbirth classes.

15. a. The period of time from fertilization to childbirth is called the gestation period.

REACTIONS: Now use the space below to respond to the following questions.

1. For how many questions were your responses correct?

2. What amazes you most about the childbirth process?

3. What did you learn about pregnancy or childbirth from the exercise? Explain.

32 | Infertility Treatment Options

PURPOSE: Every year many married couples who wish to have children find that they are not able to conceive due to a variety of reasons. Whether it is primary or secondary infertility, there are now many options open to couples to increase their chances of fertility. The majority of couples seeking fertility treatments are heterosexual; however, we realize some gay couples are seeking these options as they choose to raise children.

DIRECTIONS: Read each of the following treatments/options for infertile couples and indicate by placing an X on the line whether you think it would be *acceptable for you* if you were to find yourself part of a couple experiencing infertility. To simplify wording, these questions are written from the perspective of the female of the couple. Then if you are married or have a partner, ask your partner to respond.

	Partner	You
1. Adoption: You adopt a child of a race different from your own.	___	___
2. Adoption: You adopt a child through an open adoption arrangement where the child knows his/her birth mother and/or father.	___	___
3. Adoption: You adopt a child of your same race born to another mother and father.	___	___
4. Embryo Transfer: Your egg and your husband's sperm are fertilized in a lab dish and then the embryo is transferred into another woman's uterus. The other woman then carries the baby to term and gives the baby to you and your husband.	___	___
5. Surrogate Motherhood: Another woman's eggs (a surrogate mother) are fertilized by your husband's sperm through artificial insemination. The surrogate carries the baby to term and then gives the baby to you and your husband immediately after birth.	___	___
6. Egg Donors: Another woman donates her eggs to be fertilized by your husband's sperm in a lab dish. Then the zygote is placed in your uterus to implant and be carried to full term.	___	___
7. Gamete Intra-Fallopian Transfer (GIFT): Your eggs and your husband's sperm are placed directly in the Fallopian tube to meet and fertilize. Then the fertilized eggs travel down into the uterus and implant.	___	___

Partner   You

8. Zygote Intra-Fallopian Transfer (ZIFT): This procedure is
   similar to GIFT, but your eggs are exposed to your husband's
   sperm in the lab. Within 24 hours, the zygote is transferred
   to your Fallopian tube.   _____   _____

9. In Vitro Fertilization (IVF): Eggs are surgically removed from
   your body, fertilized in a lab dish, then placed back in your uterus. _____   _____

10. Embryo Freezing: Your eggs that have been surgically removed
    are fertilized with sperm and then frozen as embryos to be
    transferred into the uterus in future ovulation cycles.   _____   _____

11. Artificial Insemination with Donor Sperm: Sperm is placed in
    your vagina or uterus by a medical procedure during your fertile
    time. The donor sperm is from a man other than your husband.   _____   _____

12. Artificial Insemination with Husband's Sperm: Sperm from your
    husband is placed in your vagina or uterus by a medical
    procedure during your fertile time.   _____   _____

13. Hormone Treatments for Men: Men take hormones to stimulate
    sperm production when sperm counts are low.   _____   _____

14. Fertility Drugs for Women: Women take hormones orally or by
    injection to increase stimulation of the ovaries to ovulate. _____   _____

15. Remaining Childless: You as a couple make a decision after
    some fertility testing and treatment to not pursue having children. _____   _____

REMINDER: Couples and physicians alike have varying opinions on fertility procedures. If and when the time comes to determine the best procedure for you, become informed of all risks, benefits, and applicability of the procedure for your particular situation. In the more advanced fertility treatment there are issues such as: What do you do with leftover fertilized eggs? Do you freeze eggs for use later? What if you have multiple eggs that implant? Are you willing to donate eggs to someone else? For further information consult a physician who specializes in fertility.

REACTIONS: Use the space provided to respond to the following questions.

1. Which of the fertility options do you feel most strongly about using and not using? Briefly explain your rationale.

2. Which of the fertility options listed in your response above do you think you might change your opinion about over time? Briefly explain.

33

Reproduction: Future Aspects

DIRECTIONS: If you had the ability to award large sums of money for research on reproduction, rank-order the priorities you would use for funding research proposals (with 1 ranking the highest priority for funding and 17 the least). Include your reason for assigning each rank.

Research Proposal	Rank	Reason
Addicted babies		
Amniocentesis		
Artificial insemination		
Birth defects		
Ectopic pregnancy		
Embryo transplants		
Female contraception		
Genetic engineering		
HIV-positive babies		
Infertility		
Male contraception		
Midwife training		
Miscarriages		
Premature births		
Prenatal nutrition		
Surrogate mothering		
Test-tube babies (in vitro fertilization)		

REACTIONS: Use the space provided to respond to the following questions.

1. Which of the research areas have you changed your attitude about in the last five years? What caused the change?

2. Which of the research areas do you think the general population is likely to place the most emphasis upon in the next five years? Why?

3. Discuss these rankings with your partner or significant other. Upon which issues do you disagree? Are they issues upon which it is possible to "agree to disagree" or do they affect your relationship?

SECTION V

COMMUNICATION AND SEXUAL AROUSAL

Sexual communication can contribute greatly to the satisfaction of an intimate relationship. Talking about sex is a unique kind of communication that presents a variety of challenges. The presence of warmth, caring, and openness in a relationship is no guarantee that the couple has good sexual communication. In addition, even knowledge of effective communication skills is no guarantee that a couple will apply them in a relationship. It is our opinion that effective sexual communication begins with mutual empathy, the underlying knowledge that each partner in a relationship cares for the other and knows that this care is reciprocated. We hope that the inventories and strategies in this section will be helpful.

Communication and Sexual Arousal exercises include:

34 | Do You Know Your Level of Communication?

PURPOSE: This exercise is designed to provide some indication of the level of communication in your relationship with your partner or a close friend.

DIRECTIONS: With one person in mind, respond to each of the following questions by writing YES or NO in the blank to the right.

1. Do you feel that your partner does not understand you? _____

2. Do you know how to dress to please your partner? _____

3. Are you able to give constructive criticism to each other? _____

4. In appropriate places, do you openly show your affection? _____

5. When you disagree, does the same person usually give in? _____

6. Are you able to discuss money matters with each other? _____

7. Are you able to discuss religion and politics without arguing? _____

8. Do you often know what your partner is going to say before he/she says it? _____

9. Are you afraid of your partner? _____

10. Do you know where your partner wants to be in five years? _____

11. Is your sense of humor basically the same as your partner's? _____

12. Do you have the persistent feeling you do not really know each other? _____

13. Would you be able to relate an accurate biography of your partner? _____

14. Do you know your partner's secret fantasy? _____

15. Do you feel you have to avoid discussion of many topics with your partner? _____

16. Does your partner know your biggest flaw? _____

17. Does your partner know what you are most afraid of? _____

18. Do you both take a genuine interest in each other's work? _____

19. Can you judge your partner's mood accurately by watching his/her body language? _____

20. Do you know who your partner's favorite relatives are and why? _____

21. Do you know what it takes to hurt your partner's feelings deeply? _____

22. Do you know the number of children your partner would like to have after getting married? _____

SCORING: Look over your responses and give yourself one point for each YES response for numbers 2, 3, 4, 6, 7, 8, 10, 11, 13, 14, and 16 to 22 and one point for each NO response to 1, 5, 9, 12, and 15.

If you scored:

1–5: This indicates there is little communication between you and your partner. However, you are together, so you must be fulfilling some need through your relationship. Perhaps the two of you simply need to develop better communication.

6–9: Your relationship is lacking in communication but perhaps you are trying to increase the communication.

10–14: There are weak areas in your relationship, but you probably know they exist. Just keep working on the development of open and honest communication.

15–18: You have a great relationship as it is, but you do have your differences. With open communication you are learning to deal with your differences, which will strengthen the relationship.

19–22: You may be in love; at least you have a great understanding of what it takes to make a relationship continue growing and endure.

REACTIONS: Use the space provided to respond to the following questions:

1. Do you feel your score accurately represents your level of communication with the person you have in mind? Why or why not?

2. Do you and/or your partner wish to increase your level of communication? If so, what steps will you take to increase your level of communication?

35 | Strengthening Communication

PURPOSE: This exercise is designed as an opportunity to practice the communication techniques needed for developing a deeper level of intimacy and understanding with another person. Any type of relationship at any contour is enhanced if those involved periodically take a close look together at who they are and where their relationship is going.

DIRECTIONS: This exercise consists of a series of open-ended statements. One person begins by completing the first statement; then the same statement is completed by the other person. Each person has the option to decline or respond to any statement. You are encouraged to expand a statement with further discussion, but only after each person has completed the statement. Be open and accepting of your partner's responses. Talk about feelings you have by using statements that begin with "I." Do not look ahead at questions; it may help to use a sheet of paper to cover the page and uncover questions one at a time. This can be an *excellent opportunity to share information and feelings*. Complete this exercise when you have at least one hour of uninterrupted time together.

STATEMENTS:

1. The first time I saw you I . . .
2. The length of time we have really known each other is . . .
3. Now the type of relationship we have is . . .
4. We are different in that . . .
5. We are alike in that . . .
6. If our relationship were a book, it would be titled . . .
7. A growth experience in our relationship was . . .
8. A part of my past I wish I could share with you is . . .
9. When I am feeling tense in a new situation, I . . .
10. When I introduce you to people I know, I . . .
11. When we are in a social setting together, I feel . . .
12. Our craziest time together was . . .
13. The needs you fulfill in me are . . .
14. Something that always brings you to mind is . . .

Because half this exercise involves active listening, it is advantageous to stop occasionally to check on how well you understand what your partner is saying. After the first person completes a sentence, the second person repeats in his or her own words what the first speaker has just said. The first speaker must be satisfied that he/she has been heard correctly.

15. I feel your friends are . . .
16. I like to be just a follower when . . .
17. The emotion I find most difficult to control is . . .
18. When I think of growing old, I feel . . .
19. When I am alone I usually . . .
20. Your greatest asset is . . .
21. I am proud of you when . . .
22. You have helped me to learn that . . .
23. I am uncertain when . . .
24. I often assume you know that . . .
25. One thing I would never change about you is . . .
26. I am afraid when . . .

NOW: How well are you listening?
      How open and honest have you been?

27. I am disturbed when you . . .
28. I wish I had never . . .
29. A habit of mine I would like to change is . . .
30. If I did not have to worry about money, I would . . .
31. A fantasy I have had about you is . . .
32. Our intellectual discussions . . .
33. Something that is helping us grow closer is . . .
34. Something I avoid discussing with you is . . .
35. One thing I have always wondered about is . . .
36. I would like to be more like you in that . . .
37. I feel inferior to you when . . .
38. I am most ashamed of . . .
39. This experience . . .

NOW: Can you make your partner smile without talking? Try!!

40. I need you when . . .
41. When you are hurt, I . . .

42. I feel you are unfair when . . .

43. When you are quiet, I . . .

44. I became defensive when you . . .

45. The time I was most angry with you was . . .

46. When we disagree . . .

47. I sometimes feel you do not give me a chance to . . .

48. I find that being open with you is . . .

49. One thing I have always wanted to talk more about is . . .

50. I think it would be fun to . . .

51. My idea of a lazy afternoon is . . .

52. I feel most affectionate when . . .

53. The part of my body I am uncomfortable about is . . .

54. My favorite part of my body is . . .

55. What I like most about your body is . . .

56. I like it when you touch me . . .

57. Right now I am feeling . . .

58. Premarital sex is . . .

59. Extramarital sex is . . .

60. I have feelings of jealousy when . . .

61. What I like best about our relationship is . . .

62. In the future, I would like our relationship . . .

63. What I value most in life is . . .

64. In six months I see us . . .

65. In three years I see us . . .

REACTIONS: The real value of this exercise can only be determined by you and your partner. Use the space provided to respond to the following questions.

1. How did you feel about doing this exercise? How did your partner feel?

2. Was it helpful in opening up channels of communication? Why or why not?

3. Did it broaden your understanding of each other? Why or why not?

4. Did this exercise bring you closer together? If so, how? If not, explain.

5. Ideally, your discussion will have gone beyond the statements. You may even have discovered that you now have your own list of topics you wish to discuss further. What are some?

36 Individual Needs: Sharing and Relating

PURPOSE: Many of us do not share enough information about ourselves with those close to us to help them meet our needs. In addition, we are often negligent in recognizing signs of another person's needs or asking what we can do to meet these needs. This exercise is designed to help you improve your sharing and relating.

DIRECTIONS: Choose a person you are close to and respond to the following questions in relation to that person. The person can be a spouse, boy/girl friend, roommate, parent, child, etc.

A. List ten things this person does that please you.

1.   6.

2.   7.

3.   8.

4.   9.

5.   10.

B. List three things you would like this person to do more often. Be *specific* and *positive*. For example, don't say, "Stop being so self-centered and pay more attention to me," which is negative and vague. Instead say, "Listen and respond as I talk about the day's activities and my feelings at dinner every night," which is positive and specific.

1. _____

_____

This happened _____ times in the past week. I consider this:

_____ crucial

_____ important

_____ not too important

2. _____

_____

This happened _____ times in the past week. I consider this:

_____ crucial

_____ important

_____ not too important

3. _____

_____

This happened _____ times in the past week. I consider this:

_____ crucial

_____ important

_____ not too important

C. List three things which this person would like *you* to do more often. Be specific and positive. Discuss this with the other person to get his/her point of view.

1. _____

_____

This happened _____ times in the past week. I consider this:

_____ crucial

_____ important

_____ not too important

2. _____

_____

This happened _____ times in the past week. I consider this:

_____ crucial

_____ important

_____ not too important

3. _____

_____

This happened _____ times in the past week. I consider this:

_____ crucial

_____ important

_____ not too important

D. Ask the person you identified to do the same exercises above, and then share your responses with each other.

REACTIONS: Use the space provided to respond to the following questions.

1. How did you feel about doing this activity?

2. What was your partner or friend's reaction?

3. How do you feel now?

Now complete the following statements.

1. I learned . . .

2. I was surprised that . . .

3. I'm going to . . .

SOURCE: Reprinted from *Health Behaviors* by Rosalind Reed-Flora and Thomas Lang. Copyright © 1982 by West Publishing Company. All rights reserved.

37 | Active Listening Exercise

PURPOSE: The purpose of this exercise is to provide an opportunity for you and a significant other (spouse, partner, brother, sister, parent) to practice your listening skills.

DIRECTION: Find a quiet place where the two of you can talk without interruption. Take a tape recorder with you to tape your conversation. Pick a topic the two of you wish to discuss. This exercise works best if your topic of conversation is a real issue, not something contrived for the activity, so that you can talk for at least 15 minutes. Start the recorder to record your discussion.

Nature of issue _____ How long did you talk? _____

UPON COMPLETION OF DISCUSSION: Read the following paragraphs describing active listening elements.

Active Listening Elements

When communicating, both a talker and a listener are needed. One of the biggest problems in communication is that both people involved want to talk and neither want to really listen. This can be helped by emphasizing **active listening,** which involves attending behavior, acknowledgments, feedback (paraphrasing), door openers, and silence.

Attending behavior indicates nonverbally that you are paying attention to the person. It can be indicated by such things as orienting your body toward the person, maintaining eye contact, and not having distractions available while you are listening (put down the newspaper or turn off the TV while they are talking).

Acknowledgments are any indication that the communication is coming across to you. It can include nodding your head or saying things like "Ah-huh" to let the person know you are listening.

Feedback or paraphrasing are ways of making sure that you really understood what the person said. Essentially, it summarizes the message you think you heard. It may be phrased as a question: "So you're saying that. . . ?" or "You mean that. . . ?" These are good ways to begin feedback or to paraphrase a message. Then the speaker can either verify that you have heard correctly or correct any miscommunication that has occurred, and communication can continue.

Concentrating on giving feedback also reduces the tendency of the listener to try to think up answers or replies to give the speaker when she or he needs to listen.

Door openers are invitations to talk. It can be openers like "Is something bothering you?" or "It seems like you want to talk about something." If the person does not want to talk about anything at the time of the first invitation, a door opener can be given for sometime in the future, "If you want to talk later on, I will be available." This does not close off communication just because the person doesn't want to talk at that time.

Silence also indicates receptiveness to the communication, but it doesn't mean that you can't give acknowledgments like "ah-huh." If you are the speaker, you are not doing a good job of listening.

Now Rewind the Tape: Listen to your discussion while reviewing the elements of active listening. Record with slash marks how many times each element was practiced in the discussion. If you do not feel you or your partner made adequate use of the listening skills, you may wish to repeat the exercise to see if you can improve.

Active Listening Skills Practiced

	You	Partner
Attending behavior (this is nonverbal so you each be the judge of the other)	___	___
Acknowledgments	___	___
Feedback or paraphrasing	___	___
Door openers	___	___
Silence (when appropriate)	___	___

Reactions: Now use the space below to respond to the following questions.

1. How would you evaluate your active listening skills in this discussion? What do you need to do to improve?

2. How would you evaluate your partner's active listening skills in this discussion? What does your partner need to do to improve?

3. Is the discussion you had for the exercise your usual way of listening? Explain why or why not.

4. How did using your active listening skills affect the communication process and/or outcome? Explain.

SOURCE: David A. Gershaw, PhD, Psychology Department, Arizona Western College, and Sandra K. Kammermann, MS, EdS, School of Medicine, University of South Carolina. Copyright © 1996 by Valois, Kammermann, & Associates. All rights reserved. Used with permission of the authors.

38

Delivering Criticism: Now What Do I Say?

PURPOSE: This exercise is designed as an opportunity to practice communication techniques for delivering criticism to a partner or friend.

SITUATION: You can't believe it! You've been waiting for an important business call, and it came. There's only one hitch: Your partner was home at the time—you were out—and your partner's not sure *who* called. If only your partner would be more responsible and write down messages! You can't let it go this time. You're bound and determined to say something. But what?

Now What Do I Say?

DIRECTIONS: Note some possible responses in the spaces provided, and then see the following for some suggestions.

1. _____
_____
_____
_____

2. _____
_____
_____
_____

3. _____
_____
_____
_____

Delivering criticism is tricky. Your goal should be to modify your partner's behavior without arousing extremes of anger or guilt. Consider these guidelines:

1. Be specific to communicate what *behavior* disturbs you. Don't insult your partner's personality. Say something like "Please write down messages for me," —not "You're totally irresponsible."

2. Express dissatisfaction in terms of your own feelings. Say "You know, it *upsets me* when something that's important to me gets lost, or misplaced," —not "*You* never think about anybody but yourself."

3. Keep complaints to the present. Say "This was a very important phone call." It may not be helpful to say "Last summer you didn't write that message from the computer company and as a result I didn't get the job."

4. Phrase the criticism positively, and combine it with a concrete request. Say something like "You know, you're usually very considerate. When I need help, I always feel free to ask for it. Now I'm asking for help when I get a phone call. Will you please write down the message for me?"

REACTIONS: Compare your written responses with the guidelines and decide which is your usual way of delivering criticism. Explain whether or not your approach is usually positive.

SOURCE: Excerpts adapted from S. A. Rathus and J. S. Nevid, *Adjustment and Growth: The Challenges of Life*, 5th ed. Copyright © 1992, Holt, Rinehart & Winston, Inc. Reprinted by permission of the publisher.

39 | Receiving Criticism: Now What Do I Say?

PURPOSE: This exercise is designed as an opportunity to practice communication techniques for receiving criticism from a partner or friend.

Honest criticism is hard to take, particularly from a relative, a friend, an acquaintance, or a stranger. Franklin P. Jones

SITUATION: You're having dinner one evening when your partner surprises you with, "You've got to do something about your hair." You're threatened and peeved, but you stop and think before answering.

Now What Do I Say?

Note some possible responses in the spaces provided, and then see the following for some suggestions.

1. _____
_____
_____
_____

2. _____
_____
_____
_____

3. _____
_____
_____
_____

Although delivering criticism is tricky, taking criticism can be even more difficult. Your objectives should be to learn about your partner's concerns, keep the lines of communication open, and find ways of changing the troublesome behavior. Here are some ideas for responding to "You've got to do something about your hair."

1. When we deliver criticism, it helps to be aware of our motives. In receiving criticism, it helps to be aware of the motives of others. Is your partner's concern limited to your hair, or is this criticism only the opening salvo of a war that's about to erupt? When you're not sure, you can help your partner be specific by asking clarifying questions. For example, "Could you tell me exactly what you mean?" or "My hair?"

2. As with being a good listener in general, you can acknowledge the criticism even if you do not agree with it by saying something like, "I hear you," or "I know you're not thrilled with this style, but it's impossible to control when it gets longer."

3. If you have been letting your hair go because you've been busy, you can accept the criticism by saying something like, "I know. It was my day/week to tidy up, and I blew it."

4. You can follow acceptance of criticism (as in response 3) with a request for help. For example, "Do you suppose you'd be willing to look over the styles with me so that we can settle on something we both can live with?"

5. If none of these responses work, it is possible that you partner has a *hidden agenda* and is using the remark about your hair as an opening. You can then try something like, "I'm trying to find ways to help the situation, but they don't seem to be working. Is there something else on your mind?"

6. Notice that we have not seized the opportunity to retaliate with something like, "You're worried about my hair? What about your teeth and that beach ball you're trying to hide under your shirt?" Although it can be tempting to retaliate, we're assuming that it might be better for the relationship, and for you in the long run, to try to resolve conflict, not heighten conflict.

REACTIONS: Compare your written responses with the guidelines and decide which is your usual way of responding. Explain whether or not your responses are usually positive.

SOURCE: Excerpts adapted from S. A. Rathus and J. S. Nevid, *Adjustment and Growth: The Challenges of Life*, 5th ed. Copyright © 1992, Holt, Rinehart & Winston, Inc. Reprinted by permission of the publisher.

40 | Focusing on Your Problem

PURPOSE: Over the span of your adult life, there may be a time when you have a sexual difficulty or problem. The following inventory is intended as a guide to pinpointing the problem(s) or potential problems and then understanding yourself as a sexual human being.

DIRECTIONS: Keep in mind this guide is intended to be *used,* not just read. We suggest that you first read it over. Then write out your answers to all the questions. If you have a partner and he or she also completes this inventory, refrain from discussing the questions or your responses with him or her until you complete each section. If you already know specifically what your problem is, you can proceed to look at it from various perspectives, starting with defining it and then exploring its history.

1. What, specifically, do you think is your problem?

2. When does the problem occur? With whom? In any particular place or under any particular circumstances?

3. Who, besides you, is complaining about your problem? Does he or she see your problem the same way that you do?

4. When did the problem first occur? What were the circumstances? How old were you? Did it come on suddenly or at a specific time? What do you think brought it on?

5. What have been the results of your having this problem? What has happened to you or your partner because of it?

6. Has the problem changed over time? Has it gotten worse or better? When did it become worse, and when better?

7. Do you think that your sexual problem is in any way related to other aspects of your life? How?

8. What do you think caused the problem in the first place?

9. Have you tried to work on the problem yourself? Has it helped? If not, why do you think it didn't?

10. Have you ever tried to get help for the problem? From whom? When? What kind of treatment did you receive? Did it help? If not, why do you think it didn't?

11. Are you currently experiencing problems in other aspects of your life that may affect your sexual life?

12. Are you experiencing any physical illnesses that may have an effect on your sexual activities? Are you under medical treatment? Are you taking any medication that may have a bearing on your sexual adjustment? If you're not sure, check with your physician.

13. How do you hope your sex life and life in general will be improved if you are successful in treating yourself? Does your partner share your goals? (If you don't know, ask.)

REACTIONS: Now look at your responses to the above questions. If your partner responded to the questions, you may want to discuss each question. Once you find your problem, it is beneficial to explore it further to aid you in working out a resolution. Don't forget to look at the positive as well and find your good points. Then you can build on the positive to overcome your problem.

SOURCE: Harvey L. Gochros and Joel Fischer, *Treat Yourself to a Better Sex Life.* © 1980 by Prentice-Hall, Inc., Englewood Cliffs, NJ 07632.

41 How Jealous Are You?

PURPOSE: One feeling that often causes conflict between two people is jealousy, perhaps because men and women often experience and express jealousy in different ways. If partners are unable to communicate openly about an issue, a conflict may result. The following exercise is designed to help bring to light your experiences with jealousy so that you may better understand yourself and your partner. If you currently do not have a partner, simply respond to the questions in terms of your last relationship or a hoped-for future one.

DIRECTIONS: Read each statement carefully, then respond YES or NO in the blank following the statement.

1. You have found at times that you actually like feeling jealous. _____

2. Your spells of jealousy seem to follow a pattern, one after another. _____

3. Sometimes you get so jealous that you lose your appetite or you overeat. _____

4. When you hear about, or think about, your partner's former lovers, you are jealous. _____

5. You avoid close relationships with people other than your partner because such situations may cause your partner to be jealous. _____

6. You are very jealous of your partner's friends, yet you tell people you are not the jealous type. _____

7. You are apt to display fits of jealousy with no apparent cause. _____

8. You are often jealous of your partner's friends even when you know your partner has no romantic feelings toward them. _____

9. At social gatherings you are aware of every move your partner makes. _____

10. Jealousy has led you to spy on your partner. _____

11. You want to know where your partner is at all times. _____

12. It would definitely be a crisis if you discovered your partner had one sexual encounter with another person. _____

13. The feeling of loneliness is common to you. _____

14. You have thought of taking revenge on a person you felt was a rival. _____

15. You feel that jealousy is proof of your love for your partner. _____

16. You are jealous of your partner's hobbies. _____

SCORING: If you have responded YES to *more than five of these statements,* you are allowing jealousy to control your life. To continue in this way is to leave yourself open to considerable pain and anguish. When jealousy arises, talk about it and reaffirm your commitment to your partner. You need to listen to each other.

REACTIONS: Use the space provided to respond to the following questions.

1. Which statements, to which you responded YES, are of most concern to you? After discussing them with a friend or partner, explain what you plan to do differently.

2. Do you feel you are trying to control this person who is important to you? Why or why not?

42 | Constructive Fighting

PURPOSE: People who are closely involved, whether as a family, good friends, or partners, often find it difficult to resolve disagreements. One person may try to ignore a problem until it becomes very obvious and is forced into the open. Then when the issue is discussed, the people involved are often dissatisfied with the outcome and the feelings they are left with. However, there are constructive methods of fighting to solve problems. This may seem too technical or mechanical, yet people find some guidelines for constructive fighting are practical, and the outcome of constructive fighting often enhances the relationship. This inventory will give you an opportunity to check your fighting style.

DIRECTIONS: Read each question carefully and respond by writing a YES or NO in the blank to the right. Respond in terms of a present relationship or a significant one from the past.

1. When your anger surfaces, do you take time to look at where it is coming from? _____

2. Whenever you argue, do you make "I" statements to explain how the other person's behavior makes you feel? _____

3. Do you say directly what change you would like to see in the current situation? _____

4. Are you sensitive to the hints your partner sends out when he/she is not happy with a situation? _____

5. Do you know what you and your partner expect of your relationship? _____

6. Do you threaten infidelity, divorce, violence, or telling others of your disagreement? _____

7. Are you dependent on your partner to fulfill many of your needs? _____

8. Are you aware of tensions that naturally occur when major lifestyle changes are made? _____

9. Do you feel that "winning" an argument is important to your self-image? _____

10. Do you keep score of who "wins" arguments? _____

11. Do you regard compromising as losing? _____

12. Are you afraid of being rejected by your partner? _____

13. Do you bring up problem areas as they arise instead of storing grudges to release all at once?   _____

14. Do you belittle your partner in an attempt to control him/her?   _____

15. Do you set aside a time and place where both you and your partner can discuss a problem without distractions?   _____

16. Do you confine your discussions about problems to the current issue and not bring up past issues?   _____

17. Are there recurring themes behind your disagreements?   _____

18. If you are not sure of your partner's message, do you repeat it in your own words and ask if you understand correctly?   _____

19. Do you feel you learn something from your disagreements?   _____

20. Are you uneasy with the changes that may result from an argument?   _____

SCORING: The questions above actually list many suggestions for constructive fighting. The correct answers are as follows:

1. YES. When you feel anger rising, it is helpful to stop to think about what is causing the anger. You need to realize that you yourself created the anger. Then ask yourself why you feel this way; it may be a result of unfair demands or expectations.

2. YES. You do not have the right to make assumptions about your partner's feelings and thoughts. Therefore, it is important to learn to begin statements with "I feel . . ." to let your partner know your feelings. Statements that begin "You . . ." tend to make assumptions and put your partner on the defensive.

3. YES. Learn to say directly what changes in the current situation you would like to see. After your partner has given his/her viewpoint, you can explore which options are fair or possible. Try to be positive in your statements, saying what you "do want" instead of focusing on the negative and what you "do not want."

4. YES. If you can understand your partner's nonverbal communication, you can ask what he/she is feeling. Your partner may want your help or support but may feel uncomfortable telling you so.

5. YES. If you have not recently discussed your expectations of your relationship, you may have conflicting ideals. Review them together to decide if any need to be changed. Do not expect your partner to change just for you.

6. NO. Threats will not solve the conflict. Remember: Threats are most effective if seldom used. Use them only if you feel the action is absolutely necessary and you are willing to carry it through.

7. NO. Any overdependence on your partner can cause conflict. Your partner may feel he/she is giving more than receiving. Take a look at your needs and reevaluate how to meet them.

8. YES. Many lifestyle changes naturally result in more tension and stress. Be aware of those situations and avoid blaming your partner for the stress.

9. NO. If you feel you must "win" an argument to keep your self-image, think about where your real happiness in the relationship comes from. Solving the problem that caused the conflict is the most important factor.

10. NO. Do not keep score of who "wins." Again the real issue is that the conflict is resolved. Keeping score tends to make people want to "get even." Stable relationships involve cooperation.

11. NO. Again, the real issue is that the conflict is resolved. A compromise is usually best since there is no "loser" whose feelings are hurt.

12. NO. If communication is open in your relationship, your partner will not reject you because you do not always agree. In fact, couples often find conflict resolution serves to strengthen a relationship.

13. YES. It is easier to find a compromise for problem issues if they are discussed and resolved one at a time as they arise. If one partner holds grudges for a period of time, it may cause conflicts in other areas.

14. NO. Attempting to belittle your partner is likely to put him/her on the defensive. In addition, the real concern should be reaching a compromise together.

15. YES. When a conflict needs to be resolved, one partner may want to make an appointment with the other. Discussion should not take place while either partner is tired, rushed, or under the influence of alcohol or drugs. Both partners need to be able to devote their full attention to the issue. If one person has an important presentation to make or paper to write, the discussion may need to be delayed for a reasonable length of time.

16. YES. Discussions should be limited to the current problem since it is better to deal with one issue at a time. If an unresolved issue is brought up, agree to discuss it at a later time.

17. NO. If the same arguments or variations on the same theme keep recurring, perhaps you need to look at your process for conflict resolution. Ask yourself if any positive changes have been made since the last time you discussed the issue.

18. YES. This is a basic rule of good communication. Restate what you heard your partner say but in your own words. This helps to clear up misunderstandings before they become problems.

19. YES. When fighting is constructive, both partners will learn something about themselves and their partner. This new information can then be applied to similar situations that arise in the future. Thus, no conflict would result.

20. NO. Both partners should feel fairly comfortable with the changes agreed upon, although it often takes time for people to feel completely comfortable if they are changing habits developed over several years. Both partners need encouragement and positive strokes when making changes.

Now that you have evaluated your fighting style, try to practice these suggestions the next time you feel angry or disagree with someone. Remember, these basic guidelines can be applied to disagreements with anyone—partner, mate, co-worker, or family member. However, if you cannot solve the problem, seek professional help. Friends and family may be able to help some, but a potentially long-term relationship is too important to trust to well-meaning friends. Seek professional help together. Once you resolve the conflict, put the problem behind you and have some fun!

REACTIONS: Use the space provided to respond to the following questions.

1. How constructive is your fighting with your partner, family, or friends?

2. What changes do you need to make your "fighting" or disagreements more constructive? How do you plan to do this?

43

Sexual Arousal Scale

PURPOSE: Arousal is the magic key to sexuality and is a powerful persuader. We've included two versions of the Arousal Scale since men and women seem to be turned on by very different types of stimuli. If you have someone special in your life the two of you may want to take the tests together and compare levels of arousal. Then look over the specific things that you each find stimulating. Using our research group we were able to pinpoint the six strongest (and weakest) turn-ons for **heterosexual** men and for women. Take the test first, then see how you compare.

INSTRUCTIONS (MEN): In the Arousal Scale for men, below, you'll find a list of 40 items or images that you may find sexually stimulating. Read each description and choose the number from the scale below that represents your level of arousal. Write your response next to each item, then turn the page to find your score.

Doesn't Turn Me On	A Little Turn-on for Me	A Pretty Good Turn-on for Me	Turns Me On a Great Deal
1	2	3	4

____ 1. A passionate couple in public

____ 2. The smell of perfume

____ 3. Romantic music

____ 4. The feel of lingerie

____ 5. An extremely intelligent woman

____ 6. Driving fast

____ 7. Wet bodies

____ 8. A woman in leather clothing

____ 9. A woman without a bra running across the street

____ 10. Tan lines

____ 11. A see-through blouse

____ 12. A crowded elevator

____ 13. The feel of a cashmere sweater

____ 14. Long hair

____ 15. Large breasts

____ 16. Tight jeans and T-shirts

____ 17. An aggressive woman

____ 18. A woman in a tight skirt

____ 19. A silk blouse

____ 20. A woman in velvet

____ 21. Pearls around a woman's neck

____ 22. A woman driving a powerful car

____ 23. Freckles on a woman's chest

____ 24. Painted toenails

____ 25. Small, firm breasts

____ 26. A pregnant woman

____ 27. A very tall woman

____ 28. A woman driving a motorcycle

____ 29. Very high heels

____ 30. A pleasingly plump woman

____ 31. Tall boots

____ 32. A nubile adolescent girl

____ 33. Erotic talk

____ 34. The nape of a woman's neck

____ 35. Long legs

____ 36. A woman executive

____ 37. A pantyhose commercial on television

____ 38. A woman in sunglasses

____ 39. An athletic woman

____ 40. Following a woman up stairs

INSTRUCTIONS (WOMEN): In the Arousal Scale for women, below, you'll find a list of 40 items or images that you may find sexually stimulating. Read each description and choose the number from the scale below that represents your level of arousal. Write your response next to each item, then turn the page to find your score.

Doesn't Turn Me On	A Little Turn-on for Me	A Pretty Good Turn-on for Me	Turns Me On a Great Deal
1	2	3	4

____ 1. An erotic romantic photograph

____ 2. The smell of fresh sweat

____ 3. Sounds of lovemaking from next door

____ 4. A men's underwear commercial on television

____ 5. Eye contact

____ 6. Dancing

____ 7. Watching a space launch

____ 8. A man in dark sunglasses

____ 9. Spending his money

____ 10. A good sense of humor

____ 11. A celebrity or movie star

____ 12. A male jogger in tight shorts

____ 13. A sexy passage in a romantic novel

____ 14. A vampire story

____ 15. An erotic conversation

____ 16. A male stripper

____ 17. A man in tight jeans

____ 18. Flirtation

____ 19. Drinking champagne

____ 20. Knowing that I look good

____ 21. A bubble bath

____ 22. Well-manicured hands on a man

____ 23. A man wearing a wedding band

____ 24. Having a man give me flowers

____ 25. A beautiful woman

____ 26. A thoughtful and supportive man

____ 27. A man enjoying children

____ 28. Undressing in front of a full-length mirror

____ 29. A warm summer night

____ 30. A man with a foreign accent

____ 31. A man in a tuxedo

____ 32. An attractive doctor

____ 33. A man with muscles

____ 34. A moustache or beard

____ 35. A really smart man

____ 36. The smell of a man's cologne

____ 37. Wearing lingerie

____ 38. An athletic man

____ 39. A man in uniform

____ 40. A man with a hairy chest

SCORING: To find your score on the Arousal Scale, simply add up all your numerical responses and write the total in the box below.

Total Score

INTERPRETATION: Arousal is in the mind of the beholder. At least that's what we would like to think, but one session with the television set tells us that whoever creates the commercial view of reality is attempting to establish fixed standards for the so-called turn-on.

If one is to believe what television and magazines constantly tell us, the Western world, in particular, idolizes certain physical attributes. Women are told to hide their panty lines as well as their facial lines. Men are promised sexual prowess if they use the right deodorant and drink the right brew—in that order, of course. The commercial world, fortunately, isn't the real world—at least not for most of us.

There do seem to be certain characteristics that are more of a turn-on for some people than for others—and there certainly are differences between the types of things that turn men on and what works for women. In 1972, research was published that presented some interesting insights into the differences between the sexes. These seemed to be the four characteristics that people most desire in a partner:

What Men Want in Women	What Women Want in Men
1 Physical attractiveness	1 Achievement
2 Erotic ability	2 Leadership
3 Affectional ability	3 Occupational ability
4 Social ability	4 Economic ability

These findings suggest that for women, in their thinking about men, beauty is only skin deep—but this isn't so for men when they think about what they want in a woman.

Now let's examine the current data from the Arousal Scale, which you just took. The responses from men tell us that things haven't changed much since 1972 (or since the Stone Age for that matter).

Highest		Lowest	
1	Tight jeans and T-shirts	40	A woman in sunglasses
2	A see-through blouse	39	A crowded elevator
3	Long legs	38	A pantyhose commercial on television
4	Erotic talk	37	A woman driving a powerful car
5	Small, firm breasts	36	A pregnant woman
6	A woman in a tight skirt	35	A pleasingly plump woman

These results are consistent with what many sex therapists regard as a major problem in sexual relationships. Few women meet these standards, yet most try to and then worry about losing their partners when they fail to measure up.

The Arousal Scale results for women tell us that women have changed—somewhat. If women in 1972 wanted achievement and leadership, today's women are turned on by the personality of the man doing the achieving and leading. The highest- and lowest-ranked characteristics that arouse women are as follows:

Highest		Lowest	
1	A good sense of humor	40	A man wearing a wedding band
2	A thoughtful and supportive man	39	A vampire story
3	Flirtation	38	Watching a space launch
4	Knowing that I look good	37	A men's underwear commercial on television
5	A really smart man	36	Spending his money
6	A sexy passage in a romantic novel	35	A man in dark sunglasses

As far as women are concerned, it looks as though Johnny Carson (with his late-night sense of humor) is right and Sigmund Freud (with his sexual symbology typified by a space launch) is wrong. Because what women want in men are intangible qualities, men find it difficult to grasp and embody the desires of women. Even Freud lamented, "What do women want?"

The differences in what arouses men and women are much clearer and easier to state than the reasons that the differences exist at all. Some psychologists, such as sex therapists Drs. Zella Luria and Mitchel Rose, see the differences as proof of the continued power of sex role socialization in our culture. We're conditioned by our society to be roused by certain characteristics. Other scientists, notably ethologist Desmond Morris, argue that the differences are biologically based. He believes that certain physical characteristics of women act as innate releasers of sexual energy in men, although the same biological forces don't act the same way in women. The argument rages on.

The Norms Tables will show you where you score in terms of arousal intensity and frequency. The *average scorer* is indicating healthy feelings of arousal in his or her day-to-day life. Most of us score here. The *high scorer* is easily turned on and probably finds sexual undertones in many varied situations. Men who score high indicate strong requirements for body contact, but our research also reveals that these men express high levels of sexual satisfaction. Women who score in this range show low levels of inhibition, but also indicate they have an external locus of control, meaning that they rely on outside influences for their sexual motivations. The *low scorer* is turned on by few things on the scale. It could be that the specific qualities that serve as turn-ons for low scorers may not have been included. Or the few high-ranking items chosen by a low scorer may be even more arousing than the scale indicates.

Problems can arise if high and low scorers are partners in a sexual relationship: One can't understand why the other is always so turned on; the second can't see (or accept) why the first is not. When partners have very different levels of arousal, a discussion of these differences may not be enough. The sex differences in the types of characteristics that trigger arousal also need to be understood—and accepted—by both. Arousal may be in the mind of the beholder, but meaningful communication can be the glue that holds the beholders together.

NORMS TABLE—MEN

Very Low	Low	Average	High	Very High
64 and below	65–74	75–76	88–100	101 and above

NORMS TABLE—WOMEN

Very Low	Low	Average	High	Very High
62 and below	63–73	74–92	93–102	103 and above

REACTIONS: Use the space provided to respond to the following questions.

1. How do you feel about your score on the Arousal Scale?

2. Explain (if applicable) how you feel about your partner's score.

44 | Sex Talk Quiz

PURPOSE: This quiz is designed to test your knowledge about male and female communication.

DIRECTIONS: With no one person in mind, respond to each of the following questions by marking TRUE or FALSE in the space provided.

1. Women are more intuitive than men. They have a sixth sense, which is typically called "women's intuition." _____

2. At business meetings, co-workers are more likely to listen to men than they are to women. _____

3. Women are the "talkers." They talk much more than men in group conversations. _____

4. Men are the "fast talkers." They talk much quicker than women. _____

5. Men are more outwardly open. They use more eye contact and exhibit more friendliness when first meeting someone. _____

6. Women are more complimentary. They give more praise than men. _____

7. Men interrupt more and will answer a question even when it is not addressed to them. _____

8. Women give more orders and are more demanding in the way they communicate. _____

9. In general, men and women laugh at the same things. _____

10. When making love both men and women want to hear the same things from their partner. _____

11. Men ask for assistance less often than women do. _____

12. Men are harder on themselves and blame themselves more often than women. _____

13. Through their body language women make themselves less confrontational than men. _____

14. Men tend to explain things in greater detail when discussing an incident. _____

15. Women tend to touch others more often than men. _____

16. Men appear to be more attentive than women when they are listening. _____

17. Women and men are equally emotional when they speak. _____

18. Men are more likely to discuss personal issues. _____

19. Men bring up more topics of conversation. _____

20. Today, we tend to raise our male children the same way we do our female children.   _____

21. Women tend to confront problems more directly and are likely to bring up the problem first.   _____

22. Men are livelier speakers who use more body language and facial animation.   _____

23. Men ask more questions than women.   _____

24. In general, men and women enjoy talking about similar things.   _____

25. When asking whether their partner has had an HIV test or when discussing safe sex, a woman will likely bring up the topic before a man.   _____

Answers to the Sex Talk Quiz

1. FALSE — According to studies there is no truth to the myth that women are more intuitive than men. However, research has shown that women pay greater attention to "detail." For instance, according to world-renowned anthropologist Ashley Montagu, women have a greater sensitivity and acuity for color discrimination than men. Linguist Robin Lakoff, in her classic book, *Language and Woman's Place* (Harper Colophon, 1975), also confirms this and states that women tend to use finer descriptions of colors. For instance, they will use words like cinnabar, bone, persimmon, and ebony. This attention to detail makes women seem more intuitive because they often notice characteristics others might miss, such as a person's body language, vocal tones, and facial expressions. This finding is apparent in early-childhood development studies which have shown that baby girls seem to be more aware of parents' and others' facial expressions than baby boys. This may be carried over into adulthood, and thus explain why women can oftentimes better perceive a person's mood and present emotional state than men. As a result of their conditioning, women have also been found to have greater acuity and sensitivity to "nonverbal communication" than men, which also makes them "appear" to be more intuitive.

2. TRUE — Men are listened to more often than women. In their study, "Sex Differences in Listening Comprehension," Kenneth Gruber and Jacqueline Gaehelein (*Sex Roles,* vol. 5, 1979) found that both male and female audiences tended to listen more attentively to male speakers than to female speakers. The audience also tended to remember more information from the presentations given by male speakers, even when the presentation was identical to a female's. Another study showed there was less noise in the room, as measured by decibels of audience talking or shuffling papers, when men spoke as compared to when women spoke at a scientific conference. An explanation for this finding may be due to a person's voice control and vocal pitch. A high-pitched, little girl's voice tends to "turn the audience off" and prevent them from actually hearing the information that the women had presented.

3. FALSE — Contrary to popular stereotype it is men—not women—who talk more. Studies like the one done by linguist Lynette Hirshman ("Analysis of Supportive and Assertive Behavior in Conversations," Linguistic Society of America, 1974) show that men far outtalk women. In fact, women tend to ask more questions, while men tend to give more answers which are lengthier and more involved than the questions they are asked. One

study found that women only spoke an average of 3 minutes when asked to describe a painting, while men averaged 13 minutes when asked to describe the same painting. Several studies from Fred Strodtbeck's study (*American Sociological Review*, 1951, 468–473) to Marion Wood's 1966 study to Marjorie Swacker's study (*Language and Sex: Difference and Dominance*, Newbury House Publishers, Inc., 1975) all confirm that women speak less than men in mixed-sex conversations.

4. FALSE — Although several studies show that women talk at a more rapid rate, it doesn't necessarily mean that women talk extremely fast. It is just that women, according to a 1973 study by W. Starkeweather, tend to articulate more precisely and more quickly than men. Perhaps this is because men tend to interrupt more, and women want to hurry up and get all their information out before they are interrupted.

5. FALSE — Numerous studies show that it is women and not men who tend to maintain more eye contact and facial pleasantries. A study by Dr. Albert Merhabian showed that in positive interactions, women increased their eye contact while men tended to be more uncomfortable in these interactions and, in essence, decreased their eye contact. Other studies by Dr. Albert Merhabian (*Nonverbal Communication*, Aldine Atherton, Inc., 1972), as well as Dr. Nancy Henley's chapter "Power, Sex, and Non-Verbal Communication" in *Language and Sex: Difference and Dominance* (Newberry House Publishers, 1975, 184–203), show that women exhibit more friendly behavior such as smiles, facial pleasantries, and head nods than men. This is especially true when first meeting someone, as research indicates. Even though women were found to smile 93 percent of the time, they only received approximately 67 percent of their smiles returned by men.

6. TRUE — Studies show that women are more open in their praise and give more "nods of approval" than men. They also use more complimentary terms throughout their speech according to Peter Falk, in his book *Word-Play: What Happens When People Talk* (Knopf, 1973), who studied the vocabulary of men and women. Linguist Robin Lakoff found that during conversational speech, women tend to interject more "uhm uhms" as an indicator of approval when listening to members of either sex.

7. TRUE — At the University of California researchers Donald Zimmerman and Candace West conducted a study in 1975 on how often interruptions occurred when men and women conversed. These results showed that 75 to 93 percent of the interruptions were made by men. In another study they found that in eleven conversations between men and women, there was only one conversation where the woman interrupted the man, and ten conversations where the man interrupted the woman. Oftentimes they found that after being interrupted by the man, the woman became increasingly quiet, pausing more than usual after speaking again. Dr. Zimmerman and Dr. West believe that the reason men tend to interrupt is because interrupting may be a way of establishing dominance. This conversational "dominance" is also verified in Judy Kester's 1978 observations which found that men are more likely to answer questions that are not even addressed to them.

8. FALSE — It is men who use more command terms or imperatives, which makes them sound more demanding. In essence, several researchers have concluded that women tend to be more polite in their speech. According to University of California's Mary Ritchie Key, an expert on women's speech, women tend to be more "tentative" when they speak because they generally communicate from a position where they are not the decisionmakers (*Male/Female Language*, Scarecrow Press, 1975). Robin Lakoff in her book *Language*

and Women's Place reveals her classic discovery of women's use of "tag endings": asking a question after a declarative statement is made, such as, "It's a nice day, isn't it?" This adds to the image of women as more tentative and less sure of themselves in their conversation. She also found that women are less likely to make use of command terms. They will often appear to command with terms of politeness or endearment such as, "Honey, would you mind closing the door?" as opposed to a more direct, "Close the door," which is a typical command a man will use without even thinking about it. This may be conditioned early in childhood as researchers Daniel Maltz and Ruth Borker's study, *A Cultural Approach of Male-Female Miscommunication in Language and Social Identity* (Cambridge University Press, 1982), shows. They contend that little boys and girls differ in the way they talk to their friends. Little girls don't give orders like boys, who often will say, "Give me that," or "Get out of here." Instead, girls tend to use suggestions in order to express themselves such as, "How about doing that," or "Let's do this."

9. FALSE — Men and women definitely differ in their sense of humor according to researcher Carol Mitchell's 1985 study, *Differences in Male and Female Joke Telling* (*Women's Folklore, Women's Culture*, Philadelphia Press, 1985); women are more likely to tell jokes when there is a small, nonmixed sex group, while men are even more likely to tell jokes in a larger, mixed sex group. Linguists Robin Lakoff and Nancy Henley both discovered that women tell jokes less frequently than men. Psychologist Paul McGhee's research (*Humor: Its Origin and Development*, W. H. Freeman, 1979) indicates that male humor tends to be more hostile, abrasive, and sarcastic than women's humor. Men also tend to joke around with one another as a "bonding" technique or to establish camaraderie with one another according to Robin Lakoff, while women don't use jokes in this way.

10. FALSE — In a survey conducted for the Playboy Channel, people were asked what they wanted to hear when making love. In general, women wanted to be told they were beautiful and loved, while men wanted to hear how good they were in bed, and how they pleased their woman. In a recent Gallup poll only 30 percent of the men and women surveyed were pleased with what they heard from the opposite sex while making love. Fewer women than men were found to like what was being said to them in bed.

11. TRUE — Deborah Tannen in her book, *You Just Don't Understand: Women and Men in Conversation* (William Morrow, 1990), found that men usually will not ask for help by asking for directions while women will. She explains this is due to the fact that men are usually "givers" of information, while women are "takers." As "givers" of information, men are proclaimed the experts and superiors in knowledge, while women are considered "uninformed" and "inferior."

12. FALSE — Several surveys and numerous psychotherapists' observations have indicated that women tend to be more self-critical and more apt to blame themselves than men. Women tend to be more self-deprecating and apologetic when things go wrong. Women also often personalize a problem, take responsibility for it, or blame themselves when they may not even have instigated it. Deborah Tannen's findings confirm this as she states that women also tend to use more "apologetic phrases" in their conversations such as, "I'm sorry," "I didn't mean to," or "Excuse me."

13. TRUE — Naturalist Charles Darwin stated that making oneself appear smaller by bowing the head to take up less space can inhibit human aggression. This observation can also be supported by the research of Ray Birdwhistall (*Kinesics and Context*, U of PA Press, 1970,

39–46), Albert Merhabian (1972), and Marguerite Piercy (*Small Changes*, Doubleday, 1973), who found that women tend to inhibit themselves by crossing their legs at the ankles or knees or keeping their elbows to their sides. Since women tend to take up less room in terms of their body language, they tend to make themselves less available for confrontation than men. According to linguists, this body language tends to reflect less power and status.

14. FALSE — Women tend to be more detailed and more descriptive than men in what they say and in how they explain things. As Robin Lakoff's research shows, women tend to use more description in word choices. They describe things in greater detail by their use of certain adjectives and intensifiers such as "so," "vastly," "immensely. " Observations of male-female communication patterns also indicate that women tend to speak less concisely. They go into greater detail about an incident than men, which oftentimes sidetracks the conversation. This result is substantiated in a survey conducted for this quiz which indicates that men are most frustrated by women going on and on, "beating around the bush," and not "getting to the point" quickly enough.

15. FALSE — Men tend to touch more than females. According to several researchers such as Stanley Jourard, Jane Rubin, and Barbara and Gene Eakins, women are more likely to be physically touched by men who guide them through the door, assist them with jackets and coats, and help them into cars. Nancy Henley's research also substantiates these findings. Her study showed that in a variety of outdoor settings, men touched women four times as much as women touched men. Men have also been shown to touch one another (i.e., backslapping and handshakes) during participation in various sports.

16. FALSE — Women, not men, appear to be more attentive when listening. Studies consistently show that women exhibit greater eye contact and express approval by smiling and head-nodding as a form of attentiveness and agreement. Sally McConnell-Ginetts' research at Cornell University found that women are more inclined to say "uhm hum" than men when listening to another person speak in order to monitor the flow of the conversation.

17. TRUE — Men and women are equally emotional when they speak. However, women appear to sound more emotional according to researchers such as Robin Lakoff because they use more psychological-state verbs: I *feel, I think, I hope,* and I *wish.* Women also have a greater variety of vocal-intonation patterns. Nancy Henley and Barrie Thorne's research (*Beyond Sex Roles*, West Publishing Co., 1977), as well the research done by Robert Luchsinger and Geoffrey Arnold, showed that women use approximately five tones when expressing themselves, while men only use three tones. This makes them sound more monotonous and unemotional than women. Also, men have been observed to express their emotions through increased vocal intensity such as loudness, yelling, or by using swear words. Women, on the other hand, express themselves by getting more quiet, exhibiting a shaky voice quality, or letting out tears.

18. FALSE — In general, men tend to bring up less personal topics than women. Women tend to discuss people, relationships, children, self-improvement, and how certain experiences have affected them. Men, on the other hand, tend to be more "outer directed" as they originate discussions about events, news, sports-related issues, and topics related to more concrete physical tasks.

19. FALSE — Even though men do not bring up as many subjects of conversation as women, men interrupt more, which ultimately gives them control of the topics which are raised by

women. A study done by Pam Fishman of Queens College in New York verified this finding. She discovered that over 60 percent of the topics which were introduced into conversation were done so by women. However, even though women introduced subjects more often, this may have been due to the fact that men tended to interrupt more, thus making the conversation change continually. According to the research by Don Zimmerman and Candace West (*Language and Sex: Difference and Dominance*, Newbury House Publishers, Inc., 1975), men usually interrupted as a way of controlling the topics of discussion which women originated.

20. FALSE — Even though there are many progressive and socially enlightened parents in the modern world, parents still treat their male children differently than their female children. They tend to communicate differently to their children according to their sex, which in turn, induces sex-stereotyped behaviors. For example, a recent Harvard University study showed that mothers are generally more verbal toward their daughters than they are toward their sons. Current studies have also shown that boy infants are handled more physically and robustly and are spoken to in louder tones than girl infants.

21. TRUE — Even though men make more direct statements, a recent survey conducted for this quiz indicated that women tend to confront and bring up a problem more often than men. In a survey of 100 men and women between the ages of 18 and 65, over 70 percent of the women stated that they would be the ones to confront a problem, while only about 40 percent of the males claimed that they would make the first move. Even though women bring up a problem more often, they tend to be more indirect and polite, as Deborah Tannen relates in her book. This also can be seen in the Gallup poll results which reveal women are more likely than men to confront issues such as AIDS, sexually transmitted diseases, or safer sex.

22. FALSE — In several studies, it was determined that women are more animated and livelier speakers than men. According to anthropologists at the University of California at San Francisco, women are more facially animated. Studies also show that women make more eye contact, use more body movement, use more intonation, have a more varied pitch range, and use more emotionally laden words and phrases than men.

23. FALSE — Just as women bring up more topics of conversation, they also ask more questions. According to researchers, this is usually done to facilitate the conversation.

24. FALSE — Men and women usually talk about different things. Studies indicate that women enjoy talking about diet, personal relationships, personal appearance, clothes, self-improvement, children, marriages, personalities of others, actions of others, relationships at work, and emotionally charged issues that have a personal component. Men, on the other hand, enjoy discussing sports, what they did at work, where they went, news events, mechanical gadgets, latest technology, cars, vehicles, and music.

25. TRUE — In a recent Gallup poll survey commissioned for this book, it was found that women rather than men were more likely to introduce the topic of HIV testing and safer sex.

SCORING: Add up your number of correct responses and place that number in the space provided.

Total Correct: _____

INTERPRETATION: If you had between 18–25 correct responses you have a good understanding of male and female communication. A score of 9–17 represents a fair level of understanding and 1–8 reflects a poor perspective on male/female communication dynamics.

REACTIONS: Use the space provided to respond to the following questions.

1. Do you feel that your score accurately represents your level of understanding about male-female communication differences? Why or why not?

2. Would your score on this quiz have been different three year ago? Explain.

3. Do you feel you personally fit the typical male or female communication style? Explain why or why not. If applicable, explain the differences in the typical style and yours.

SOURCE: Reprinted/adapted by permission of The Putman Publishing Group, from *He Says, She Says,* by Lillian Glass, Ph.D. Copyright © 1992 by Lillian Glass, Ph.D.

VI

SEXUAL ATTITUDES, PERCEPTIONS, AND BEHAVIOR

Sexual activity occurs for different reasons: procreation, demonstration of emotional warmth and intimacy, or pure pleasure, among others. Any single sexual experience can have one or many reasons as its motivating force. Our media tend to bombard us with sexual messages both explicit and subliminal. The commercialization of sex cannot only muddy the picture of a healthy sexual experience, it can lessen an individual's confidence. Today people are engaging in sexual practices at younger ages and tend to be performance- or goal-oriented in their sexuality. The effects of sexual activity can range from intense pleasure to dejection. Your sexual beliefs and behaviors can enhance your self-image or decrease your personal effectiveness. The consequences of your sexual expression are farreaching indeed. Completing this section on sexual activity will help you analyze your sexual attitudes, clarify your value system, examine your sexual communication skills, sharpen your decision-making skills, and reach a better understanding of human behavior in our culture.

Sexual Attitudes, Perceptions, and Behavior exercises include:

45. Muehlenhard-Quackenbush Sexual Attitude Scale
46. Sexual Fantasies
47. Rate Your Level of Desire
48. The Alligator River Story
49. The Uses of Sex
50. Sexual Anxiety Inventory
51. Sex Myths: The Old and the New
52. Sexual Pressures: How to Make the Right Decisions for You
53. Masturbation Attitude Scale
54. Sexual Decisions: Autosexual Behavior
55. Sex and Drugs: Test Your Knowledge

45 Muehlenhard-Quackenbush Sexual Attitude Scale

PURPOSE: This exercise is designed for you and your partner or friend to examine some of their attitudes about male and female sexuality.

DIRECTIONS: Read each of the statements below carefully and respond using the scale provided. If you have a friend, roommate, or partner who would like to take this scale, cover your answers and compare them, if desired, when completed.

A = Agree Strongly	B = Agree Mildly	C = Disagree Mildly	D = Disagree Strongly

	You	Partner/Friend
1. It's worse for a woman to sleep around than it is for a man.	___	___
2. It's best for a guy to lose his virginity before he's out of his teens.	___	___
3. It's okay for a woman to have more than one sexual relationship at a time.	___	___
4. It is just as important for a man to be a virgin when he marries as it is for a woman.	___	___
5. I approve of a 16-year-old girl having sex just as much as a 16-year-old boy having sex.	___	___
6. I kind of admire a girl who has sex with a lot of guys.	___	___
7. I kind of feel sorry for a 21-year-old woman who is still a virgin.	___	___
8. A woman having casual sex is just as acceptable to me as a man having casual sex.	___	___
9. It's okay for a man to have sex with a woman with whom he is not in love.	___	___
10. I kind of admire a guy who has had sex with a lot of girls.	___	___
11. A woman who initiates sex is too aggressive.	___	___
12. It's okay for a man to have more than one sexual relationship at a time.	___	___
13. I question the character of a woman who has had a lot of sexual partners.	___	___
14. I admire a man who is a virgin when he gets married.	___	___

15. A man should be more sexually experienced than his wife. _____ _____

16. A girl who has sex on the first date is easy. _____ _____

17. I kind of feel sorry for a 21-year-old man who is still a virgin. _____ _____

18. I question the character of a guy who has had a lot of sexual partners. _____ _____

19. Women are naturally more monogamous (inclined to stick to one partner) than are men. _____ _____

20. A man should be sexually experienced when he gets married. _____ _____

21. A guy who has sex on the first date is easy. _____ _____

22. It's okay for a woman to have sex with a man she is not in love with. _____ _____

23. A woman should be sexually experienced when she gets married. _____ _____

24. It's best for a girl to lose her virginity before she's out of her teens. _____ _____

25. I admire a women who is a virgin when she gets married. _____ _____

26. A man who initiates sex is too aggressive. _____ _____

SCORING: Convert your A's to zero, your B's to 1's, your C's to 2's, your D's to 3's.

Computing your total involves some simple mathematics:

#4 + #5 + #8 + (3 − #1) + (3 − #15) + (3 − #19) + (#24 − #2) + (#3 − #12) + (#6 − #10) +

(#7 − #17) + (#22 − #9) + (#26 − #11) + (#18 − #13) + (#14 − #25) + (21 − #16) +

(#23 − #20) = YOUR TOTAL: _____

INTERPRETATION: The actual name of this scale is the Sexual Double Standard Scale. A person having identical sexual standards for women and men should score zero. **A score greater than zero** reflects more restrictive sexual standards for women than for men; the highest possible score is **48. A score less than zero** reflects more restrictive sexual standards for men than for women; the lowest possible score is −30.

From a sample of college students at a large southwestern university researchers found a mean score for women to be 11.99 ($N = 461$) and a mean score for men to be 13.15 ($N = 255$).

REACTIONS: Use the space provided to respond to the following questions.

1. Do you think that the sexual double standard plays a role in the traditional sexual script, in which a woman is expected to refuse a man's sexual advances if she wants to have sex? Explain why.

2. If a woman wants to engage in sexual intercourse with a new partner, and if she believes that her partner accepts the double standard, what are her options?

3. Do you think that the sexual double standard and the "token resistance" to sex can play a role in rape? Explain why.

4. Do you think that the sexual double standard can put women at risk for sexually transmitted diseases, including HIV? Explain why.

SOURCE: Charlene L. Muehlenhard and Debra M. Quackenbush, *The Sexual Double Standard Scale*. Department of Psychology and Women's Studies, University of Kansas. Reprinted with permission.

46 Sexual Fantasies. . . ?

Many people feel that a sexual fantasy is an expression of an actual desire to participate in or experience a given situation. Masters and Johnson have demonstrated that most people with recurrent sexual fantasies feel neither the desire nor the need to act on them in real life.

PURPOSE: Sometimes our sexual values and our sexual fantasies seem to be in conflict, or on a collision course. The exercise that follows provides you with an opportunity to juxtapose your values and your sexual fantasies. It is designed to help you steer a safer course by recognizing conflicts.

DIRECTIONS: Indicate your response to the following statements by circling the appropriate response.

SA = Strongly Agree	AS = Agree Somewhat	UN = Undecided	DS = Disagree Somewhat	SD = Strongly Disagree

1. A thought is not equivalent to an act.   SA AS UN DS SD

2. A person who has "immoral" sexual daydreams or desires is as sinful as a person who acts upon them.   SA AS UN DS SD

3. Any fantasy that portrays anything other than heterosexual acts that lead to coitus is an immature or deviant expression of the sex drive.   SA AS UN DS SD

4. Sexual fantasy that provokes sexual desire should be stopped immediately and thoughts shifted to other things.   SA AS UN DS SD

5. Sexual fantasy is necessary for sexual arousal.   SA AS UN DS SD

6. Sexual fantasies shouldn't necessarily be shared between sexual partners.   SA AS UN DS SD

7. A sexual partner should be willing to play out the fantasy of the other partner.   SA AS UN DS SD

8. Sexual fantasies that are unpleasant and unwanted and that produce stress when they recur could benefit by counseling.   SA AS UN DS SD

9. Sexual fantasies can serve to boost self-confidence.   SA AS UN DS SD

10. Sexual fantasies can increase sexual excitement.   SA AS UN DS SD

11. Sexual fantasies provide a safety valve for pent-up feelings and discharge inner tensions.   SA AS UN DS SD

12. Sexual fantasies combined with masturbation provide a source of turn-on when a partner is unavailable.   SA   AS   UN   DS   SD

13. Sexual fantasies that occur while making love with someone else can enhance the sexual response level.   SA   AS   UN   DS   SD

14. Sexual fantasies allow the fantasizer to direct the action of the script and the key players.   SA   AS   UN   DS   SD

15. Sexual fantasies are an effective means to rehearse for an anticipated sexual encounter.   SA   AS   UN   DS   SD

16. Sexual fantasies express an actual desire to participate in the situation or act out the fantasy in real life.   SA   AS   UN   DS   SD

17. Our sexual fantasies are a reflection of our sexual values.   SA   AS   UN   DS   SD

18. People with sexual fantasies that involve physical or nonphysical force may be prospective rapists or sadomasochists.   SA   AS   UN   DS   SD

19. Sexual fantasies of extrarelational or extramarital sex result in guilt feelings.   SA   AS   UN   DS   SD

20. Women who fantasize about rape are really yearning for such an event to occur.   SA   AS   UN   DS   SD

SCORING: Questions 1, 6, 8, 10, 11, 12, 13, 14, 15 are scored
SA = 1, AS = 2, UN = 3, DS = 4, SD = 5.   Subtotal _____

Questions 2, 3, 4, 5, 7, 16, 17, 18, 19, 20 are scored
SA = 5, AS = 4, UN = 3, DS = 2, SD = 1.   Subtotal _____

     TOTAL _____

If your score is **below 50,** you probably will experience little conflict; if your score is between **51 and 69,** you are in the neutral area; if your score is **70 or above,** you might want to think about the probability of some conflict between fantasies and values. You might also find that discussing your feelings about sexual fantasies with your partner and significant others can be helpful in clarifying your values.

REACTIONS: Use the space provided to respond to the following questions.

1. Considering your score, do you feel comfortable with your sexual fantasies? Why or why not?

2. Do you think sexual fantasies can be a positive aspect of your life? Explain.

47 Rate Your Level of Desire

PURPOSE: This inventory is designed to give you some indication of your level of sexual desire.

DIRECTIONS: Decide how well each of the following statements applies to your life on a scale of 1 to 9, where **1 = doesn't apply at all, 5 = somewhat or sometimes applies, and 9 = strongly or always applies.** Circle the number that best represents your response to each statement.

1. I think about sex on a daily basis.		1 2 3 4 5 6 7 8 9
2. Sex is very satisfying for me.		1 2 3 4 5 6 7 8 9
3. I initiate lovemaking.		1 2 3 4 5 6 7 8 9
4. I am receptive to my partner's overtures to make love.		1 2 3 4 5 6 7 8 9
5. I feel attractive and desirable.		1 2 3 4 5 6 7 8 9
6. I masturbate on a regular basis.		1 2 3 4 5 6 7 8 9
7. I find it easy to block out mental distractions when making love.		1 2 3 4 5 6 7 8 9
8. I'm a very passionate person.		1 2 3 4 5 6 7 8 9
9. My sex drive is as strong as my partner's.		1 2 3 4 5 6 7 8 9
10. I would be very unhappy if sex wasn't a part of our relationship.		1 2 3 4 5 6 7 8 9
11. I have sexual fantasies.		1 2 3 4 5 6 7 8 9
12. I don't pretend to be asleep when my partner wants to make love.		1 2 3 4 5 6 7 8 9

SCORING: Add up the numbers that correspond to your responses to questions 1 to 12 to determine your total score. Place your total score in the space provided.

Total Score = _____

INTERPRETATION: **A total score above 75** means your sexual desire and, hopefully, your satisfaction, is at a high boil. **A score from 60 to 74** means your desire for sex is simmering. While it's not occupying your every thought, sex is obviously an important part of your life. **A score from 40 to 59** raises the possibility that you may have inhibited sexual desire. But that could have more to do with your lifestyle than any real sexual problem. Since it's difficult to go from ice cold to passionate at a moment's notice, Masters and Johnson suggest scheduling "sex dates," so you can look forward to a romantic interlude all day long. Another way to rev things up is to get some exercise. One study found that men and women who work out regularly had a stronger sex drive and had sex more often than nonexercisers. **Total scores below 40** indicate that you probably have inhibited sexual desire, although a diagnosis can't be made from a paper-and-pencil test. There are numerous causes for low sexual desire: Depression, stress, anemia, and certain drugs—such as medications for high blood pressure or anxiety—can interfere with libido. Don't be shy about discussing such concerns with your doctor. Obviously, problems in a relationship can also take a toll on desire. In those cases, therapy can help—but only if both partners really want to change the situation. If a lack of sexual desire is a problem for you, you might consider seeing a sex therapist. For a list of qualified therapists in your area, contact the American Association of Sex Educators, Counselors, and Therapists at P.O. Box 238, Mt. Vernon, Iowa 52314, (319) 895-8407.

REACTIONS: Use the space provided to respond to the following questions.

1. Do you feel that your score accurately represents your level of sexual desire? Why or why not?

2. Do you or your partner wish to increase or decrease your level of sexual activity? If so, what steps would you take to make these changes?

SOURCE: Adapted excerpt, "Rate Your Level of Desire," from *Heterosexuality* by William Masters, Virginia Johnson, and Robert Kolondy. Copyright 1994 by the authors. Reprinted by permission of HarperCollins Publishers, Inc.

48 The Alligator River Story

Every day, every one of us meets life situations that call for thought, opinion forming, decisions, and action. Some of our experiences are familiar, some novel; some are casual, some of extreme importance. Every decision we make and course of action we take is based on consciously or unconsciously held beliefs, attitudes, and values.

PURPOSE: Your responses to the behavior of the characters in the following story will reveal some of your values and attitudes.

DIRECTIONS: Read the story carefully and then at the space provided at the bottom rank the five characters, from the one whose behavior you most respect to the one whose behavior you least respect. Rank the five characters from this story from the the one you MOST RESPECT in terms of his/her behavior, to the one you LEAST RESPECT. Give a brief explanation of why you ranked each character in their respective positions.

Once upon a time there was a woman named Abigail who was in love with a man named Gregory. Gregory lived on the shore of a river. Abigail lived on the opposite shore of the river. The river that separated the two lovers was teeming with man-eating alligators. Abigail wanted to cross the river to be with Gregory. Unfortunately, the bridge had been washed out. So she went to ask Sinbad, a river boat captain, to take her across. He said he would be glad to if she would consent to go to bed with him preceding the voyage. She promptly refused and went to a friend named Ivan to explain her plight. Ivan did not want to be involved at all in the situation. Abigail felt her only alternative was to accept Sinbad's terms. Sinbad fulfilled his promise to Abigail and delivered her into the arms of Gregory.

When she told Gregory about her amorous escapade in order to cross the river, Gregory cast her aside with disdain. Heartsick and dejected, Abigail turned to Slug with her tale of woe. Slug, feeling compassion for Abigail, sought out Gregory and beat him brutally. Abigail was overjoyed at the sight of Gregory getting his due. As the sun sets on the horizon, we hear Abigail laughing at Gregory.

Most Respect

1. _____ Explain why you ranked this character first.

2. _____ Explain why you ranked this character second.

3. _____ Explain why you ranked this character third.

4. _____ Explain why you ranked this character fourth.

5. _____ Explain why you ranked this character fifth.

Least Respect

INTERPRETATION: Compare your results with those of your friends or partner. Discuss the similarities and differences among your reactions to the different characters in the story. The characters in this story, to some extent, represent personality or character traits of other people that you like or dislike:

Ivan — Independence, intellect, loner, self-centered

Sinbad — Manipulator, businesslike, identifies with power

Abigail — Impatient, quick to compromise, romantic lover

Gregory — Righteous, uncompromising, moralistic

Slug — Bully, opportunist

SOURCE: Adapted by permission of A&W Publishers, Inc., from *Values Clarification: A Handbook of Practical Strategies for Teachers and Students*. Revised Edition by Sidney B. Simon, Leland W. Howe, and Howard Kirschenbaum. Copyright © 1972 and 1978, Hart Publishing Company.

49 The Uses of Sex

People engage in sexual activity for many reasons, some of which are more acceptable in our society than others. Each individual evaluates sexual behavior according to his or her own morals and values. Thus, it is difficult to decide objectively which expressions of sexual activity and purposes are "right" and which ones are "wrong."

PURPOSE: This exercise is intended to aid you in analyzing how you use sexual behavior.

Directions: Read the list below, and place a check mark next to those phrases that represent how you sometimes use sex.

_____ Sex as purely playful activity.

_____ Sex as a way to have babies.

_____ Sex as fun.

_____ Sex as an expression of hostility.

_____ Sex as punishment.

_____ Sex as a mechanical duty.

_____ Sex as an outlet from physiological or psychological tension.

_____ Sex as a protection against alienation.

_____ Sex as a way of overcoming separateness or loneliness.

_____ Sex as a way to communicate deep involvement in the welfare of others.

_____ Sex as a form of "togetherness."

_____ Sex as a reward.

_____ Sex as a revenge.

_____ Sex as an act of rebellion.

_____ Sex as an experiment.

_____ Sex as an adventure.

_____ Sex as a deceit.

_____ Sex as a form of self-enhancement.

_____ Sex as an exploitation for personal gain.

REACTIONS: Use the space provided to respond to the following questions.

1. Review the list and circle those uses you checked with which you are not happy. Why are you not happy with these? Explain.

2. How will you attempt to change your behavior as a result of this activity?

SOURCE: J. L. Malfetti and E. M. Eidlitz, "The Uses of Sex," in *Perspectives on Sexuality.* New York: Holt, Rinehart and Winston, 1972.

50 Sex Anxiety Inventory

PURPOSE: This exercise is designed to provide some indication of your current level of sex anxiety.

DIRECTIONS: Write the letter of the alternative that comes closest to describing your feelings in the space provided. If you are in a relationship have your partner complete this inventory in the column provided. Compare your answers if you are comfortable sharing this information.

You Partner

____ ____ 1. Extramarital sex

a. is okay if everyone agrees.

b. can break up families.

____ ____ 2. Sex

a. can cause as much anxiety as pleasure.

b. on the whole is good and enjoyable.

____ ____ 3. Masturbation

a. causes me to worry.

b. can be a useful substitute.

____ ____ 4. After having sexual thoughts

a. I feel aroused.

b. I feel jittery.

____ ____ 5. When I engage in petting

a. I feel scared at first.

b. I thoroughly enjoy it.

____ ____ 6. Initiating sexual relationships

a. is a very stressful experience.

b. causes me no problem at all.

You   Partner

____ ____ 7. Oral sex

      a. would arouse me.

      b. would terrify me.

____ ____ 8. I feel nervous

      a. about initiating sexual relations.

      b. about nothing when it comes to members of the opposite sex.

____ ____ 9. When I meet someone I'm attracted to

      a. I get to know him or her.

      b. I feel nervous.

____ ____ 10. When I was younger

      a. I was looking forward to having sex.

      b. I felt nervous about the idea of sex.

____ ____ 11. When others flirt with me

      a. I don't know what to do.

      b. I flirt back.

____ ____ 12. Group sex

      a. would scare me to death.

      b. might be interesting.

____ ____ 13. If in the future I committed adultery

      a. I would probably get caught.

      b. I wouldn't feel bad about it.

____ ____ 14. I would

      a. feel too nervous to tell a dirty joke in mixed company.

      b. tell a dirty joke if it were funny.

You   Partner

____ ____ 15. Dirty jokes
          a. make me feel uncomfortable.
          b. often make me laugh.

____ ____ 16. When I awake from sexual dreams
          a. I feel pleasant and relaxed.
          b. I feel tense.

____ ____ 17. When I have sexual desires
          a. I worry about what I should do.
          b. I do something to satisfy them.

____ ____ 18. If in the future I committed adultery
          a. it would be nobody's business but my own.
          b. I would worry about my spouse's finding out.

____ ____ 19. Buying a pornographic book
          a. wouldn't bother me.
          b. would make me nervous.

____ ____ 20. Casual sex
          a. is better than no sex at all.
          b. can hurt many people.

____ ____ 21. Extramarital sex
          a. is sometimes necessary.
          b. can damage one's career.

____ ____ 22. Sexual advances
          a. leave me feeling tense.
          b. are welcomed.

____ ____ 23. When I have sexual relations
          a. I feel satisfied.
          b. I worry about being discovered.

You   Partner

____   ____ 24. When talking about sex in mixed company
              a. I feel nervous.
              b. I sometimes get excited.

____   ____ 25. If I were to flirt with someone
              a. I would worry about his or her reaction.
              b. I would enjoy it.

SCORING: For each item, one alternative indicates a response associated with anxiety, and the other a nonanxiety response. Each anxiety response is scored as 1 point. The anxiety response is "a" for items 2, 3, 5, 6, 8, 11, 12, 13, 14, 15, 17, 22, 24, and 25. For the remaining items, "b" is the anxiety response. The possible score ranges from 0 to 25.

INTERPRETATION: In general, the higher one's score, the more sex guilt is indicated. Scoring between 1–7 could be considered low sex guilt, 8–14 could be considered average, and 15–25 could be considered high sex guilt. In a 1980 study of undergraduate psychology students at Old Dominion University, Janda and O'Grady found a significant difference between men's and women's scores. The mean score for men was 8.09, with a standard deviation of 5.19. For women, the mean was 11.76, with a standard deviation of 5.31.

REACTIONS: Use the space provided to respond to the following questions.

1. Do you feel your score accurately represents your level of sex anxiety? Explain why or why not.

2. Do you feel that you would like to decrease you level of sex anxiety? If so, what steps do you think are appropriate?

SOURCE: L. H. Janda and K. E. O'Grady, "Sex Anxiety Inventory," *Journal of Consulting and Clinical Psychology*, vol. 48, pp. 169–175, 1980. Copyright 1980 by the American Psychological Association. Adapted with permission.

51 | Sex Myths: The Old and the New

Human sexuality is an area of excitement, mystery, and uncertainty; because of this, myths and misconceptions exist and evolve much the same as our sexuality.

PURPOSE: This exercise is designed to help you examine some past and present fallacies about sexuality in our culture.

DIRECTIONS: Read each set of paired statements carefully and make your own evaluation as to why they are misconceptions. Refer to the condensed explanations at the end of the exercise and to your textbook for further information.

1. OLD MYTH: Unusual sexual fantasies indicate mental disturbance.

   NEW MYTH: All sexual fantasies are healthy.

   Why are these misconceptions?

   _____

   _____

2. OLD MYTH: Masturbation is a harmful and immature sexual act.

   NEW MYTH: Masturbation is a more fulfilling sexual experience than intercourse.

   Why are these misconceptions?

   _____

   _____

3. OLD MYTH: Female orgasm is perverse or a rare occurrence.

   NEW MYTH: Female orgasm is a joyous experience that changes a woman's life.

   Why are these misconceptions?

   _____

   _____

4.   OLD MYTH: In-depth, prolonged therapy is necessary to cure sex problems.

NEW MYTH: Sex problems are now cured by simple tricks.

Why are these misconceptions?

_____

_____

5.   OLD MYTH: Love is an essential element to satisfying sex.

NEW MYTH: Love is irrelevant to sex. Technique and a philosophy of play are everything.

Why are these misconceptions?

_____

_____

6.   OLD MYTH: Vaginal orgasms are superior to clitoral orgasms.

NEW MYTH: Women experience no difference between clitorally and vaginally induced orgasms.

Why are these misconceptions?

_____

_____

7.   OLD MYTH: Homosexuals are "sick people," and they all lead miserable lives.

NEW MYTH: Homosexuality is equally as rewarding as heterosexuality.

Why are these misconceptions?

_____

_____

8.   OLD MYTH: Women are basically disinterested in sex.

NEW MYTH: Women are now more sexually aggressive than men.

Why are these misconceptions?

_____

_____

9.   OLD MYTH: Simultaneous orgasms are the best sexual experiences for a couple.

NEW MYTH: Sequential orgasms are best.

Why are these misconceptions?

_____

_____

10. OLD MYTH: A large penis is essential to satisfy a woman.

    NEW MYTH: Penis size has no relevance to female pleasure.

    Why are these misconceptions?

    _____

    _____

11. OLD MYTH: Well-adjusted people are pure and innocent.

    NEW MYTH: Promiscuity is rampant among contemporary adolescents.

    Why are these misconceptions?

    _____

    _____

12. OLD MYTH: Any woman who is raped was probably looking for it.

    NEW MYTH: Many women fantasize about rape and therefore must enjoy it.

    Why are these misconceptions?

    _____

    _____

13. OLD MYTH: The larger her breasts, the more sexually aroused a woman is capable of
    becoming.

    NEW MYTH: Breast size is totally irrelevant to male sexual pleasure.

    Why are these misconceptions?

    _____

    _____

14. OLD MYTH: Lower-class people have a much more active and varied sexual life.

    NEW MYTH: An extraordinary sexual lifestyle is the domain of the upper classes.

    Why are these misconceptions?

    _____

    _____

15. OLD MYTH: An orgasm is necessary for an ovary to release an egg.

    NEW MYTH: There is a female ejaculation during orgasm.

    Why are these misconceptions?

    _____

    _____

CONDENSED EXPLANATIONS:

1. Sexual fantasy is a universal phenomenon. Fantasies themselves are not harmful but can be disturbing to someone who does not understand them or has not come to terms with them. If a fantasy bothers you, find a qualified person you can talk to about it. Oftentimes a fantasy that you find disturbing is only a small internal conflict that needs to be worked out. Sexual fantasy can tell you and your partner much about what arouses you and can enhance a sexual relationship or self-stimulation, whatever be the case.

2. Masturbation is the most sensible form of self-discovery a person can experience. Research by Masters and Johnson did find, based on objective measures of physiological rather than emotional responses, that masturbation induced a more intense response. Masturbation is only one small part of a person's sexuality. Relationships involving sexual contact between two people take preference over solitary masturbation.

3. There has been an increase in the number of women who recognize their capacity for orgasm and multiple orgasm and who expect more out of sex. Some women have unrealistic expectations about orgasm, which cause a degree of difficulty. The role of sex therapy is to foster a proper, realistic perspective toward orgasm and make it easier for a woman to achieve her desired reaction.

4. People with sex problems do not "have to just live with them" nor do they have to go through prolonged psychoanalysis, as of yesteryear. The "squeeze technique" or sensate focus are not simple tricks that offer quick cures to sexual problems. Helping people with sexual problems involves changing their attitudes and behavior. Some problems require extensive psychoanalysis; others can be cured with a few sessions of therapy. Some people require either marital or individual therapy as part of their sexual therapy.

5. Sexual technique is important in some ways. However, the interpersonal relationship of the people involved will determine the quality of sex. Today, some of our popular adult media communicate the feeling that sex is only fun. Sex can have a variety of meanings to different people. It can represent a strong bond, a source of intimacy, and at a different time a playful endeavor. Basically, sexual relationships entail a combination of joy, animalistic impulses, and also quiet thoughtful moments.

6. Research shows all orgasms are the same: no matter where the stimulation, the vagina contracts at the rate of less than once per second during orgasm. However, some research in recent years suggests that psychological and physical factors combine subjectively to produce various kinds of orgasm. It is not uncommon for women to report a sharper, more intense orgasm from clitoral stimulation alone, whereas an orgasm stimulated by intercourse often involves the entire body. Women vary widely in their preferences for stimulation to orgasm and also in the subjective sensations they report.

7. Homosexuality is no longer considered a mental illness or a deviance by the American Psychiatric Association. Homosexuals who are troubled by their preference should not be characterized as persons with a sexual orientation disturbance. Research has shown that many homosexuals, especially lesbian women, lead healthy, happy, productive lives. What is rewarding in a sexual relationship will depend on the people involved and their expec-

tations of satisfaction and pleasure. Whether one sexual orientation or lifestyle is equal in reward to another depends on what the people involved consider rewarding.

8. Disinterest in sex is an individual function. There is no database to support the notion that impotence and premature ejaculation are increasing. Individual cases may exist where the male experiences anxiety due to pressure to perform, resulting in sexual problems.

9. There are advantages and disadvantages to both; which is best depends on what the people involved enjoy in a particular situation. It can be pleasurable to have sequential orgasms and enjoy your partner's experience; on the other hand, simultaneous orgasms can be just as enjoyable. Sexual pleasure should be free from the pressure of orgasm as a goal.

10. Research has shown that the sensation areas of the female genitalia include the breasts, mons veneris, clitoris, labia, vaginal entrance, and the first one-third of the vaginal canal. Therefore, deep penetration by the male is not required. Some women report that a small penis can deny the feeling of fullness in the vagina. However, a very large penis can cause some discomfort if caution is not exercised. A majority of women report that penis size does not make much difference. Circumference of the penis is usually more a concern than length, again, because it affects the feeling of fullness. Penis size may be a psychological factor in foreplay and arousal. However, a majority of women are not as aroused by the physical characteristics of the male as men are by those of females.

11. Due to the increasing openness about sex in our culture, speculations about sexual practices of young people are somewhat overstated. There are many adolescents who do not exercise their sexuality, and a good percentage who have experienced intercourse before marriage.

12. Rape is an act of violence, not the result of an uncontrollable sex drive. Regardless of what a woman "wears or does," no one has the right to assault her. Women may fantasize about the use of force or coercion, yet there are two important elements present in a fantasy that are very much absent in actual rape. First, the woman remains in complete control of the situation, and second, she feels no threat of harm. These myths are currently under attack, and good progress is being made in changing the public attitude on this topic.

13. Physiologically, breast size is unrelated to sexual arousal in the female. Psychologically, breast size can be a factor in male arousal if the individual considers large or small breasts more desirable.

14. This myth arises from the fact that the incidence of premarital intercourse at lower-class levels is higher than at upper-class levels. However, if you look at other sexual behavior such as foreplay, masturbation, and intercourse positions, you find more varied behavior among the upper-class levels than among the lower-class levels The rich and powerful have been known for making their own sexual rules. As one of Murphy's laws puts it: Whoever has the gold makes the rules.

15. An ovary or ovaries usually release an egg about 14 days prior to menstruation. The release of the egg is not dependent upon female orgasms nor is it caused by a female orgasm. New research studies do suggest the possibility of a female ejaculation through the urethral opening from the Grafenberg spot during orgasm. However, the research is still inconclusive as to the existence of the Grafenberg spot or its ability to produce an ejaculate.

REACTIONS: Use the space provided to respond to the following questions.

1. Why do you think some of these myths continue to exist today? How does it help you to know these are not true?

2. What can you as an individual do to dispel the myths?

52 Sexual Pressures: How to Make the Right Decisions for You

Purpose: The decision to have or not to have intercourse for the first time is a serious one. No one can tell you whether or not you should, but perhaps you can decide for yourself by considering these questions.

Directions: Read each set of questions carefully. Your responses should go further than a yes or no. This is a highly personal topic and decision process, so it should be given careful consideration.

1. Do you know why your parents and/or religion have taught that intercourse should wait until marriage? Do you accept these ideas? If so, then you would be creating a lot of inner turmoil to go against your own beliefs.

2. If you do accept the beliefs you were taught, is it only at their intellectual level? Do you feel really comfortable and firm in your own beliefs? Try to imagine how you would feel about losing your virginity. Would it make you feel less valuable, less lovable, less good? If so, it is a bad "bargain." This is not to say that an emotional reaction to first intercourse is a sign of trouble. On the contrary, it is a very important moment and an outpouring of feelings can be expected—feelings of joy and sadness, pleasure, and disappointment.

3. Have you said no to intercourse not out of moral consideration but out of fear? Many people have fears about sex, especially first intercourse. Do you fear pain and/or bleeding? Do you think there is some reason you would have an unusually difficult time? Are you afraid you would be unable to respond sexually? Are you afraid your parents would find out? A moral decision made out of fear or ignorance is not really moral. You must understand your own feelings and try to find someone (perhaps a doctor) who can hear your concerns and help answer your questions.

4. Are you yielding to group pressure from your friends against what you feel is right for you? Don't dismiss this question lightly. Most people don't recognize the full extent of the influence exerted on them by peers. It is easy to feel you are "hung up" or abnormal when your way is against most of the people around you. Remember also that some friends may be giving the impression that they are more sexually experienced than they actually are.

5. Are you expecting too much from intercourse? If you believe that intercourse will transport you to the stars, make you overnight into a "real person," it won't. Try to get your expectations down to earth before you decide.

6. What does intercourse mean to you—permanent commitment for life? Fidelity for both partners? Love?

7. However you answer question 6, does your current relationship meet these criteria? Does your partner understand what it means to you and do you understand your partner's feelings?

8. Would you feel comfortable being naked with your partner, touching his/her genitals, and having your partner touch your genitals, seeing your partner reach orgasm, allowing yourself to respond sexually with your partner? If not, slow down and go through the stages of physical intimacy at a pace that feels right to you before intercourse.

9. If applicable, can one of you get effective contraception and will you both use it responsibly and correctly?

10. If applicable, are you both prepared to a face a pregnancy should your contraception fail?

11. Is your current relationship emotionally intimate and open? Could you tell your partner you were scared or if something hurt? Could your partner tell you he or she never had intercourse before and was really nervous? You are much more likely to have a satisfactory experience if the relationship is at this level before you have intercourse.

12. Together, do you have the opportunity for uninterrupted privacy, free from the fear of being heard or intruded upon?

REACTIONS: Use the space provided to respond to the following questions.

1. If you do not feel comfortable discussing sexual intercourse with your partner, let this questionnaire be your opening for a discussion. Are you comfortable discussing the topic of sexual intercourse and all it involves with your partner or others? Why or why not?

2. This is a lot to ponder. Did you learn anything new about your attitudes and beliefs from these questions? Is so, what?

SOURCE: Adapted from Lorna and Philip M. Sarrel, "Sexual Pressures: How to Make the Right Decisions for You," *Glamour*, August 1974, pp. 58+.

53 | Masturbation Attitude Scale

DIRECTIONS: Complete this questionnaire by indicating the degree to which you agree or disagree with each of the following statements, using the scale below.

SA = Strongly Agree	AS = Agree Somewhat	UN = Undecided/ No Opinion	DS = Disagree Somewhat	SD = Strongly Disagree

_____ 1. People masturbate to escape from feelings of tensions and anxiety.

_____ 2. People who masturbate will not enjoy sexual intercourse as much as those who refrain from masturbation.

_____ 3. Masturbation is a private matter which neither harms nor concerns anyone else.

_____ 4. Masturbation is a sin against yourself.

_____ 5. Masturbation in childhood can help a person develop a natural, healthy attitude toward sex.

_____ 6. Masturbation as an adult is juvenile and immature.

_____ 7. Masturbation can lead to homosexuality.

_____ 8. Excessive masturbation is physically impossible, so it is a needless worry.

_____ 9. If you enjoy masturbating very much, you may never learn to relate to the opposite sex.

_____ 10. After masturbating, a person feels degraded.

_____ 11. Experience with masturbation can potentially help a woman become orgasmic in sexual intercourse.

_____ 12. I feel guilty about masturbating.

_____ 13. Masturbation can be "a friend in need" when there is no "friend in deed."

_____ 14. Masturbation can provide an outlet for sex fantasies without harming anyone else or endangering oneself.

_____ 15. Excessive masturbation can lead to problems of impotence in men and frigidity in women.

_____ 16. Masturbation is an escape mechanism which prevents a person from developing a mature sexual outlook.

_____ 17. Masturbation can provide harmless relief from sexual tensions.

_____ 18. Playing with your own genitals is disgusting.

_____ 19. Excessive masturbation is associated with neurosis, depression, and behavioral problems.

_____ 20. Any masturbation is too much.

_____ 21. Masturbation is a compulsive, addictive habit which, once begun, is almost impossible to stop.

_____ 22. Masturbation is fun.

_____ 23. When I masturbate, I am disgusted with myself.

_____ 24. A pattern of frequent masturbation is associated with introversion and withdrawal from social contacts.

_____ 25. I would be ashamed to admit publicly that I have masturbated.

_____ 26. Excessive masturbation leads to mental dullness and fatigue.

_____ 27. Masturbation is a normal sexual outlet.

_____ 28. Masturbation is caused by an excessive preoccupation with thoughts of sex.

_____ 29. Masturbation can teach you to enjoy the sensuousness of your own body.

_____ 30. After I masturbate, I am disgusted with myself for losing control of my body.

SCORING: For statements 1, 2, 4, 6, 7, 9, 10, 11, 12, 15, 16, 18, 19, 20, 21, 23, 24, 25, 26, 28, and 30, score

  1 for Strongly Agree (SA)

  2 for Agree Somewhat (AS)

  3 for Undecided (UN)

  4 for Disagree Somewhat (DS)

  5 for Strongly Disagree (SD)

Because items 3, 5, 8, 11, 13, 14, 17, 22, 27, and 29 are worded in a different direction, score your answers in reverse:

  5 for Strongly Agree (SA)

  4 for Agree Somewhat (AS)

  3 for Undecided (UN)

  2 for Disagree Somewhat (DS)

  1 for Strongly Disagree (SD)

Now total the number of points. TOTAL: _____

Keep in mind that there are no right and wrong answers as such. Rather, the answers you gave reflect your feelings. Your feelings, regardless of what they are, are just as valid as anyone else's and no better or worse than anyone else's. A low total score indicates a negative attitude and a high score indicates a positive attitude toward masturbation. The lowest possible score is 30, and the highest 150. In a sample of 96 male and 102 female undergraduate students at the University of Connecticut in 1975, the average score for both males and females was 72. According to P. R. Abramson and D. L. Mosher, a negative attitude toward masturbation among females is related to the amount of sexual experience, frequency of masturbation per month, and maximum frequency of masturbation per day. Among males, a negative attitude toward masturbation is related only to the frequency of masturbation per month.

REACTIONS: Use the space provided to respond to the following questions.

1. Mark on the scale below where your score falls.

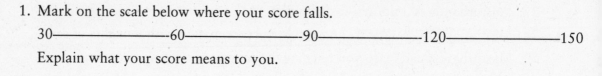

Explain what your score means to you.

2. Do you feel your score is a true reflection of your attitude toward masturbation? Why or why not?

SOURCE: P. R. Abramson and D. L. Mosher, "Development of a Measure of Negative Attitudes toward Masturbation," *Journal of Consulting and Clinical Psychology*, 1975, 43:485–490. Copyright © 1975 by the American Psychological Association. Adapted by permission of the author.

54 Sexual Decisions: Autosexual Behavior

PURPOSE: This decision story will help you examine your feelings and attitudes regarding masturbation within a marriage relationship.

DIRECTIONS: Read the paragraph below and respond to each of the questions that follow. Give each of the issues careful thought.

Beth and her husband Ray have been married a year and a half. They have made love about once every two weeks during that time. Beth is twenty-two and Ray is twenty-four. She cannot understand why they make love so infrequently, especially when she desires more. When Beth tries to initiate lovemaking, Ray tells her that aggressive females turn him off. When they finally make love, Beth either gets too excited to have an orgasm or she has one rapidly, as does Ray. This leaves no time to enjoy lovemaking as Beth would like. As a result Beth has begun to masturbate often. She enjoys it and is able to bring herself to orgasm and relieve her own tensions.

1. Should Beth continue to masturbate? Explain why or why not.

2. Would Beth be able to change Ray's behavior? How? Should Beth try to change Ray's behavior? What if she meets with no success?

3. Do you think Beth should see a doctor or therapist? Is her sexual behavior normal?

4. Should Ray see a doctor or therapist? Is his sexual behavior normal?

5. Is Ray's behavior fair to Beth? What compromises could be reached?

6. If you were in Beth's situation, how would you react?

7. If you were in Ray's position, how would you react if:
   a. Your wife was masturbating frequently?

   b. Your wife told you she was not pleased with her sex life?

Scoring: There are no right or wrong responses in this exercise. We can only point out that many people can be uncomfortable discussing masturbation. Yet masturbation is generally viewed as a normal sexual outlet and a healthy component in sexual development.

1. Is masturbation a topic you would feel comfortable discussing with your partner? Why or why not?

2. How do your religious beliefs and past education affect your attitudes toward masturbation? Explain.

55 | Sex and Drugs: Test Your Knowledge

PURPOSE: Studies have shown that drug use can be a common occurrence among college students. However, most college students have limited knowledge of the effects that certain drugs can produce, especially on their sexual behavior. This exercise is designed to increase your knowledge and awareness regarding drug choices and sexual practices.

DIRECTIONS: Read each statement or question carefully and then determine the best response. Place your response in the space provided to the left of each question. If you have a friend or partner who would like to take this quiz, cover your answers with a sheet of paper and compare them later if desired.

You   Friend

____ ____ 1. A common antibiotic Amoxicillin has what kind of effect on the human sexual response cycle when ingested in prescribed doses?

a. Delays male ejaculation and increases impotence

b. Has no measurable effect

c. Enlarges the female clitoris, making penetration very painful and decreasing female sensitivity of the genitalia

d. Increases the length of both male and female orgasms

____ ____ 2. Research has demonstrated that some men and some women users of antidepressants such as Prozac and Zoloft have increased sexual arousal.

a. True

b. False

____ ____ 3. Amphetamines (uppers) such as Benzedrine and Dexedrine (in diet pills) produce what effects on sexual arousal?

a. Dries vaginal mucous membranes and therefore produces painful female intercourse

b. Lowers inhibitions for men and women

c. Delays ejaculation for men

d. All of the above

You   Friend

____ ____ 4. After ingestion of caffeine, a well-known substance found in coffee, No-Doz, and Vivarin, a male's semen is often discolored and contains fewer sperm.

  a. True

  b. False

____ ____ 5. Which of the following pairs of natural or synthetic drugs are considered sex hormones?

  a. FSH and LH

  b. Prostaglandins and progesterone

  c. Androgens and estrogens

  d. Steroids and gonadotropin-releasing hormone

____ ____ 6. Some of the drugs used in the treatment of schizophrenia may affect sexual functioning.

  a. True

  b. False

____ ____ 7. Some of the drugs used in the treatment of hypertension can cause impotence.

  a. True

  b. False

____ ____ 8. Drinking moderate amounts of alcohol at any one time produces what effect(s)?

  a. Intensifies all sexual experiences

  b. Limits communication between partners

  c. Produces multiple orgasms for a female

  d. Reduces inhibitions

  e. Both b and d

____ ____ 9. Smoking or injecting heroin has been found to instantaneously produce a "psychological" and "pharmacogenic" orgasm.

  a. True

  b. False

You   Friend

____ ____ 10. In today's society, the most widely acknowledged aphrodisiac in drug form is:

   a. Marijuana

   b. Ecstasy

   c. LSD (acid)

   d. Alcohol

____ ____ 11. If cocaine is smoked in the form of "crack," rather than inhaled intranasally in powder form, what effect, if any, could this have on a male's erection?

   a. The erection is slower in developing.

   b. An instant erection occurs, then slowly dissipates.

   c. The erection produces no sexually stimulating effect.

   d. Males report no erection differences when smoking or snorting cocaine.

____ ____ 12. The habitual or heavy use of marijuana (cannabis, pot, or reefer) may cause sexual dysfunctions.

   a. True

   b. False

____ ____ 13. What effect does smoking tobacco have on the libido (sex drive) of both men and women?

   a. The libido is not effected for both men and women.

   b. The libido increases for both men and women.

   c. The libido increases for males but decreases for females.

   d. The libido increases for females but decreases for males.

____ ____ 14. Hallucinogens such as LSD, mescaline, and mushrooms, usually have what kind of effect(s) on the human sexual response cycle?

   a. They increase perceived awareness of sexual arousal, intensify and prolong orgasm, and increase penis circumference.

   b. They increase perceived awareness of sexual arousal and disrupts thought processes.

   c. They increase awareness of sexual arousal, disrupt the respiratory system, and enhances the frequency of ejaculation and erection.

   d. They decrease erotic feelings, male impotence, and decrease vaginal lubrication.

You   Friend

_____ _____ 15. Cantharides (Spanish fly) produce all of the following reactions *except*:

a. Inflammation of the bladder

b. Mild genital irritation

c. Enhancement of perceived sexual abilities

d. Excessive tissue destruction

_____ _____ 16. Which of the following nonprescription drugs can alter the level of mental awareness, making a person more susceptible to date rape?

a. Rohypnol

b. Alcohol

c. Demerol

d. a and b

_____ _____ 17. In general, the effects of drugs on male sexual response are better documented and understood than are the effects of drugs on the sexual response of females.

a. True

b. False

SCORING: The correct responses and explanations are listed below.

1. b. Research studies have shown that Amoxicillin and other antibiotics have no measurable effect on either male or female sexual response cycles. Antibiotics such as Amoxicillin may frequently alter vaginal flora and allow yeast infections. These yeast infections, while not causing a change in the sexual response cycle, may create discomfort during sexual intercourse until treated. It should also be noted that these medications may reduce the effectiveness of birth control pills.

2. b. Clinically controlled studies have shown that a measurable decrease in libido is a possible adverse reaction to Prozac as well as Zoloft. However, it should be noted that depression itself frequently causes a decrease in concentration, pleasure, and sexual desire. Antidepressants are primarily prescribed for episodes of depression. The relief of depression by these antidepressants may have a positive overall effect on sexual functioning. However, any improvement is not specifically due to medication, but from relief of depression. Arousal levels of both men and women do not increase with the proper use of antidepressants.

3. d. Amphetamines act upon the central nervous system as a stimulant making it difficult for a person to concentrate. Psychological effects such as an increase in perceived performance, lowered inhibitions, and an increase in awareness of mood often affect sex-

ual decision making. The physiological effects include a reduction in vaginal lubrication in women and delayed ejaculation in men. The long-term abuse of amphetamines can impair sexual functioning for both men and women.

4. b. There is no evidence that suggests that a male's semen becomes discolored or decreases in sperm count. Caffeine stimulates the central nervous system and in higher doses, caffeine may cause sleeplessness, dizziness, hallucinations, or the shakes. With an increase in dosage during sexual intercourse, a possible side effect may be an increase in heart rate or frequency in urination.

5. c. About 95 percent of the androgens produced by a male are secreted by the testes in the form of testosterone. Taking exogenous male hormones (anabolic steroids) causes testicular atrophy and with prolonged use actually can decrease libido. These steroids also cause behavior changes, increasing aggressive behavior which could be detrimental to a relationship. Birth control pills are the most commonly used female hormone, but typically they are not reported to have any physiological effects on sexual functioning. When ovaries are removed or women are postmenopausal, estrogen replacement therapy may be used. For the female, estrogens help maintain the elasticity of the vaginal lining, contribute to the production of vaginal lubricant, and help preserve the texture and function of the breasts. However, the role that ovarian estrogens play in female sexual arousal, motivation, and behavior remains a topic of ongoing debate.

6. a. A side effect of some of the drugs used in treating schizophrenia is a "dry orgasm." A dry orgasm is one in which the man produces no ejaculate.

7. a. Drugs used to treat hypertension have frequently caused impotency. Another problem with some hypertension drugs (such as beta blockers, thiazide diuretics, central acting alpha antagonists, and Reserpine) is the inhibition of sympathetic nerves which may cause ejaculatory problems for men. There are however, newer alternative hypertensive drugs (ace inhibitors, calcium channel blockers) with which sexual dysfunction is much less common. Untreated hypertension and diabetes can affect sexual functioning over time. The drugs themselves may not be the problem, but instead there may be underlying vascular problems. Men who are concerned should discuss alternatives with their physician as hypertension should not go untreated.

8. e. Even moderate alcohol consumption has a direct effect on the central nervous system as a depressant. Therefore, communication between partners, reaction times, and needed listening skills often decrease while consuming alcohol. Speech can become hindered or slurred during sexual decision making. Thus, communication signals are often misinterpreted by partners. Research studies suggest that alcohol use decreases inhibitions and also is strongly associated with violent and aggressive sexual behavior. In short, alcohol has been found to lower sexual inhibitions and decrease responsible decision making.

9. a. Some heroin users feel the initial high of injecting or smoking heroin produces a euphoric experience. These users feel the psychological state is much like that of a physical orgasm. In addition, some male users of heroin have noted an instantaneous erection during the initial injection of the heroin. Regardless of these momentary psy-

chological "highs," the overall effects and dependence upon heroin is negative to sexual functioning in the long run.

10. d. In our culture, there is widespread belief in the erotic enhancement properties of alcoholic beverages. Alcohol is used by many people. It is often perceived to lower inhibitions, prolong sexual intercourse, and enhance orgasm and ejaculation. In reality, alcohol is a general central nervous system depressant and may impair sexual functioning. If a person has aggressive tendencies, the result of alcohol abuse may be date rape instead of increased sexual functioning.

11. a. Smoking cocaine immediately affects the cardiovascular system of the human body, whereas snorting cocaine has more of an effect on the central nervous system. Most users report a loss of an initially sustained erection or the inability to achieve an erection when smoking cocaine in its "crack" form. The cardiovascular system has a direct correlation on the amount of blood flow to the penis, thus decreasing the amount of blood needed to obtain an erection. Users report that delayed ejaculation or no ejaculation is a common occurrence when using both forms of cocaine.

12. a. Many reports suggest that the use of marijuana decreases sexual functioning. One study reported lower plasma testosterone and sperm count in psychologically addicted cannabis users. Other studies have suggested that repeated and habitual marijuana users find sex disinteresting and rather boring.

13. a. Nicotine from smoking tobacco produces no evidence of any effect on either men's or women's libido. Tobacco does, however, reduce fertility in women and hastens menopause. Testosterone levels may decrease but levels will reverse within about a week after cessation of smoking. Impotence in males can improve after cessation of smoking but with severe cardiovascular damage the erectile failure is often permanent. Moreover for men, "smoking" is seen as a "high-risk" factor in relation to organic erectile failure.

14. b. Hallucinogens produce very dramatic alterations in consciousness and perception while disrupting normal thought processes. Areas of concern are emotional expression and the integration of perceptual processes. While the person generally retains his/her orientation and memory, he/she experiences a "loosening" of the cognitive inhibitory or filtering processes, resulting in being flooded with vivid images and thoughts. When a "bad trip" is experienced, naturally all interest in sexuality diminishes as the person is absorbed in fear or paranoia.

15. c. Spanish fly is derived from the ground-up bodies of a species of beetle found in southern Europe. Taken internally, it travels to the bladder and is excreted in the urine. It acts as a powerful irritant, causing acute inflammation of the lining of the bladder and urethra as it passes out of the body. This stimulation of genital structures has resulted in the myth of cantharides as a drug which enhances sexual awareness. In reality, "Spanish fly" can be extremely painful for both genders, producing effects ranging from mild irritation to extensive tissue destruction and even death, depending on the dose. It is completely useless as a sexual stimulant and its dangerous side effects make it a substance that should never be used.

16. d. Rohypnol ("Roofies") is a potent and hypnotic sedative not prescribed in the United States but relatively inexpensive on the street. It may be the "mightiest Micky Finn" ever concocted since it is a dime-size white pill that dissolves quickly in a soda. In about 10 minutes, it creates a drunklike effect that lasts several hours and then works its way out of the system within 24 hours. Rohypnol multiplies the effect of alcohol, causing loss of inhibition, extreme sleepiness, relaxation and—worst of all—amnesia. "Roofie rapes" have become a problem. The victims usually don't remember anything. A word of caution, when socializing do not accept an open drink that someone else has poured for you. Alcohol use can also alter a person's level of mental awareness and make a person more susceptible to date rape. Since alcohol lowers inhibitions, persons sometimes make choices regarding sexual behavior that they would not otherwise choose while under the influence of alcohol.

17. a. Most research is focused on male sexuality rather than female sexuality. Erection and ejaculation are certainly more readily studied than lubrication swelling, and easier to measure than the female orgasm. The effects of drugs which impair erection and emission are well understood, but there have been few comparable studies on the effects of these substances on the female sexual response. There is good evidence to suggest that drugs that affect sexual interest by acting on the brain, either as stimulants or depressants, have similar sexual effects on both genders.

SUMMARY AND ASSESSMENT OF DRUG EFFECTS: The effects of drugs on sexual behavior are difficult to assess accurately and reliably because a person's response to a drug represents multiple factors. The factors may include the pharmacological action of the drug and the dose, as well as situational psychological forces such as the person's expectations of what the drug will do, his/her mental state, his/her relationship with a partner(s), and his/her personality characteristics. Since the drug is only one variable in a complex system, the same drug may produce different sexual effects depending on the input of the other forces. You need to be careful about self-medicating.

In summary, health care professionals would not recommend the use of nicotine, amphetamines, marijuana, hallucinogens, cocaine, Spanish fly, or Rohypnol. Furthermore, alcohol should be used with caution. Any problems with prescription drugs should be discussed with your health care professional—physician, nurse practitioner, pharmacist, or counselor. If there is a problem, you should seek help from an appropriate health professional to find a solution instead of covering up the symptoms.

REACTIONS: Use the space provided to respond to the following questions.

1. What did you learn about the effects of drugs on sexuality? How will this information help you in a present situation or in the future?

2. Have you ever used drugs before, during, or after a sexual experience? How did the drug(s) change your sexual experience? Was it a good or bad experience? Why? What would you do differently now?

3. Do you feel comfortable with communicating to your partner the choices regarding drug use and sexuality issues? Why or why not?

4. What complications, problems, or frustrations do you have when drugs are used to promote images of either positive or negative sexuality?

SOURCE: Developed by Sandra K. Kammermann, M.S., Ed.S., and Charles T. McElmurray, MD, University of South Carolina School of Medicine; Kenneth C. Traum, M.P.H., and Robert F. Valois, PhD, MPH, University of South Carolina, School of Public Health, "How Much Do You Know About Sex and Drugs." Copyright © by Valois, Kammermann & Associates, May 1996. All rights reserved. Used with permission of the authors.

SECTION VII

DATING AND RELATIONSHIPS

Relationships present many challenges. At the onset there is the challenge of building a positive relationship with oneself, then with family, friends, co-workers, and others within an individual's social network. We also have the challenge of developing special, intimate relationships with friends and, when we desire them, sexual relationships. This section presents a variety of inventories and strategies to help you examine dating and relationship dynamics.

Dating and Relationships exercises include:

56. Index of Sexual Satisfaction
57. Trust Scale
58. Are You Inhibited?
59. Relationship Vulnerability Scale
60. Power in Relationships: Is Yours in Balance?
61. Sexual Decisions: Sex in Dating
62. Interracial Dating
63. Your Personal Commitment Levels
64. Can Your Relationship Go the Distance?
65. Issues in Human Sexuality: Cohabitation
66. How to Live together . . . and Live to Talk About It
67. Sexual Decisions: Extramarital Sex

56

Index of Sexual Satisfaction

PURPOSE: This questionnaire is designed to measure the degree of satisfaction you have in a sexual relationship with your partner.

DIRECTIONS: Answer each item as carefully and accurately as you can. Place the number that represents your response in the space provided. Then ask your partner to complete the questionnaire while covering your responses.

1 = Rarely or none of the time

2 = A little of the time

3 = Some of the time

4 = A good part of the time

5 = Most of the time

You   Partner

_____ _____ 1. I feel that my partner enjoys our sex life.

_____ _____ 2. My sex life is very exciting.

_____ _____ 3. Sex is fun for my partner and me.

_____ _____ 4. I feel that my partner sees little in me except for the sex I can give.

_____ _____ 5. I feel that sex is dirty and disgusting.

_____ _____ 6. My sex life is monotonous.

_____ _____ 7. When we have sex it is too rushed and hurriedly completed.

_____ _____ 8. I feel my sex life is lacking in quality.

_____ _____ 9. My partner is sexually very exciting.

_____ _____ 10. I enjoy the sex techniques that my partner likes or uses.

_____ _____ 11. I feel that my partner wants too much sex from me.

_____ _____ 12. I think that sex is wonderful.

_____ _____ 13. My partner dwells on sex too much.

_____ _____ 14. I feel that sex is something that has to be endured in our relationship.

_____ _____ 15. My partner is too rough or brutal when we have sex.

_____ _____ 16. My partner observes good personal hygiene.

_____ _____ 17. I feel that sex is a normal function of our relationship.

You   Partner

____ ____ 18. My partner does not want sex when I do.

____ ____ 19. I feel that our sex life really adds a lot to our relationship.

____ ____ 20. I would like to have sexual contact with someone other than my partner.

____ ____ 21. It is easy for me to get sexually excited by my partner.

____ ____ 22. I feel that my partner is sexually pleased with me.

____ ____ 23. I feel that I should have sex more often.

____ ____ 24. I feel that my sex life is boring.

SCORING: Follow these steps:

First, be sure you have responded to all the items.

Second, you have to rescore some of the items because they are worded in a different direction than the others. Change the scores for items 1, 2, 3, 9, 10, 12, 17, 19, 21, 22, 23 as follows:

Change an answer of 5 to a 1.

Change an answer of 4 to a 2.

A 3 remains a 3.

Change an answer of 2 to a 4.

Change an answer of 1 to a 5.

Third, after rescoring, add these scores for all 24 items and from the total subtract 20. This is your Total Score: _____.

Fourth, the possible range of scores is from 0 to 100. This exercise, of course, is not absolute, but only an indication of the magnitude of sexual satisfaction in a two-person relationship. A **low score** would indicate a very small or no sexual problem existing in your relationship with this person and a **high score** would indicate the presence of a sexual problem to some degree. You should keep in mind that a "sexual problem" will be relative to the personality dynamics of the individuals involved in the relationship.

REACTIONS: Use the space provided to respond to the following questions.

1. Considering the range of scores from 1 to 100, how does your score fall in the range? What do you think that means?

2. What did you learn about yourself or your partner?

3. Review your responses and look for ways to improve the sexual aspect of your relationship with your partner. List two goals you are setting to improve the sexual aspect of your relationship.

4. If your partner completed the questionnaire, how do you feel about the comparison of your scores and responses?

SOURCE: W. W. Hudson, D. F. Harison, and P. C. Crosscup, "A Short-Form Scale to Measure Discord in Dyadic Relationships," *Journal of Sex Research,* 1981, 17, p. 160. Reprinted by permission of the *Journal of Sex Research,* a publication of the Society for the Scientific Study of Sex.

57 | Trust Scale

PURPOSE: This exercise is designed to provide some indication of the level of trust in your relationship with your partner or a close friend.

DIRECTIONS: Read each of the following statements and decide whether it is true of your relationship with you partner or friend. Indicate how strongly you agree or disagree by choosing the appropriate number from the scale below and placing it in the space provided in the left-hand margin.

1 = strongly disagree

2 = moderately disagree

3 = mildly disagree

4 = neutral

5 = mildly agree

6 = moderately agree

7 = strongly agree

Initial Score   Final Score

_____   1. I know how my partner is going to act. My partner can always   _____
              be counted on to act as I expect.

_____   2. I have found that my partner is a thoroughly dependable   _____
              person, especially when it comes to things that are important.

_____   3. My partner's behavior tends to be quite variable. I can't always   _____
              be sure what my partner will surprise me with next.

_____   4. Though times may change and the future is uncertain, I have   _____
              faith that my partner will always be ready and willing to offer
              me strength, come what may.

_____   5. Based on past experience I cannot, with complete confidence,   _____
              rely on my partner to keep promises made to me.

_____   6. It is sometimes difficult for me to be absolutely certain that my   _____
              partner will always continue to care for me; the future holds so
              many uncertainties and too many things can change in our
              relationship as time goes on.

_____ 7. My partner is a very honest person and, even if my partner were to make unbelievable statements, people should feel confident that what they are hearing is the truth. _____

_____ 8. My partner is not very predictable. People can't always be certain how my partner is going to act from one day to another. _____

_____ 9. My partner has proven to be a faithful person. No matter who my partner was married to, she or he would never be unfaithful, even if there was absolutely no chance of being caught. _____

_____ 10. I am never concerned that unpredictable conflicts and serious tensions many damage our relationships because I know we can weather any storm. _____

_____ 11. I am very familiar with the patterns of behavior my partner has established, and he or she will behave in certain ways. _____

_____ 12. If I have never faced a particular issue with my partner before, I occasionally worry that he or she won't take my feelings into account. _____

_____ 13. Even in familiar circumstances, I am not totally certain my partner _____ will act in the same way twice.

_____ 14. I feel completely secure in facing unknown new situations because _____ I know my partner will never let me down.

_____ 15. My partner is not necessarily someone others always consider reliable. I can think of some times when my partner could not be counted on. _____

_____ 16. I occasionally find myself feeling uncomfortable with the emotional investment I have made in our relationship because I find it hard to completely set aside my doubts about what lies ahead. _____

_____ 17. My partner has not always proven to be trustworthy in the past, _____ and there are times when I am hesitant to let my partner engage in activities that make me feel vulnerable.

_____ 18. My partner behaves in a consistent manner. _____

SCORING: This is how to score yourself: For questions 3, 5, 6, 8, 12, 13, 15, 16 and 17, reverse the numbers. That is, if you put down a 1, change it to a 7 and write this in the space provided in the right-hand margin. In the same way, if you scored a 2, change it to a 6, change 3 to a 5, 5 to a 3, 6 to a 2, and 7 to a 1. A neutral score of 4 remains unchanged. When you have reversed the scoring for the items listed above, take the scores for the remaining items and write them in the right-hand margin just as they are. Add all the scores

in the right-hand margin to obtain your final trust score. If you are interested, you can add up the scores for the following questions to arrive at a score for each subscale of trust:
Predictability: Add scores for questions 1, 3, 8, 11, 13, and 18.
Dependability: Add scores for questions 2, 5, 7, 9, 15, and 17.
Faith: Add scores for questions 4, 6, 10, 12, 14, and 16.

INTERPRETATION: The trust scale is an attempt to measure trust in terms of predictability, dependability, and faith. Clearly, such a brief scale cannot capture all the subtleties and nuances in a concept as complex as trust. Nevertheless, the following interpretation should offer some insight as to your current level of trust.

Total Trust Score = _____

High Trust: If your total trust score exceeds 110, you have described yourself as being a very trusting person. Such people typically feel that they are involved in a very successful relationship and that their love for their partner is very strong. People with high faith scores in particular believe that both they and their partner are motivated by unselfish concerns. Their relationship is seen as valuable in and of itself, and they share a strong sense of attachment and emotional closeness. Trusting people seem to approach interactions and discussions in a uniquely positive, tolerant manner. First, they expect their partner to behave in a positive way toward them.

Low Trust: People who score below 90 on the Trust Scale fall into the low-trust category. The characteristic profile for such people is fairly simple to describe: It is generally the opposite of the high-trust group. It should come as no surprise that a relationship in which partners have difficulty trusting one another is a relationship in trouble. Of the three groups, these people report the greatest number of problems and are the most poorly adjusted and least satisfied in their relationships. In particular, people scoring low on faith express less love for their partner and are less inclined to see their relationship as one of mutual giving. Their emotional attachment is likely to be rather fragile, and they may fear the risks of being close to and dependent on their partner.

Hopeful Trust: The group of individuals scoring in the middle range, between 90 and 100, is perhaps the most interesting group. By most standards these people are involved in a successful relationship. In their feelings of love for their partner, the number of problems they report, and their marital adjustment, they fall between the trusting and untrusting groups, but in an important way they tend more toward the trusting end. The emotional bonds many of these people feel may be just as intense as those of trustful couples. To a large extent these hopefuls also believe that both they and their partner are involved in the relationship because it is of value in and of itself. Yet somehow they lack the assurance that could allow them to fully accept their partner's demonstrations of unselfish concern without hesitation. In general, one might consider these couples as having relatively good relationships but definitely with room for improvement.

REACTIONS: Use the space provided to respond to the following questions.

1. Do you feel your score accurately represents your level of trust with the person you have in mind? Why or why not?

2. Do you and/or your partner or friend wish to increase your level of trust? If so, what steps will you take to improve your trust level?

SOURCE: Reprinted with permission from *Psychology Today* magazine, Copyright © 1986 (Sussex Publishers, Inc.).

58 | Are You Inhibited?

PURPOSE: This quiz is designed to give some indication of your level of sexual inhibition.

DIRECTIONS: Answer each of the questions below by circling your response.

1. You are looking around a crowded room, you meet the eye of an attractive person—would you smile or wink?
   a. Yes
   b. No

2. If someone caught your eye across a crowded room, would you walk over and start a conversation?
   a. Yes
   b. No

3. Would you ask out on a date a person you have met only once?
   a. Yes
   b. No

4. Would you be comfortable initiating physical contact, such as a touch on the arm, asking for a dance, or giving a hug or kiss?
   a. Yes
   b. No

5. You are going out to dinner with someone special for the first time—where would you tend to go?
   a. A small, quiet, out of the way place
   b. A restaurant that was downtown or near a busy shopping mall

6. How would you dress for a dinner date with someone for the first time?
   a. Extra attractive
   b. Somewhat modest

7. Would you accept an invitation to come in for a drink after the first date?
   a. Yes
   b. No

8. When the time and situation were right, would you start a discussion about the future of a relationship?
   a. Yes
   b. No

9. When the time and situation were right, would you start a discussion about sex?
   a. Yes
   b. No

10. Would you ever suggest viewing an erotic film together?
    a. Yes
    b. No

11. When the time and situation were right, would you start a discussion about safer sex?
    a. Yes
    b. No

12. If your friend offered to have "you for dessert" in a restaurant bathroom right after dinner, would you agree?
    a. Yes
    b. No

SCORING: Each answer of "a" is worth one point. Add up the number of "a" answers and place your score in the space provided. Scores range from 0 to 12.

Your score _____

INTERPRETATION: Keep in mind that this is a short quiz and a general indication of your level of sexual inhibition.

If you scored:

9–12: This would suggest very little, if any sexual inhibition. You are more than likely to be very comfortable with your sexuality and that of your partner.

5–8: This would suggest some situational sexual inhibition and an average level of sexual comfort.

0–4: A score in this range would suggest that you are relatively modest and somewhat sexually inhibited in certain situations.

REACTIONS: Use the space provided to respond to the following questions.

1. Do you think your score is an accurate reflection of your level of sexual inhibition? Why or why not?

2. Would your score have been different three years ago? Explain.

3. To which specific items do you wish you could respond "yes"? How would those changes affect your relationship(s) with a significant other?

59 Relationship Vulnerability Scale

PURPOSE: People begin and continue relationships for a variety of reasons. Sometimes these motives are not mutual. A person can be taken advantage of and eventually hurt in the process. Relationships can sometimes evolve into dominant and submissive roles, without either person realizing it. This inventory is designed to help you evaluate your relationship and determine, to some degree, your chances of being in a vulnerable situation.

DIRECTIONS: Read each question carefully while reflecting on your present or most recent relationship. Check YES or NO as either relates to your situation.

	Yes	No
1. Is your partner often unavailable for phone calls at home or work?	____	____
2. Does he/she ask about the amount of money you earn or your parents earn, or try to get involved with your financial planning?	____	____
3. Does your partner ever belittle your efforts and/or ideas?	____	____
4. Has your partner ever disappeared for any length of time (overnight, several days, a week) and not informed you of his/her whereabouts?	____	____
5. Does he/she live with you and contribute little or nothing to household maintenance?	____	____
6. Does your partner borrow money and seldom bother to repay it, or frequently ask you to buy him/her things, or always use your car?	____	____
7. Has he/she had one or more tragic misfortune(s) that needed your financial assistance?	____	____
8. Has your partner told you early in your relationship that he/she would like to be married and described a life of love and luxury for both of you but made no definite steps in that direction?	____	____
9. Do you stop your present activity or postpone your plans when he/she calls to do something on the spur of the moment?	____	____
10. Is he/she the only person in your life?	____	____
11. Do you allow your partner to take the "upper hand" in your affairs?	____	____

12. Have you ever noticed any discrepancies concerning what your partner has told you in regard to his/her name, job, background, family, etc.? _____ _____

13. When you go out does your partner avoid socializing with his/her or your family and friends? _____ _____

14. Do you usually wait for others to introduce you to potential partners instead of taking the initiative to meet new people on your own? _____ _____

15. When your partner describes his/her future goals, does it seem unclear as to where you fit in the future? _____ _____

16. Do you feel that you should be married to be happy? _____ _____

SCORING: Give yourself one point for each "yes" response to the questions.

Your score: _____

13–16: You are very vulnerable to being in a lopsided relationship, which may result in hurt feelings in the future. You should seriously examine the contour and direction of your relationship with your partner. For you to continue with your present situation is almost certain to be a waste of time and energy.

9–12: You are vulnerable to being taken advantage of. Stop and ask yourself if you are getting out of this relationship what you are putting into it.

5–8: You are somewhat vulnerable to being hurt. Your relationship probably has potential but needs to be evaluated. You and your partner should discuss your future to determine what type of lifestyle you both desire.

1–4: You do not seem vulnerable to being dominated in your relationship. Keep the statements to which you responded "yes" in mind, and openly discuss them with your partner.

REACTIONS: After scoring yourself on this inventory, respond to the following questions:

1. What are some of the factors that cause you to get hurt in relationships? Explain.

2. What can happen in a relationship when one person demands and the other complies most of the time? Explain.

3. What can eventually happen in a relationship when one person has been in a vulnerable position for five or more years? Explain.

4. Do you feel you are vulnerable in your current relationship? Explain. If not applicable, think about a past relationship and explain.

60

Power in Relationships: Is Yours in Balance?

PURPOSE: This exercise is designed for you to take a preliminary look at the balance of power in your relationship.

DIRECTIONS: Read carefully each of the questions below. Mark YES or NO in the space provided. Cover your answers or have your partner complete this inventory on a separate sheet of paper.

You Partner

_____ _____ 1. When I am really bothered by some aspect of my partner's behavior, I feel free to speak my mind without serious fear of losing this person's love and affection.

_____ _____ 2. I can share my accomplishments/strengths with my partner.

_____ _____ 3. I can share my shortcomings/weaknesses with my partner.

_____ _____ 4. We discuss financial matters that affect both of us, and usually find a compromise or agree to disagree without malice.

_____ _____ 5. We discuss the use of our recreation/free time that affects both of us, and usually find a compromise or agree to disagree without resentment.

_____ _____ 6. We discuss our needs and obligations for socializing that affect both of us, and usually find a compromise or agree to disagree without any bitterness.

_____ _____ 7. My partner respects my educational pursuit and the time I devote to my studies (or my career pursuit and the extra hours I spend at work).

_____ _____ 8. Discussions take place in advance about the possible effects of individual decisions on our life as a couple.

_____ _____ 9. Most of the time, when angry, I communicate this directly instead of avoiding an issue or punishing my partner indirectly.

_____ _____ 10. The basis of our relationship, those behaviors agreed upon, can be renegotiated without risking our love for each other.

SCORING: Add up the number of "yes" responses for you and your partner and place them in the space provided.

Your Total Score: _____ **Partner's** Total Score: _____

INTERPRETATION: If you both scored between **7** and **10** on this exercise there is evidence that power is equally distributed in your relationship with some room for improvement. A score between **4** and **6** for both of you would suggest that you have the potential for balancing power in your relationship and you should work on it. If both of you scored between **1** and **3** an equal distribution of power seems questionable at this time.

REACTIONS: Use the space provided to respond to the following questions.

1. Do you feel you and your partner's scores accurately represent the balance of power in your relationship. Explain why or why not.

2. No relationship is perfect. Discuss areas where you feel the balance of power could be improved.

61 | Sexual Decisions: Sex in Dating

PURPOSE: Your response to the behavior in the following situation could offer you some valuable insight into your own feelings as well as those of your partner.

DIRECTIONS: Read the following paragraph carefully and respond to the questions that follow.

Peter and Marcia had been dating steadily for several months. Marcia was very much in love with Peter and he seemed to like her too. Peter was very popular, and he was friendly and outgoing. Marcia was flattered that he dated her, as she had always felt herself to be unattractive. Marcia was only a little bit surprised when Peter gave her an ultimatum: Either they have sexual intercourse or he would not see her any more. Marcia valued her virginity, but she valued her relationship with Peter more, so her decision was not too difficult. Marcia did as Peter asked.

1. Should Marcia have responded as she did? Why?

2. What effect might Peter's ultimatum have on their relationship? Why?

3. Is Peter being fair with Marcia? Is he respecting her personal rights? Why or why not?

4. What can happen in a relationship when one person demands and the other complies?

5. Is Marcia giving up a big part of herself or is this sort of give-and-take a reality in any relationship? Why?

REACTIONS: Peter and Marcia may want to take into consideration that "sex changes things" in a relationship. When sexual intercourse is added to a relationship, the relationship will never be the same again. It is not necessarily bad, nor good—just different. Both partners need to be ready to admit that they will not be the same people.

1. Do you think Peter and Marcia have considered that "sex changes things"? Why or why not?

2. Do you agree with the statement that "Sex changes a relationship?" Why or why not?

3. If you agree, how does this philosophy affect your relationships?

62 | Interracial Dating: What's Your Opinion?

PURPOSE: As we move toward the turn of the century society continues to become more pluralistic. Nonetheless, interracial dating continues to be controversial. This exercise is designed for you to express your opinion on a variety of aspects of interracial dating.

DIRECTIONS: Use the space provided to respond to the following statements about interracial dating. "Interracial" in this exercise refers to races.

1. Do you approve of interracial dating?

   Yes _____ No _____ Undecided _____

   If yes or no, please explain why.

2. Do you consider people who date interracially sellouts or traitors to their respective race?

   Yes _____ No _____ Undecided _____

   If yes or no, please explain why.

3. Do you think mixed-race couples can overcome the problems inherent in such a relationship?

   Yes _____ No _____ Undecided _____

   If yes of no, please explain why.

4. Have you ever been romantically involved in an interracial relationship?
   Yes _____ No _____ Currently dating someone of another race _____

5. If yes, how difficult was the relationship due to outside pressure?
   Very difficult _____ Moderately difficult _____ Not difficult at all _____

6. If you have dated interracially, by your perception, who gave you the most difficulty?
   Men of your same race _____
   Women of your own race _____
   Men of your partner's race _____
   Women of your partner's race _____
   Other situations (briefly explain)

7. Would you marry someone of another race?
   Yes _____ Currently married to someone of another race ___
   No _____ Undecided _____
   If yes or no, please explain.

8. Would you choose to have children with someone of another race?
   Yes _____ Have children with someone of another race _____
   No _____ Undecided _____
   If yes or no, please explain.

9. If you are currently dating someone of another race, what attracted you to this person?

10. Do you (now or in the past) date only individuals outside your own race? (Check all that apply.)

Yes _____

No _____

A mixture of races _____

11. Do you think most interracial relationships are doomed to failure? Why or why not?

12. In your opinion, what would it take in a variety of aspects for a long-term interracial relationship to be successful? Explain why.

REACTIONS: If desired, use the questions from this exercise to trigger a discussion regarding interracial dating with a partner or a friend or friends of similar or different races.

63 | Your Personal Commitment Levels

PURPOSE: The inventory that follows will help you set standards for yourself concerning your sexual behavior as it relates to another person. Every relationship between you and another person has some level of commitment. When you make a commitment, you agree to take personal responsibility for your sexual behavior and for the rights and feelings of another individual.

DIRECTIONS: Below are listed various forms of sexual behavior. In the blank to the right of each behavior, write the letter(s) corresponding to the levels of commitment you think are appropriate for the behavior described. Respond according to your own thoughts and feelings, not according to what you feel is "correct." Include all the levels of commitment that apply for each behavior by writing the corresponding letters on the line.

Levels of Personal Commitment

a. Casually attracted   e. Exclusively dating

b. Good friends   f. Engaged

c. Casually dating   g. Living together

d. Steadily dating   h. Married

1. Light embracing or fond holding of hands   _____
2. Casual good-night kissing   _____
3. French kissing   _____
4. Petting over clothes, standing or sitting   _____
5. Horizontal embrace with some petting but not undressed   _____
6. Petting of partner's breast from outside clothing   _____
7. Petting below the waist of partner outside clothing   _____
8. Petting below the waist of partner under clothing   _____
9. Petting below the waist of both partners under clothing   _____
10. Nude embrace   _____
11. Oral sex   _____
12. Sexual intercourse   _____

SCORING: A level commitment of (e) or higher on any item could indicate a considerable degree of sexual-emotional involvement. The unspoken message to your partner may be that you are committed to him/her in some manner due to the nature and amount of sexual contact. However, it could mean little or no commitment other than sexual experimentation or sex play.

APPLICATION: After you have completed your response to all the behaviors, read through the levels of commitment carefully. You may want to discuss these thoughts regarding commitment levels with your friends, your partners, or your teacher. Such a discussion may enable you to further clarify your feelings on the issue. Remember these are your personal standards which may help you guide your sexual behavior.

1. Ask yourself how "committed" you would want your partner to be to you to engage in each behavior. Is it the same as what you have listed?

2. Do you think young people are consistent between their sexual feelings and their actual sexual behaviors? Explain.

SOURCE: Sandra K. Kammermann, MS, EdS, "Your Personal Commitment Levels," in Kammermann, Doyle, Valois, and Cox, *Wellness R.S.V.P.*, 2d ed., Benjamin/Cummings Publishing Co, Inc., Menlo Park, CA. Reprinted by permission of the authors. Copyright © 1986 by the authors. All rights reserved.

Can Your Relationship Go the Distance?

PURPOSE: This exercise is designed to give you some idea of the situations you could face if you were to venture into a long-distance relationship. The type of questions you should ask yourself are outlined here. This also gives you the opportunity to identify how realistic you are about a possible separation and shows you how to analyze a long-distance relationship you are already in.

DIRECTIONS: Read each question carefully and place your answer in the space provided. Cover your responses and have your partner do the same. After completion, identify your situations and score yourself. You may wish to compare and discuss your reactions to these statements with your partner.

You   Partner

_____ _____ 1. You have been dating/living with/married to your partner for a year. A fabulous career or college opportunity is offered, and you must live 600 miles apart for the next year. Who is making the move?

   a. You

   b. Your partner

_____ _____ 2. Until now, your relationship has been:

   a. Strong and growing

   b. Comfortable and convenient

   c. Bordering on shaky

   d. Shaky

   e. Exciting but not exactly stable

_____ _____ 3. Before you make the move, you have the expectations of what it's going to be like during the separation. You have discussed the career advantages of the move, and:

   a. Have had some serious discussion about changes in lifestyle, dating other people, and the fears involved

   b. Have not yet discussed the interpersonal aspects of the separation

   c. Adopted the philosophy of "it will work out for the best"

   d. Have touched on ideas such as weekends together, vacations, and seeing other people, and have concluded that you will probably live together after the year

____ ____ 4. Suddenly you have much more time for yourself. You decide to:

    a. Try to take that fitness course that did not fit your schedule last year

    b. Catch up on all the reading you have put aside

    c. Experience some growth from your new sense of freedom and privacy

    d. Sit around and alternate between feelings of depression and appreciating your new freedom

____ ____ 5. How will you deal with seeing other people?

    a. Not try the singles scene or become a hermit, but see friends on a casual basis

    b. Plan not to date unless someone really interesting comes along

    c. Decide that neither you nor your partner will date anyone

    d. Take the opportunity to have an affair while your partner is working

____ ____ 6. How will the distance affect your financial situation? You decide to:

    a. Write letters and not call unless it is very urgent

    b. Save up all your dining-out money for a few big weekends together

    c. Cut back sharply on all expenses and save up for a romantic vacation for the two of you

    d. Call collect

    e. Use the telephone freely and not worry about costs

____ ____ 7. Your partner is traveling and has developed some new friends and a lifestyle that you have not been able to share. In your letters and phone calls you:

    a. Keep him/her informed of the news at home and explain honestly that you cannot really appreciate much of what is told to you because you really do not know these new friends

    b. Try to spend as much time understanding his/her new experiences as you do keeping your partner current on shared ones

    c. Simply remind him/her of the good times you have had together

    d. Just try to keep him/her informed of all the news back home

____ ____ 8. You have grown accustomed to cooking and playing tennis with your partner as a means of releasing tensions. Now that he/she is traveling, you will probably:

   a. Take up swimming

   b. Find a new tennis partner

   c. Not know exactly what to do

   d. Become a little bitter about his/her not being there

____ ____ 9. You are used to sharing with your partner the problems and accomplishments from daily school and/or work, but it no longer costs a dime to make that call. You will:

   a. Probably make too many long-distance phone calls

   b. Share your ups and downs with your friends

   c. Write your feelings out in long letters

   d. Probably be a little bit resentful about his/her not being there

____ ____ 10. You are prepared to spend most of your weekends:

   a. Going to parties solo and leaving the same way

   b. Thinking about how lucky other couples are and feeling a little bit sorry for yourself

   c. Curled up with a good book and a late movie

   d. Meeting new people and enjoying the freedom

____ ____ 11. A very attractive person asks you out. You respond by:

   a. Saying you have a commitment to someone else and stay at home

   b. Saying you are committed to someone else and walk away

   c. Saying no, and going home to your favorite fantasy

   d. Saying yes, having a good time, and not telling your partner

   e. Saying yes, having a great time, and telling your partner

SCORING: Now match your response to each question with the assigned values from the chart below. Total the values for each of your answers to obtain your overall score on the quiz.

QUESTION VALUE	QUESTION VALUE	QUESTION VALUE	QUESTION VALUE
1. a. 1	4. a. 1	7. a. 3	10. a. 2
b. 2	b. 4	b. 1	b. 2
	c. 3	c. 4	c. 2
2. a. 1	d. 2	d. 2	d. 2
b. 2			
c. 3	5. a. 1	8. a. 3	11. a. 2
d. 4	b. 2	b. 3	b. 2
e. . . . 3	c. 3	c. 1	c. 2
	d. 4	d. 2	d. 3
3. a. 1			e. 3
b. 4	6. a. 2	9. a. 1	
c. 3	b. 3	b. 3	Total Score ____
d. 2	c. 3	c. 4	
	d. . . . 3	d. 2	

INTERPRETATION:

14 or below: You have a realistic approach to handling a long-distance relationship.

15–19: You are fairly realistic about a long-distance relationship, but more communication is needed.

20–25: Be careful if you fall in this range: You could be unrealistic in your approach to a long-distance relationship.

26–31: A score this high should be a warning. Your relationship could be slipping, or if you were to enter one, it could be unstable.

32 and above: An overall score in this range indicates some real risk to your relationship. The possibility of losing each other exists, and something should be done in the near future.

REACTIONS: Use the space provided to respond to the following questions.

1. Do you think your score on this scale will change over time? Why or why not?

2. If your partner completes the questionnaire, do your scores fall in the same range? If so, is that positive? If not, is it a problem?

3. What have you learned about your relationship?

65 | Issues In Human Sexuality: Cohabitation

Should two people live together before they decide to marry?

DIRECTIONS: Read the paragraphs below carefully, making sure you clearly understand both sides of the issue before you write your reactions.

Some say yes. They argue that you never know people until you live with them, but once you do, their likes and dislikes, moods and expectations become apparent. The constant association brought about by living together serves as a trial period. It is easier to dissolve this relationship than a legal marriage, and there is little chance of having children, because not being married and living together might necessitate the use of contraception. If such a living arrangement works out, there is good reason to believe a marriage would be successful.

Others maintain that people are always changing, and there is no way of knowing if you can live with someone in the future—in spite of being able to live with that person right now. They argue that a successful arrangement now doesn't imply a successful marriage later. They further oppose living together because sex before marriage is prohibited by religious teaching. Besides, they believe that this arrangement represents "playing at" marriage and is therefore immature.

REACTIONS: Use the space provided to respond to the following questions.

1. With which viewpoint do you agree? Why?

2. How do your parents and other family members feel about people living together before marriage? Do their feelings influence yours?

3. Does your current partner or significant other agree with you? Would you consider living together prior to marriage?

SOURCE: George B. Dintiman and Jerrold S. Greenberg, *Health Through Discovery*, p. 353. © 1983, Addison-Wesley Publishing Company, Inc, Reading, MA

66

How to Live Together . . . and Live to Talk About It

PURPOSE: If marriage or any other personal arrangement were considered similar to a management and labor union situation, many partners would be on strike continuously. Unfair labor practices, emotional blackmail, fraud, malfeasance, bribery, perjury, and vindictiveness would all be on the list of grievances.

Most couples, however, never recognize that their unions are governed by management-labor rules that they themselves unknowingly have established together. This seems to be true whether people choose to live together for reasons of economic necessity, passion, companionship, trial marriage, or marriage. Sharing household tasks, deciding financial arrangements, determining child-rearing practices, and agreeing on sexual habits are part of a system of giving and receiving. The couples who are aware that something is always given or received for something else—whether or not the outcome is always satisfactory—understand that fairness can be negotiated. This kind of partnership is less likely to lead to an emotional trap.

If you're in the early stages of your partnership, or if you're in the process of renegotiating an old agreement, here are six questions that form the basis for some ground rules for living together that work.

DIRECTIONS: Read each question carefully and respond by writing a YES or NO in the blank under the YOU column. After you have responded to each statement, cover your responses and have your partner respond with a YES or NO in the PARTNER column.

	Partner	You
1. Have you developed a comfortable contract?	_____	_____
a. Do you feel power is distributed?	_____	_____
b. Do you share financial resources?	_____	_____
c. Is decision making the responsibility of both partners?	_____	_____
2. Have you built trust and respect into your relationship?	_____	_____
3. Do you remember the nonnegotiables such as loving or compassionate feelings?	_____	_____
4. Have you both learned to bargain or negotiate in your relationship?	_____	_____

5. Have you built on each other's interests and accomplishments?   _____   _____

6. Have you evaluated your relationship with these questions?   _____   _____
    a. Are roles, responsibilities, and rituals mutually satisfying?   _____   _____
    b. Are emotional expectations gratifying to both?   _____   _____
    c. Are needs and drive acceptably matched?   _____   _____

SCORING: When both you and your partner have responded to the questions, compare your responses. You may wish to discuss each item. The following paragraphs will give some further explanation and guidelines regarding each issue.

1. **Develop a comfortable contract.** Real commitment can only come after two people understand the fine print or implications of their relationship. A workable contract can be relatively simple and manageable. There should be four elements to this verbal agreement.

   a. *Power must be distributed.* As with any political system, power can corrupt and absolute power can corrupt absolutely when held by only one partner; distribution of power offers a system of checks and balances. One companion cannot be trusted with complete dominance, even though he or she has the best interests of the other at heart.

   b. *Financial resources must be shared.* Money is a potent symbol of power and love in an intimate union. In the past the breadwinner had an advantage in this regard, but today, sharing resources can be more clearcut because both partners often earn money. However, it is still a problem when finances are not pooled into one account. A joint banking account is a good test of a pair's credibility with each other.

      Couples can have separate funds for their personal needs, but a joint account indicates good faith in sharing collective expenses. Some working women consider their funds as supplemental income. This assumption is a mistake for both partners because it often breeds a resentful feeling expressed this way by one husband: "She can do what she wishes with her money, but my money is supposed to be 'ours.'" Women who are full-time housewives and mothers can take consolation in the fact that their total managerial skills would cost at least $25,000 in the marketplace. This should make both companions aware that executive management, even in a home, does not come cheap.

   c. *Decision making is the responsibility of both partners.* Making decisions about living arrangements, vacation plans, automobile purchases, the children's education, retirement goals, and necessary cutbacks in expenses are tasks to be undertaken jointly. When two people begin a relationship respecting each other's desires and priorities, this task is easier. Moreover, regrets and recriminations are less likely to occur when both enter enthusiastically into the decision making and both strongly voice their opinions.

   d. *Tasks should be assigned on a rational basis.* Day-to-day duties should be apportioned on the basis of expertise—not dictated by male or female stereotypes. Even when one partner has an exaggerated sense of his or her own competence, it does not mean he or she has the knowledge and talent to do everything.

A contract that is comfortable for two people contains at least these four elements and should be renegotiated as changes seem necessary. Such an informal agreement can help keep the practical realities of living together separate from issues of the heart.

2. **Build trust and respect.** Most partners assume that they deserve trust and respect simply because they live with each other. But realistically, it doesn't work that way. Both trust and respect must be earned over a period of time. Some people foster mistrust through deception or unfulfilled promises, even those made in good faith. When a husband who is always detained at work promises time after time to come home by a certain hour but never does so, his wife feels deceived and angry. All he really has to do is stop promising specific time and call to say he'll be late. Promising gets more companions into trouble than the dastardly deed that brought on the promise. Pledges to lose weight; to give up smoking, drinking, or marijuana; to end any annoying personal habits; to be less argumentative or misleading; to be more loving, thoughtful, or considerate; to be less demanding sexually only disappoint when they are not kept.

3. **Remember the nonnegotiables.** In any contract or agreement, a pair often assumes that loving and compassionate feelings go with the bargain. Unfortunately, they don't. It is unrealistic to expect them to do so. As with anything truly valuable in life, these feelings must be given freely. Can't one beg or force a mate to show love? The answer is an unequivocal no. The situation requires a positive approach. When one mate shows that he or she cares, the other is more likely to respond in kind. All the repetitious, tired phrases people use to elicit desired reactions from a partner are futile: "If you loved me you would," "Why don't you tell me you love me," "All I want is consideration," "You're never around when I need you," "All you think about is yourself." Such remarks are often made in anger, frustration, anxiety, or grief—hardly the state of mind to trigger a positive reaction from someone you love. To receive compassion, show it first. What kinds of feelings are nonnegotiable? Deciding whether to have guests for the weekend is negotiable. Thoughtfulness and concern are nonnegotiable. Deciding whether to live in a house or an apartment is negotiable. All the human emotions that make one feel secure, loved, or accepted cannot be bartered. They must be given freely.

When a union is gloomy, worrisome, sour or generally unhappy, one partner often expects the other to set things right, much as one would expect repair of a leaky faucet or a broken vacuum cleaner. Afraid of rejection or stubbornly insisting it is a mate's fault that life together has gone awry, partners often resist taking the first positive step toward reconciliation.

More marriages than people care to admit have broken up for this simple reason—waiting for a partner to go first in expressing feelings, either an apology or any show of affection.

4. **Learn to bargain.** Some people are good hagglers. Others are only moderately skilled or don't care to dicker at all. However, haggling is a necessary part of any agreement between two people living together. Without negotiation, a pair risks repressing desires, misunderstanding each other's intentions, or crowding each other's living space.

What is bargained? Responsibilities in living together, conflicts between separate and joint interests, acceptable behavior on the part of both, and important changes in circumstances. Changes in career interests, lifestyles, living with and then without children, as well as changes in external circumstances, make it imperative to renegotiate periodically.

Establishing negotiation as a principle of living together from the very beginning allows both partners to surface their sources of discontent with less of a feeling of being personally threatened. It also enables each to be more calm in the bargaining process because it will generally occur when both are in an amicable, rather than an irritable, mood.

5. **Build on each other's interests and accomplishments.** There is a false dichotomy that companions establish for themselves in their life together. A stimulating career, an all-consuming hobby, a fascinating community of friends or a challenging civic project is perceived as taking away from one's relationship with a partner. Ultimately, such a view forces a choice between a mate and a special interest. The assumption is similar to the one established through a management training exercise called the "zero-sum game," which essentially says that when there are two competing business managers, the achievement of one takes away from that of the other.

A valid, workable, and fair agreement between two people today should include just the opposite premise: The accomplishment of either person should be thought of as adding to the total enjoyment of both. Direct participation in a partner's activity is unnecessary, but supporting his or her involvement in it is important. Unless both are supportive of each other in this way, the relationship will be marred by competition, malice, and jealousy.

For a relationship to work, companions need not be equal in achievements or abilities. It is enough that each one feels that he or she has something to contribute to their joint happiness. When one's only goal in life is holding on to a mate, a union becomes burdensome for both. When couples have no sources of stimulation outside themselves, they will feed emotionally on one another and their relationship will close in on them in a suffocating way. But when a pair understands that outside interests add to their common pleasure, a union can prosper and grow. Nothing has to be denied or hidden. Everyone knows that new experiences are appreciated more when they are shared with someone. That someone can easily be one's lifelong companion.

6. **Evaluate your contract on three levels.** Every couple's idea of happiness is different from that of all other pairs, but all can ask the same three questions to evaluate their relationship.

a. *The three r's: Are roles, responsibilities, and rituals mutually satisfying?* (These include careers, household duties, finances, sex, parenting roles, friends, social activities, relatives, mealtimes, bedtimes, and lifestyle.)

b. *The rainbow's end: Are emotional expectations gratifying to both?* (Companionship, flexibility, affection, security, consideration, fairness, trust, bargaining, respect, and care.)

c. *The hidden powerhouse: Are needs and drives acceptably matched?* (Control, intimacy, dependence, passivity, independence, inclusion, assertiveness, and sexuality.)

A love relationship always begins with two distinct sets of assumptions held by the two companions. Terence Rattigan, the English playwright, sensitively portrayed these assumptions in his play "Separate Tables." True coupling occurs as each gives up his "separate table" and joins the other.

The six ground rules described here can make combining tables and living together not only intimate and loving but practical and fair, too.

REACTIONS: Review your responses to the questions above and then use the space provided to respond to the following questions.

1. In what two areas do you feel you and your partner could improve? Why? Does your partner feel the same?

2. In what two areas are you and your partner doing very well? Why? Does your partner agree?

SOURCE: Herbert G. Zerof, *Finding Intimacy: The Art of Happiness in Living Together.* Copyright © 1978 by Herbert G. Zerof. Adapted by permission of Random House, Inc.

67

Sexual Decisions: Extramarital Sex

PURPOSE: Your response to the behavior described in the following situation could offer you some valuable insight into your own feelings as well as your partner's.

DIRECTIONS: Read the paragraph below carefully, and respond to the questions that follow.

Bob and Mary have been married for almost seven years. Mary grew up knowing she was an unwanted child and was always neglected. She married Bob because he provided her with all the love, affection, and attention that she needed but had never received from her family.

Bob, however, had been raised in a family that stressed education and achievement and as a result had become very achievement-oriented. He had gone through law school and was now a lawyer with a very busy private practice. He has very little time left for Mary. Mary still loves Bob but finds she needs many things that he no longer provides. Mary works in an office where Scott, a co-worker, constantly pays attention to her. When she is depressed, he cheers her up. He takes her to lunch and keeps her laughing and enjoying herself. They have also had some serious talks about Mary's relationship with Bob. Scott wants the relationship to go further, but until now Mary has refused.

1. Should Mary continue seeing Scott outside the office? Why or why not?

2. Should Mary talk with Bob to try to change his behavior? What should she say?

3. Should Mary resign herself to the situation and seek fulfillment in some hobby? Should she see a therapist? How would either choice affect her life?

4. Could Bob modify his needs for achievement? Could Mary modify her needs for love and affection? How might these modifications take place?

5. Are Scott's actions fair to Mary? Why or why not?

6. Place yourself in Bob's or Mary's shoes and discuss what you might do. Be specific.

SECTION VIII | LOVE AND INTIMACY

*L*ove and intimacy are important and complex aspects of people's lives. The joys and sorrows of love and intimacy have inspired many people of various cultures. Everyone's life has been influenced in significant ways by love, beginning with the love we received as children and infants. A person's best and worst moments in life may be tied to a love relationship. Although love is of great concern to humankind, little is conclusively known about it. In this section we offer you the opportunity to explore various aspects of love and intimacy.

Love and Intimacy exercises include:

68 Rate Your Romantic Attraction

PURPOSE: This scale is designed for you to rate your level of romantic attraction to your partner.

DIRECTIONS: For each of the following statements rate the strength of your feeling about your partner. Use the scale of 1 to 5, circling a "5" to represent strong agreement with the statement and a "1" to represent strong disagreement. If you are uncertain of an answer circle a "3." After completing this exercise cover your answers and have your partner respond to each statement and compare scores if desired. Please respond as you personally feel and use the following letter code for your answers:

SD = Strongly Disagree	D = Disagree	U = Uncertain	A = Agree	SA = Strongly Agree

	SD D U A SA	You	Partner
1. I feel very lucky to know her (him).	1 2 3 4 5	_____	_____
2. There was something unusual and very special between us at our very first meeting.	1 2 3 4 5	_____	_____
3. We often have a very good time even when we are not doing anything grand.	1 2 3 4 5	_____	_____
4. I don't really miss him (her) a great deal when we are apart.	1 2 3 4 5	_____	_____
5. Her (his) approval is very important to me.	1 2 3 4 5	_____	_____
6. I get a thrill from just looking at him (her).	1 2 3 4 5	_____	_____
7. I want this relationship to be permanent.	1 2 3 4 5	_____	_____
8. I am happiest when we are together.	1 2 3 4 5	_____	_____
9. Being with her (him) is far more important to me than where we are or what we are doing.	1 2 3 4 5	_____	_____
10. I enjoy him (her) in many ways other than just sharing affection.	1 2 3 4 5	_____	_____
11. I feel that we were meant for each other.	1 2 3 4 5	_____	_____

	SD	D	U	A	SA	You	Partner

12. She (he) is a beautiful person. 1 2 3 4 5 _____ _____

13. I enjoy planning things that we will be doing together. 1 2 3 4 5 _____ _____

14. I am not curious about why and how much he (she) is interested in me. 1 2 3 4 5 _____ _____

15. I want our attraction to be mutual. 1 2 3 4 5 _____ _____

16. I would still consider looking for another romantic partner. 1 2 3 4 5 _____ _____

17. I get something very special from her (him) that I do not experience with anyone else. 1 2 3 4 5 _____ _____

18. I am not willing to keep this relationship even if he (she) makes changes in himself (herself). 1 2 3 4 5 _____ _____

19. I love to surprise her (him) with a card, letter, or gift. 1 2 3 4 5 _____ _____

20. I can forgive him (her) almost instantly. 1 2 3 4 5 _____ _____

21. I have a feeling of excitement when we are together. 1 2 3 4 5 _____ _____

22. I want to occupy my own, unique place in her (his) life. 1 2 3 4 5 _____ _____

23. I would have to search for a long time to find someone I enjoy so much and so consistently. 1 2 3 4 5 _____ _____

24. Physical affection with him (her) is something very different and quite unparalleled. 1 2 3 4 5 _____ _____

25. She (he) is a great companion. 1 2 3 4 5 _____ _____

26. He (she) has an attractive personality. 1 2 3 4 5 _____ _____

27. I like doing things for her (him). 1 2 3 4 5 _____ _____

28. Our relationship has something that is splendid and very hard to find. 1 2 3 4 5 _____ _____

29. He (she) is often on my mind. 1 2 3 4 5 _____ _____

30. There is something almost mystical in our eye-to-eye contact. 1 2 3 4 5 _____ _____

	SD	D	U	A	SA	You	Partner

31. I experience unusual and pleasantly exciting feelings when I am with her (him).   1   2   3   4   5   _____   _____

32. I am not willing to continue this relationship in spite of all the pleasantness.   1   2   3   4   5   _____   _____

33. When there are tasks to be done, I prefer that we do them alone.   1   2   3   4   5   _____   _____

34. I have made efforts to change in order to be more pleasing to him (her).   1   2   3   4   5   _____   _____

35. I enjoy discussing a wide variety of subjects with him (her).   1   2   3   4   5   _____   _____

36. She (he) is my favorite person to be with.   1   2   3   4   5   _____   _____

37. We have something that could be described as spiritual intimacy.   1   2   3   4   5   _____   _____

38. I get a very strange feeling when I meet him (her) unexpectedly.   1   2   3   4   5   _____   _____

39. I would not feel jealous if she (he) became strongly interested in another person.   1   2   3   4   5   _____   _____

40. I am, or could easily become, totally committed to this relationship.   1   2   3   4   5   _____   _____

41. I enjoy being with him (her) even when we are silent.   1   2   3   4   5   _____   _____

42. I want her (him) to respect me for my abilities.   1   2   3   4   5   _____   _____

43. When things are going well between us, I have a sense of completeness and well-being.   1   2   3   4   5   _____   _____

44. It means a lot to me when he (she) does something special for me.   1   2   3   4   5   _____   _____

45. At times I wish she (he) would know and accept me completely.   1   2   3   4   5   _____   _____

46. I would like to know what he (she) finds attractive about me.   1   2   3   4   5   _____   _____

47. I like to touch and be touched by her (him).   1   2   3   4   5   _____   _____

48. I am attracted in a way that others do not understand.   1   2   3   4   5   _____   _____

	SD	D	U	A	SA	You	Partner

49. There are so many things I wish we could do together, if only there were enough time. 1 2 3 4 5 _____ _____

50. If he (she) were criticized by others, I would defend him (her). 1 2 3 4 5 _____ _____

51. I am not quite willing to do things for her (him) without having to know the reason why. 1 2 3 4 5 _____ _____

52. I have a protective interest in his (her) well-being. 1 2 3 4 5 _____ _____

53. The pleasure I get from this relationship is well worth the price I pay. 1 2 3 4 5 _____ _____

54. She (he) has a great deal of influence over me. 1 2 3 4 5 _____ _____

55. I often wonder what he (she) is thinking. 1 2 3 4 5 _____ _____

56. It's easy for me to say "no" to her (him). 1 2 3 4 5 _____ _____

57. I like to think up lovely surprises for him (her). 1 2 3 4 5 _____ _____

58. I am happy when she (he) is pleased with me. 1 2 3 4 5 _____ _____

59. This relationship is not really my strongest interest in life. 1 2 3 4 5 _____ _____

60. This is the man (woman) with whom I would prefer to grow old. 1 2 3 4 5 _____ _____

SCORING: Your score is determined for this scale by first reverse-scoring ten of the items. For items 4, 14, 18, 32, 33, 38, 39, 51, 56, and 59:

Change an answer of 1 to a 5.

Change an answer of 2 to a 4.

A 3 remains a 3.

Change an answer of 4 to a 2.

Change an answer of 5 to a 1.

Write the number score for each question in the column to the right.

Now add up your rating points and place your total in the space provided.

Total Score = _____

INTERPRETATION: **220 and up:** Strong chance for a satisfying longer-term relationship if scored by both parties.

200–219: You and/or your partner appear to have some doubts and/or questions about the relationship that you need to evaluate.

Under 200: You and your partner are probably better suited for friendship than for a long-term romantic relationship.

REACTIONS: Use the space provided to respond to the following questions.

1. Do you feel that your score accurately represents your level of romantic attraction? Why or why not?

2. Do you think your responses to this inventory will change six months from now? Explain.

3. Do you see a long-term relationship with this person? Why or why not?

69

How Well Do You Know Your Partner?

PURPOSE: Have you ever stopped to think—really think—about how well you know your partner. How much do you know about his/her childhood, likes, dislikes, fears, or favorites? This test gives you an idea of where to start.

DIRECTIONS: Find a time when you and your partner can be alone and feel free to talk about yourselves. Each of you should take this test on separate sheets of paper and compare your answers afterwards to see how you have done.

1. What is his/her birth date?
2. How many brothers and sisters does he/she have?
3. Where do his/her parents live?
4. Name two of his/her best friends.
5. What is his/her favorite color?
6. What is his/her favorite kind of music?
7. What would embarrass him/her most?
8. What really makes him/her angry?
9. Who is his/her greatest hero/admired person?
10. What is his/her biggest fear?
11. What does he/she like most about his/her job/studies in school?
12. What does he/she like least about his/her job/studies in school?
13. Of what accomplishment is he/she proudest?
14. Name one pet he/she had as a child?
15. What would his/her choice be for a vacation: a camping trip, visit to a big city, a boat trip, or to stay at home?
16. What nicknames was he/she called in school?
17. What is his/her favorite food?
18. Which type of pet would he/she prefer: a cat, a dog, a bird, or fish?
19. What is his/her most prized possession?
20. What would he/she dislike most: drying the dishes, cleaning the bedroom, doing laundry, or getting gas in the car?
21. What book has he/she most recently read?

22. What is his/her favorite family occasion?

23. What is his/her favorite free time activity?

24. If he/she could buy anything in the world what would be his/her first choice?

25. If he/she could move, in what city or what area would he/she most like to live?

SCORING: Give yourself a point for each similar answer you have for your partner. The most points you could possibly have would be 25.

20–25 You are a top-notch observer and more than likely listen well to the likes and needs of your partner. Good job and keep it going.

14–19 Although you know quite a bit about your partner, perhaps you need to improve your fine tuning.

0–14 Your communication, both listening and sharing, appear to be lacking. Perhaps you have been preoccupied with your own concerns, or your partner may be unexpressive. Now is the time to be talking over dinner, during walks, or at other opportune times.

REACTION: Use the space provided below to respond to the following questions.

1. Did you have any fun doing this? Explain.

2. Did you learn anything new or significant about your partner that you did not know before?

3. Were you comfortable doing this exercise with your partner? Explain. Do you think your partner was comfortable doing this exercise?

70 Just How Sexy Are You?

PURPOSE: What do we mean when we say a person is sexy? Reference is often made to a person's physical appearance, dress, or body language. Some people say that sexiness is a state of mind and the ability to communicate that state of mind to others. The nature of this exercise is to help you clarify what you feel sexiness is and how sexy you feel you are. Keep in mind that our sexual standards and customs are changing all the time, and most are relative to you, your lifestyle, and your social environment.

DIRECTIONS: Read each of the following statements and write either "A" for Agree or "D" for Disagree in the space provided according to whether you tend to agree or disagree with the statement. If you are in doubt, force yourself to decide whether Agree or Disagree is more applicable in your case.

_____ 1. The opposite sex will respect you more if you are not too familiar with them.

_____ 2. Sex without love is highly unsatisfactory.

_____ 3. All in all I am satisfied with my sex life.

_____ 4. Everything has to be "just right" before I can get sexually excited.

_____ 5. I do not feel that I am deprived sexually.

_____ 6. I do not need to respect or love a sexual partner in order to enjoy intercourse with him or her.

_____ 7. If I love a person I could do anything with them.

_____ 8. I know that I am sexually very attractive.

_____ 9. I have very many friends of the opposite sex.

_____ 10. It doesn't take much to get me excited sexually.

_____ 11. Sex contacts have never been a problem to me.

_____ 12. I would like to take part in a sex orgy.

_____ 13. I feel there is something lacking in my sex life.

_____ 14. I enjoy having sexual intercourse with a partner of a different skin color or racial background.

_____ 15. I have strong feelings but when I get a chance I can't seem to express myself.

_____ 16. A woman should sometimes take the dominant role or be sexually aggressive.

_____ 17. I believe in taking my pleasures where I find them.

____ 18. My sex behavior often causes me unhappiness.

____ 19. Young people should be allowed to behave more or less as they please regarding sexual matters.

____ 20. My love life is just great.

____ 21. I have never been involved with more than one sex affair at the same time.

____ 22. Sex should be used only for the purpose of reproduction, not for personal pleasure.

____ 23. I prefer to have intercourse under the bedcovers and with the lights off.

____ 24. I deliberately try to keep sex out of my mind.

____ 25. It is all right to seduce a person who is old enough to know what he or she are doing.

____ 26. I get sexually aroused only at night, not in the day.

____ 27. My parents' influence did not inhibit me sexually.

____ 28. Intercourse should not take place outside marriage.

____ 29. I make lots of vocal noises during intercourse.

____ 30. My religious beliefs are against sex.

____ 31. I have had a number of both homosexual and heterosexual relationships.

____ 32. There are some things I only do because they please my sex partner.

____ 33. I wouldn't change my sex life in any significant way.

____ 34. I would not enjoy watching my usual partner having intercourse with someone else.

____ 35. I always know for sure when I have had an orgasm.

____ 36. My sex partner does not satisfy all my physical needs.

____ 37. I would never vote for a law permitting polygamy.

____ 38. Being good in bed is very important to my partner.

____ 39. Sex is not all that important to me.

____ 40. I would like to have a new sex partner every night.

____ 41. I don't enjoy a lot of precoital love play.

____ 42. I find it difficult to tell my sex partner what I like or I don't like about lovemaking.

____ 43. Sex is more exciting with a stranger.

____ 44. To me physical factors in my sex partner are more important than psychological ones.

____ 45. I would like my sex partner to be more explicit.

____ 46. I would never dream of taking part in group sex.

____ 47. I sometimes feel like scratching or biting my partner during intercourse.

____ 48. No one has ever completely satisfied me sexually.

____ 49. Illicit relationships do not excite me.

____ 50. I believe my sexual activities are average.

____ 51. Romantic love is just childish illusion.

_____ 52. I can't stand people touching me.

_____ 53. I feel sexually less competent than I think most of my friends are.

_____ 54. I would be bothered if my sex partner had sexual relations with someone else.

_____ 55. Physical sex is the most important part of marriage.

_____ 56. I am a bit afraid of sexual relationships.

_____ 57. I don't like to try different positions in lovemaking.

_____ 58. The need for birth control upsets my lovemaking because it makes everything so cold-blooded.

_____ 59. Physical attraction is not important to me.

_____ 60. I love physical contacts with the opposite sex.

SCORES

	Agree	Disagree		Agree	Disagree		Agree	Disagree
1.	–1S	0	21.	0	1P	41.	0	1S
2.	0	1P	22.	–1S	0	42.	0	1C
3.	1C	0	23.	–1S	0	43.	1P	0
4.	–1S	0	24.	–1C	0	44.	0	–1S
5.	1C	0	25.	1P	0	45.	–1C	0
6.	1P	0	26.	–1S	0	46.	0	1P
7.	1S	0	27.	0	–1C	47.	1S	0
8.	1P	0	28.	0	1P	48.	–1C	0
9.	1P	0	29.	1S	0	49.	0	1P
10.	1S	0	30.	–1C	0	50.	1C	0
11.	1C	0	31.	1P	0	51.	1P	0
12.	1P	0	32.	–1S	0	52.	–1S	0
13.	–1C	0	33.	1C	0	53.	–1C	0
14.	1P	0	34.	0	1P	54.	0	1P
15.	–1C	0	35.	0	–1S	55.	1S	0
16.	0	–1S	36.	0	1C	56.	0	1C
17.	1P	0	37.	0	1P	57.	0	1S
18.	0	1C	38.	1S	0	58.	–1C	0
19.	1P	0	39.	–1C	0	59.	0	1S
20.	1C	0	40.	1P	0	60.	1S	0

SCORING: Three dimensions of your sexual behavior are marked by the letters P, S, and C.

Step 1: Add up all the P points you scored.

Step 2: Add up all the S points you scored.

Step 3: Add up all the C points your scored.

Step 4: Subtract minus-S scores from your S totals.

Step 5: Subtract minus-C scores from your C totals.

This question allows you to evaluate your sex life and behavior along three important dimensions—**Promiscuity, Contentment,** and **Sensuality** (P, C, and S)—considered by psychologists to be important aspects in your sex life.

Remember, when you assess your score, that there is nothing right or wrong about any score you achieve—this merely gives you an indication of what kind of person you are in the important field of sexual relationships. An extreme score will simply mean that you are not characteristic of the majority of other people in this respect. It does not mean that you are bad or good, moral or immoral, mentally balanced or unbalanced.

On the whole, **the higher your P score,** the more **promiscuous** a person you are—the more likely you are to be involved in large numbers of sexual relationships. Bear in mind, however, that while this means you are leading an active sex life, it does not necessarily imply that you are particularly happy with it. Often a high level of promiscuity brings more problems with it than pleasures in the long run.

The **C,** or **contentment,** scale gives a closer picture of whether your love life is a happy and satisfactory one. Most people will end up with a fairly low C score (whether on the plus or minus side) and it is fair to say that those scoring very high in Cs are really having a satisfactory love life, whereas those with high minus-Cs are certainly disappointed or discontented.

The **S score** refers to the dimension of **sensuality,** a term in some ways exchangeable with sexiness, but which in all is probably related to the individual's interest in the purely physical side of sex. Of course, sexual intercourse is impossible without a strong physical component, but psychological factors are important as well. People vary in the amount of weight that they attach to the physical and psychological aspects. Those with a high S score tend to find the former dominant in their lives, and the opposite is true for those with a high minus-S score.

For more specific information on how you rate, look at the detailed comments in the analysis. You will end up with three scores, of course, which may all be high, all low, or balanced among the categories. There are no hard and fast rules as to how to interpret the combination of scores; do this yourself.

ANALYSIS

Your P Rating

0P to 5P This represents an average rating, which suggests that you are not in any sense of the word a promiscuous person, although you have a normal person's interest in the realities of sex and appreciate that it would be a peculiar person indeed who did not at some time in his or her life feel a sexual attraction to more than one individual at any one time. If your score lies in this range and you have a C rating greater than 2, the chances are that you are either happily married or in the midst of a stable and satisfying relationship with someone you feel very close to.

6P to 10P Your sexual behavior is not far from average, though you have a slight but perfectly normal tendency to sexual adventuring. If you are under the age of 30 this is no more than characteristic human behavior, and if it is coupled with a C rating of greater than 4, you are probably enjoying a balanced and contented love life.

11P to 15P There's not much doubt that you have a promiscuous nature and as a result you may find your love life in a bit of a tangle. This may not upset you too much, and if you are scoring above 5 on the C rating, then there is not much doubt that you are enjoying yourself. If you have only a middle C rating, or one with some minuses in it, however, then it is very likely that your free and easy approach to sex is bringing domestic or personal problems with it.

Over 15P You have a decidedly promiscuous nature. Possibly this is the first flush of youth, and if you have a C rating of 6 or more, then you have really nothing to complain about. It may be, however, that other people are suffering because of your exceedingly casual approach to sex, and this is almost certainly the case if your C score is in the low pluses or in the minuses. If it is in the high minuses, then your promiscuity might be a flight from something and may led to conflict.

Your C Rating

7C to 10C Congratulations on having what is almost certainly a balanced and contented love life. Long may it remain so. The chances are that this is coupled with a relatively low P rating (say under 10) and very likely a plus rather than minus S rating. If your husband (wife) or lover has filled our his (her) questionnaire, too, he (she) is likely to have come out with a rather similar score.

3C to 6C These denote a high measure of contentment in one's sex life, which at any age is a bonus to life happiness in general. Like all human pleasures, sex is never 100 percent perfect, but your rating suggests that you have learned to accept these imperfections.

–2C to 2C Perhaps this is best described as an average score, suggesting that your love life on the whole is happy, though sprinkled occasionally with difficulties and small disappointments. Very possibly you move from moments of ecstasy to moments of relative indifference in your lovemaking, and this may be part of your nature and unlikely to change as the result of any conscious efforts on your part. A more passionate lover might stir things up a bit, but if you have a high P rating and also a high S rating the chances are that you have tried this without success. This may not be particularly useful advice if you are already married, except to say that perhaps you could persuade your husband [wife] to return to the passion of the past.

–3C to –6C Clearly there is some measure of disappointment and dissatisfaction in your love life. This could be due to a large number of reasons of which you are probably yourself unaware. If you have a high P rating as well, then it may be that you are seeking sexual contentment in the wrong way—through a series of whizzbang affairs which come to nothing and are in the long run deeply unsatisfying. If your low score is also coupled with a low S score (say, less than –2) then the problem may be that you are a bit inhibited and disinclined to let go of your emotions. If you are married or have a lover, the best tactic by far will be to talk over your dissatisfaction in as open a way as you can.

–7C to –10C It is quite evident that you are leading a disappointing love life, perhaps to the extent that it is making the rest of your life a bit unsatisfactory as well. There are so many possible reasons for this that one cannot offer specific advice, but if you are married you should certainly talk about this immediately and quite openly with your partner. The problem may be one of inhibition (do you have a low S rating as well?) or of sheer incompatibility and boredom—this may be reflected in a high P rating as well. Perhaps also you are trying too hard, for it is certainly true that contentment in love comes naturally and not at anyone's command. If your life is being made unhappy through disappointing love relationships, then you might consider seeking qualified medical or psychological advice.

Your S Rating

5S to 10S This denotes that you have a strongly developed nature which makes the physical side of lovemaking tremendously important to you. There are clearly no traces of sexual inhibition in your nature, and if this is coupled with a high C rating (say, over 4) then you have probably found yourself a perfect partner as well. It would be rather surprising if these high scores are also coupled with a very high P rating, unless you are a young person just experiencing the first joys of sex. If you do have high scores on all three ratings, then love may well be the most important aspect of your life. Fine, as long as you still find time and emotional energy for other things.

4S to −4S Most people will find themselves falling into this category, and scores in this range will almost invariably be coupled with plus C scores and a P rating no higher than 15. If your S score lies between 1 and 4, then you have a healthy appreciation of the physical side of love; if between 0 and −4 you may be a bit on the inhibited side. If you have an inhibited partner too, then this will be reflected in a C score in the minuses rather than in the pluses.

−5S to −10S In physical terms you are a cool person and not likely to be described as a passionate lover—unless you happen to meet exactly the right partner for you! Very likely there is some psychological inhibition here, possibly because when you were younger you were taught to believe that sex was improper and immoral. It is not easy to overcome such prejudices from the past, but the first step might be to realize that without love and sex (two of the most important drives), the human race would soon cease to exist.

REACTIONS: Now use the space provided to respond to the following questions.

1. What is your P rating and how is this information useful to you in developing relationships?

2. What is your C rating and how is this information useful to you in developing relationships?

3. What is your S rating and how is this information useful to you in developing relationships?

4. About which rating are you the most comfortable? Why?

SOURCE: *Understanding Yourself* by J. M. McCarthy with an Introduction by Dr. Christopher Evans. Copyright © 1977 Phoebus Publishing Company/BPC Publishing Limited. Reprinted by permission of A&W Publishers, Inc.

71 | Mosher Sex-Guilt Inventory

PURPOSE: This inventory is designed for you to examine a series of guilt- or nonguilt-related statements.

DIRECTIONS: This subscale consists of 50 items arranged in pairs of responses written by college students in response to sentence completion items such as "When I have sexual dreams. . . ." You are to respond to each item as honestly as you can by rating your response on a 7-point scale from 0, which means "not at all true of (for) me," to 6, which means "extremely true of (for) me." Ratings of 1 to 5 represent ratings of agreement-disagreement that are intermediate between the extreme anchors of "not at all true" and "extremely true" for you. This limited comparison is often useful since people frequently agree with only one item in a pair. In some instances, both or neither item may be true for you, but you will usually be able to distinguish between items in a pair by using different ratings from the 7-point range for each item.

Rate each of the items from 0 to 6 by circling the number. Keep in mind the value of comparing items within pairs. Please do not omit any items. Circle your response.

	0 = Not at all true for me	6 = Extremely true for me	Final Score
"Dirty" jokes in mixed company . . .			
1. do not bother me.	0 1 2 3 4 5 6		_____
2. make me very uncomfortable.	0 1 2 3 4 5 6		_____
Masturbation . . .			
3. is wrong and will ruin you.	0 1 2 3 4 5 6		_____
4. helps one feel eased and relaxed.	0 1 2 3 4 5 6		_____
Sex relations before marriage . . .			
5. should be permitted.	0 1 2 3 4 5 6		_____
6. are wrong and immoral.	0 1 2 3 4 5 6		_____
Sex relations before marriage . . .			
7. ruin many a happy couple.	0 1 2 3 4 5 6		_____
8. are good in my opinion.	0 1 2 3 4 5 6		_____

	0 = Not at all true for me	6 = Extremely true for me	Final Score

Unusual sex practices . . .

9. might be interesting. 0 1 2 3 4 5 6 _____

10. don't interest me. 0 1 2 3 4 5 6 _____

When I have sexual dreams . . .

11. I sometimes wake up feeling excited. 0 1 2 3 4 5 6 _____

12. I try to forget them. 0 1 2 3 4 5 6 _____

"Dirty" jokes in mixed company . . .

13. are in bad taste. 0 1 2 3 4 5 6 _____

14. can be funny depending on the company. 0 1 2 3 4 5 6 _____

Petting . . .

15. I am sorry to say, is becoming an
    accepted practice. 0 1 2 3 4 5 6 _____

16. is an expression of affection, which is
    satisfying. 0 1 2 3 4 5 6 _____

Unusual sex practices . . .

17. are not so unusual. 0 1 2 3 4 5 6 _____

18. don't interest me. 0 1 2 3 4 5 6 _____

Sex . . .

19. is good and enjoyable. 0 1 2 3 4 5 6 _____

20. should be saved for wedlock and
    childbearing. 0 1 2 3 4 5 6 _____

"Dirty" jokes in mixed company . . .

21. are coarse, to say the least. 0 1 2 3 4 5 6 _____

22. are lots of fun. 0 1 2 3 4 5 6 _____

	0 = Not at all true for me	6 = Extremely true for me	Final Score

When I have sexual desires . . .

23. I enjoy them like all healthy humans
    beings.   0 1 2 3 4 5 6   _____

24. I fight them, for I must have complete
    control of my body.   0 1 2 3 4 5 6   _____

Unusual sex practices . . .

25. are unwise and lead only to trouble.   0 1 2 3 4 5 6   _____

26. are all in how you look at it.   0 1 2 3 4 5 6   _____

Unusual sex practices . . .

27. are okay as long as they're heterosexual.   0 1 2 3 4 5 6   _____

28. usually aren't pleasurable because you
    have preconceived feelings about
    their being wrong.   0 1 2 3 4 5 6   _____

Sex relations before marriage . . .

29. in my opinion, should not be practiced.   0 1 2 3 4 5 6   _____

30. are practiced too much to be wrong.   0 1 2 3 4 5 6   _____

As a child, sex play . . .

31. is immature and ridiculous.   0 1 2 3 4 5 6   _____

32. was indulged in.   0 1 2 3 4 5 6   _____

Unusual sex practices . . .

33. are dangerous to one's health and
    mental condition.   0 1 2 3 4 5 6   _____

34. are the business of those who carry
    them out and no one else's.   0 1 2 3 4 5 6   _____

When I have sexual desires . . .

35. I attempt to repress them.   0 1 2 3 4 5 6   _____

36. they are quite strong.   0 1 2 3 4 5 6   _____

	0 = Not at all true for me	6 = Extremely true for me	Final Score

Petting . . .

37. is not a good practice until after marriage.   0 1 2 3 4 5 6   _____

38. is justified with love.   0 1 2 3 4 5 6   _____

Sex relations before marriage . . .

39. help people adjust.   0 1 2 3 4 5 6   _____

40. should not be recommended.   0 1 2 3 4 5 6   _____

Masturbation . . .

41. is wrong and a sin.   0 1 2 3 4 5 6   _____

42. is a normal outlet for sexual desire.   0 1 2 3 4 5 6   _____

Masturbation . . .

43. is all right.   0 1 2 3 4 5 6   _____

44. is a form of self-destruction.   0 1 2 3 4 5 6   _____

Unusual sex practices . . .

45. are awful and unthinkable.   0 1 2 3 4 5 6   _____

46. are all right if both partners agree.   0 1 2 3 4 5 6   _____

If I had sex relations, I would feel . . .

47. all right, I think.   0 1 2 3 4 5 6   _____

48. I was being used, not loved.   0 1 2 3 4 5 6   _____

Masturbation . . .

49. is all right.   0 1 2 3 4 5 6   _____

50. should not be practiced.   0 1 2 3 4 5 6   _____

SCORING: Your score is determined for this inventory (guilty script) by reverse-scoring the nonguilty alternatives (those item numbers in the following key).

To reverse the scores: 0 = 6

1 = 5

2 = 4

3 = 3

4 = 2

5 = 1

6 = 0

KEY: Reverse-score items 1, 4, 5, 8, 9, 11, 14, 16, 17, 20, 22, 23, 26, 27, 30, 32, 34, 36, 38, 39, 42, 43, 46, 47, and 49 and write the new score in the space to the right of each question. Add the new scores and write your total here.

INTERPRETATION: High guilt   = 200–300

Medium guilt = 100–199

Low guilt   = 0–99

At Texas Tech University, C. Hendrick and B. Hendrick asked 105 students to complete this inventory. They found that students tended to rate the items slightly toward the guilty side of the midpoint.

REACTIONS: Use the space provided to respond to the following questions.

1. Do you feel your score accurately represents your level of sex guilt? Explain why or why not.

2. Do you feel that you would like to decrease your level of sex guilt? If so, what steps do you think are appropriate?

Source: D. L. Mosher, Revised Mosher Guilt Inventory, in C. M. Davis, W. L. Yarber, and S. L. Davis (eds.), *Sexuality-Related Measures: A Compendium.* Lake Mills, IA: Graphic, 1988. Used by permission of the author.

72 | Body Contact Questionnaire

PURPOSE: We gave the test that follows to a group of men and women and asked them to evaluate their reactions to statements describing physical contact with others. The test attempts to measure both how comfortable the subject feels with body contact and the level of need for such contact. Incidentally, this is a good test to give to someone with whom you're romantically involved. We've included a second scoring column for that purpose.

DIRECTIONS: Below is a list of 25 statements that describe situations involving body contact. Read each one and decide how closely that statement describes your feelings. Choose a number from the scale below that indicates your response and write it in the space provided. After you've answered all 25 questions, turn the page to find the results.

1	2	3	4
Rarely	Occasionally	Frequently	Almost Always

Partner   You

1. I'm uncomfortable when I'm examined by my doctor.   1. _____ _____
2. Whenever I dance, I prefer to dance close.   2. _____ _____
3. I feel that hugging is an appropriate way to greet and say good-bye.   3. _____ _____
4. If there's a choice in a restaurant, my date and I prefer to sit next to each other rather than across the table.   4. _____ _____
5. I prefer cars with bucket seats.   5. _____ _____
6. When buying clothes, I become uncomfortable when the sales person measures me for alterations and tailoring.   6. _____ _____
7. I'm uncomfortable trying to sleep on an airplane with a stranger sitting next to me.   7. _____ _____
8. I like my lover to spend a long time exploring my entire body before we make love.   8. _____ _____
9. I like to have my back rubbed even more than I like sex.   9. _____ _____
10. There are parts of my body I don't like my lover to touch.   10. _____ _____
11. When I'm angry I like to be held.   11. _____ _____
12. In the movies I like to hold hands.   12. _____ _____

13. I hate it when people stare into my eyes.

13. _____ _____

14. I'm far more receptive to being touched when I've been drinking or taking drugs.

14. _____ _____

15. Cuddling is important to me.

15. _____ _____

16. I like taking baths and showers with my lover.

16. _____ _____

17. I like it when animals climb into my lap.

17. _____ _____

18. It takes me a long time to feel comfortable when I'm in close quarters with a person I'm just getting to know.

18. _____ _____

19. I hate it when the cashier touches my hand while giving me my change.

19. _____ _____

20. I find public telephones unsanitary and disgusting.

20. _____ _____

21. I like to be rubbed with oils or lotions.

21. _____ _____

22. After sex I feel the need to wash myself as soon as possible.

22. _____ _____

23. Being touched isn't part of what turns me on.

23. _____ _____

24. Most people I know like to touch me more than I like to touch them.

24. _____ _____

25. I find being tickled irritating and upsetting.

25. _____ _____

Scoring Key:

1. (reverse) _____	7. (reverse) _____	13. (reverse) _____	19. (reverse) _____
2. _____	8. _____	14. (reverse) _____	20. (reverse) _____
3. _____	9. _____	15. _____	21. _____
4. _____	10. (reverse) _____	16. _____	22. (reverse) _____
5. _____	11. _____	17. _____	23. (reverse) _____
6. (reverse) _____	12. _____	18. (reverse) _____	24. (reverse) _____
			25. (reverse) _____

Scoring: To find your score on the Body Contact Questionnaire, transfer your numerical responses to the Scoring Key. As you do this, reverse the values for questions 1, 6, 7, 10, and so forth, as indicated. In those cases:

4 points become 1 point

3 points becomes 2 points

2 points becomes 3 points

1 point becomes 4 points

All other point values remain the same. Once you've filled in the Scoring Key, add up your points and write the total in the box below.

Total Score

INTERPRETATION: Touching and closeness are essential parts of lovemaking—and lovemaking, according to one woman quoted in *The Hite Report*, "is 75 percent sensuality and 25 percent sexuality." The literature of sex therapy has long emphasized the importance of meaningful body contact, and some psychologists argue that touching and physical closeness deserve even higher levels of recognition for their importance to successful sexual relationships. The Body Contact Questionnaire was designed to measure your desire to feel contact with others and the degree of comfort and satisfaction that you derive from this contact.

Although one's level of desired body contact is a personal preference, many sexual relationship problems center on this issue. Sex therapist Michael Castleman writes in his book *Sexual Solutions: An Informative Guide*, "Unhurried whole-body loveplay is the solution to both men's and women's chief complaints about the other's lovestyle. Sensuality gives the men the aroused, responsive lovers they want, at the same time that it gives women the whole-body sharing they want."

An essential point made by Castleman and others is that partners in sexual relationships must communicate to each other about the amount and type of body contact they require. Poor communication about body contact desires is often the cause of later, serious problems in the relationship. Our research, for example, shows that those who indicate high levels of comfort with body contact also score high in their overall level of sexual satisfaction.

NORMS TABLE

	Very Low	Low	Average	High	Very High
MEN	61 and below	62–66	67–74	75–79	80 and above
WOMEN	60 and below	61–66	67–74	75–78	79 and above

Very Low Scores: Very low scorers on the Body Contact Questionnaire are stating their dislike of physical closeness or contact. They may, in fact, be expressing emotions very close to terror. Such fear may relate to the contact itself; perhaps they anticipate being found undesirable when someone gets physically close. Or the fear could relate to the meaning of the contact: "Sex could follow, and that terrifies me!"

Regardless of the reason, a very negative view of body contact can prevent you from finding sexual satisfaction in your relationships. It's certainly true that body contact requirements are individual preferences and that with the right partner, you may find happiness. But such a low level of need could make it difficult to find a partner who shares your tastes. If you're unhappy with your situation, therapy can help you examine why the idea of body contact is so negative for you. If you're fulfilled sexually, then you've probably found the perfect match.

Low Scores: Although low scores on the Body Contact Questionnaire indicate some discomfort with physical closeness, body contact can be negotiated between partners. Therefore, scores in this range may not present problems as clearly as do very low scores. Finding a partner who feels as you do, however, is essential. Short of a perfect match between you and your partner, you'll need to rely on clear and open communication to avoid misunderstandings and anger caused by differing views on "appropriate" body contact.

Average Scores: An average score on the Body Contact Questionnaire means that you've scored like many others in our research—it doesn't guarantee sexual happiness. What it does guarantee, however, is that many potential partners feel as you do. Take advantage of this fact and make your needs known to your partner. You'll have a much better chance of sexual happiness.

High Scores: Castleman is speaking to the high scorer on the Body Contact Questionnaire when he writes, "As time spent in sensual loveplay increases, a man's likelihood of developing sex problems decreases. And women are more likely to feel comfortable enough to reach orgasm." Your score in this range strongly suggests that you possess a high level of comfort with physical contact and an ability to draw positive feelings about yourself from that contact. High scorers in our sample also indicated high levels of sexual satisfaction, little fear of rejection, and low levels of performance anxiety. Again, however, the importance of making your strong desire for contact known to your partner is essential.

Very High Scores: Although many of the statements about high scorers on the Body Contact Questionnaire may be true for you, they must be presented under a caution flag. Your level of desire for contact is so high, it may be difficult for you—or anyone else, for that matter—to fulfill your desires. That can and probably will lead to frustration and anger at your partner and not much sexual satisfaction for either of you.

Keep in mind that body contact requirements for most people change during lovemaking. Some women and men want to be stroked and cuddled after lovemaking; others want to be left alone. Your great need for contact may make it difficult for you to tolerate a lack of desire on your partner's part. Negotiation and communication, however, can make a real difference in your potential for mutual sexual satisfaction.

Reactions: Use the space provided to respond to the following questions.

1. Explain how you feel about your score on the Body Contact Questionnaire.

2. Explain (if applicable) how you feel about your partner's score.

3. If you could change any body contact situations between you and your partner, what would they be? Explain.

SOURCE: Body Contact Questionnaire from *The Love Exam,* copyright © 1984 by Rita Aero and Elliot Weiner. Reprinted by permission of Quill, an imprint of William Morrow and Company, New York, NY.

73 | What Do You Mean by Love?

PURPOSE: People define love in many different ways. If you have a good understanding of the concept of love, you will be more likely to find it and keep it than those who don't. This exercise is designed to help increase your understanding of the diverse nature of this perennial subject.

DIRECTIONS: Read each statement carefully and answer TRUE or FALSE in terms of how you feel about the love in your present, significant past, or future relationship. You may wish to have your partner or friend do the same and place their answers in the space provided.

You   Friend

____ ____ 1. I believe that love is immediately evident, or love at first sight is possible.

____ ____ 2. I was in a relationship for quite a while before I actually realized I was in love.

____ ____ 3. When things are not going well in our relationship, I get an upset feeling in my stomach.

____ ____ 4. From a practical perspective, I have to consider what a person is going to accomplish in life before I commit myself to loving him/her.

____ ____ 5. Love cannot exist unless you have had caring for a while.

____ ____ 6. It is a good idea to keep your partner a little uncertain about how committed you are to him/her.

____ ____ 7. The first time we kissed or embraced, I felt a significant genital response (erection, lubrication).

____ ____ 8. I maintain good friendships with almost everyone I've ever been involved with in a love relationship.

____ ____ 9. I try to help my partner through difficult times, even when he/she tends to be unreasonable.

You   Friend

____ ____ 10. If illness or some misfortune were to happen to one of us, I would rather it be me than my partner.

____ ____ 11. Some of the fun of being in love is testing your skill at keeping it going smoothly and getting what you want from it at the same time.

____ ____ 12. It is in your best interest to love someone with a similar background to your own.

____ ____ 13. We kissed soon after we met because we both felt we wanted it.

____ ____ 14. If my partner doesn't pay attention to me I get a generally ill feeling all over.

____ ____ 15. I do not feel I can be truly happy unless I put my partner's happiness before my own.

____ ____ 16. The first thing I'm attracted to in another person is his/her physical appearance.

____ ____ 17. The best kind of love develops from a long friendship.

____ ____ 18. The first time I touched my partner I knew that love was a real possibility.

____ ____ 19. If my partner and I were separated, I would go out of my way to see that he/she was all right.

____ ____ 20. I have difficulty relaxing if I suspect that he/she is with someone else.

____ ____ 21. I have had to carefully plan at least once to keep two of my lovers from finding out about each other.

____ ____ 22. I have always been able to adjust quickly and easily to a terminated love affair.

____ ____ 23. The best aspect of love is living together, building a home, and raising children.

____ ____ 24. I am usually willing to sacrifice my desires to let my partner achieve his/hers.

____ ____ 25. A major concern in choosing a partner is whether he/she will be a good parent.

You   Friend

____ ____ 26. A couple should not rush into sexual activity; it should happen naturally when a deep enough intimacy has developed.

____ ____ 27. I do enjoy flirting with attractive people.

____ ____ 28. My partner would be upset if he/she knew some of the things I've done with people in the past.

____ ____ 29. Long before I fell in love, I had a pretty clear picture of what my true love would be like physically.

____ ____ 30. If my partner had a child by some other people, I would raise it, love it, and care for it as if it were my very own.

____ ____ 31. It is difficult to say exactly when I fell in love.

____ ____ 32. If I ever reached the point where I could not truly love anyone, I would not be willing to marry.

____ ____ 33. Although I have no desire to be jealous, I have difficulty controlling my feelings when my partner pays attention to someone else.

____ ____ 34. I would rather end a relationship with my partner that interferes with his/her happiness.

____ ____ 35. I would hesitate to date anyone I could not fall in love with.

____ ____ 36. At least once in my life I knew realistically I could not see a certain person again without still feeling love.

____ ____ 37. Whatever worldly possessions I own are my partner's to use however he/she pleases.

____ ____ 38. If my partner were to ignore me for a while, I would probably behave stupidly to get his/her attention back to me.

____ ____ 39. One major consideration in mate selection is how my mate will influence my career or future security.

____ ____ 40. Love relationships that last the longest are definitely the best.

SCORING: These questions have been designed to give a somewhat equal representation to six dimensions of sexual lifestyles. Only your true responses should be considered for your analysis. These dimensions are as follows:

Dimension 1: **Friendship or Best Friends type of love.** True responses to questions 2, 5, 8, 17, 23, 25, 31, and 40 would indicate that you put emphasis on friendship in a loving relationship and would probably find your lover to also be your closest friend.

Dimension 2: **Dependent on Intense Attachment type of love.** True responses to questions 3, 14, 20, 33, 36, and 38 point out that you might be dependent on, or attached to, your lover to greater degree than you realized.

Dimension 3: **Other-Directed or a Thou-Focused form of love.** True responses to questions 9, 10, 15, 19, 24, 30, 34, and 37 are indicative of love that is centered on your partner's happiness and the ability to endure and overcome obstacles in a relationship.

Dimension 4: **Romantic or Sensual Love type of love.** True responses to questions 1, 7, 13, 16, 18, and 29 are characteristic of a romantic type of love and a strong physical attraction toward your partner.

Dimension 5: **Logical or Sensible form of love.** True responses to questions 4, 12, 26, 32, 35, and 39 are indications of a logical or practical approach to the person you love and how you express your love.

Dimension 6: **Self-Directed or Games-We-Play type of love.** True responses to questions 6, 11, 21, 22, and 27 indicate a self-centered style of love that tends to lack maturity, intimacy, and security.

PERSPECTIVE: You should keep in mind that very seldom is anyone a pure example of a single love-style dimension. Your score will more than likely indicate a blend of the various dimensions, with one or two categories having a predominant number of true responses. This or any exercise can never be an absolute measure but only a relative indication of your love style in regard to your relationship.

REACTIONS: Use the space provided to respond to the following questions.

1. Which types of love dominated in your score? Do you feel this is healthy? Why or why not?

2. What happens to love relationships when respect and caring are missing elements? Explain.

3. When reviewing all the statements, to which would you like to change your response? Why? How will you do that?

74 : Love Analysis

PURPOSE: This exercise is designed to help you evaluate several different types of love and to identify whether you are well matched with the individual with whom you are in love.

DIRECTIONS: Respond to each statement as it applies to a current or former lover, or spouse. Use the following key for your responses:

A	U	R	N
Almost Always	Usually	Rarely	Never (or almost never)

You   Friend

____ ____   1. You have a clearly defined image of your desired partner.

____ ____   2. You felt a strong emotional reaction to him or her on the first encounter.

____ ____   3. You are preoccupied with thoughts about him or her.

____ ____   4. You are eager to see him or her every day.

____ ____   5. You discuss future plans and a wide range of interests and experiences.

____ ____   6. Tactile, sensual contact is important to the relationship.

____ ____   7. Sexual intimacy is achieved early in the relationship.

____ ____   8. You feel that success in love is more important than success in other areas of your life.

____ ____   9. You want to be in love or have love as security.

____ ____   10. You try to force him or her to show more feeling and commitment.

____ ____   11. You declare your love first.

____ ____   12. You are willing to suffer neglect and abuse from him or her.

____ ____   13. You deliberately restrain frequency of contact with him or her.

____ ____   14. You restrict discussion and display of your feelings with him or her.

____ ____   15. If a breakup is coming, you feel it is better to drop the other person before being dropped.

____ ____   16. You play the field and have several who could love you.

____ ____   17. You are more interested in pleasure than in emotional attachment.

____ ____   18. You feel the need to love someone you have grown accustomed to.

____ ____   19. You believe that the test of time is the only sure way to find real love.

____ ____   20. You don't believe that true love happens suddenly or dramatically.

Some researchers have identified four basic types of love: erotic, ludic, storgic, and manic. Erotic love (eros) is a passionate, all-enveloping love. The erotic lover experiences a racing heart, a fluttering in the stomach, and shortness of breath. Ludic love (ludus) is a playful, flirtatious love. It involves no long-term commitment and is basically for amusement. Ludic love is usually played with several partners at once. Storgic love (storge) is a calm, compationate love. Storgic lovers are quietly affectionate and have goals of marriage and children for the relationship. Manic love (mania) is a combination of eros and ludus. A manic lover's needs for affection are insatiable, and he or she is often racked with highs of irrational joy, lows of anxiety and depression, and bouts of extreme jealousy. Manic attachments seldom develop into lasting love.

SCORING: If you answered A or U to statements 1–8, you are probably an *erotic lover.*

If you answered A or U to statements 3–4 and 8–12, your love style tends to be *manic.*

If you answered A or U to statements 13–17 and R or N to the other questions, you are probably a *ludic lover.*

If you answered A or U to statements 17–20, together with R or N for the other statements, your love style tends to be *storgic.*

If you are currently in a relationship with someone, have that person cover your responses and complete the love analysis.

REACTIONS: Use the space provided to respond to the following questions.

1. Compare your type of love with that of the person you love. Do you both have the same expectations? Needs?

2. What do you see as the future for this relationship?

SOURCE: Adapted from: John Alan Lee, *The Colours of Love*. New Press, 1973. Reprinted by permission of the author and New Press, Toronto, Canada.

75 | What Is Your Intimacy Quotient?

PURPOSE: This exercise is designed to measure your capacity for intimacy—how well you have fared in (and what you have learned from) your interpersonal relationships from infancy through adulthood. In a general way, it helps measure your sense of security and self-acceptance, which gives you the courage to risk the embarrassment of proffering love or friendship or respect and getting no response. This exercise can provide insight and can alert you to weaknesses that may be reducing your performance in everything from business, to meeting and interacting with potential mates, to ordering food in a restaurant.

DIRECTIONS: Read each question carefully. If your response is yes or mostly yes, place a plus (+) on the line preceding the question. If your response is no or mostly no, place a minus (–) on the line. If you honestly can't decide, place a zero on the line; but try to enter as few zeroes as possible. Even if a particular question doesn't apply to you, try to imagine yourself in the situation described and answer accordingly. Don't look for any significance in the number or the frequency of plus or minus answers. Simply be honest when answering the questions.

____ 1. Do you have more than your share of colds?

____ 2. Do you believe that emotions have very little to do with physical ills?

____ 3. Do you often have indigestion?

____ 4. Do you frequently worry about your health?

____ 5. Would a nutritionist be appalled by your diet?

____ 6. Do you usually watch sports rather than participate in them?

____ 7. Do you often feel depressed or in a bad mood?

____ 8. Are you irritable when things go wrong?

____ 9. Were you happier in the past than you are right now?

____ 10. Do you believe it possible that a person's character can be read or his future foretold by means of astrology, I Ching, tarot cards, or some other means?

____ 11. Do you worry about the future?

____ 12. Do you try to hold in your anger as long as possible and then sometimes explode in a rage?

____ 13. Do people you care about often make you feel jealous?

____ 14. If your intimate partner were unfaithful one time, would you be unable to forgive and forget?

____ 15. Do you have difficulty making important decisions?

____ 16. Would you abandon a goal rather than take risks to reach it?

____ 17. When you go on a vacation, do you take some work along?

____ 18. Do you usually wear clothes that are either dark or neutral in color?

____ 19. Do you usually do what you feel like doing, regardless of social pressures or criticism?

____ 20. Does a beautiful speaking voice turn you on?

____ 21. Do you always take an interest in where you are and what's happening around you?

____ 22. Do you find most odors interesting rather than offensive?

____ 23. Do you enjoy trying new and different foods?

____ 24. Do you like to touch and be touched?

____ 25. Are you easily amused?

____ 26. Do you often do things spontaneously or impulsively?

____ 27. Can you sit still through a long committee meeting or lecture without twiddling your thumbs or wriggling in your chair?

____ 28. Can you usually fall asleep and stay asleep without the use of sleeping pills or tranquilizers?

____ 29. Are you a moderate drinker rather than either a heavy drinker or a teetotaler?

____ 30. Do you smoke not at all or very little?

____ 31. Can you put yourself in another person's place and experience his emotions?

____ 32. Are you seriously concerned about social problems even when they don't affect you personally?

____ 33. Do you think most people can be trusted?

____ 34. Can you talk to a celebrity or a stranger as easily as you talk to your neighbors?

____ 35. Do you get along well with sales clerks, waiters, service station attendants, and cab drivers?

____ 36. Can you easily discuss sex in mixed company without feeling uncomfortable?

____ 37. Can you express appreciation for a gift or a favor without feeling uneasy?

____ 38. When you feel affection for someone, can you express it physically as well as verbally?

____ 39. Do you sometimes feel that you have extrasensory perception?

____ 40. Do you like yourself?

____ 41. Do you like others of your own sex?

____ 42. Do you enjoy an evening alone?

_____ 43. Do you vary your schedule to avoid doing the same things at the same times each day?

_____ 44. Is love more important to you than money or status?

_____ 45. Do you place a higher premium on kindness than on truthfulness?

_____ 46. Do you think it is possible to be too rational?

_____ 47. Have you attended or would you like to attend a sensitivity or encounter-group session?

_____ 48. Do you discourage friends from dropping in unannounced?

_____ 49. Would you feel it a sign of weakness to seek help for a sexual problem?

_____ 50. Are you upset when a homosexual seems attracted to you?

_____ 51. Do you have difficulty communicating with someone of the opposite sex?

_____ 52. Do you believe that men who write poetry are less masculine than men who drive trucks?

_____ 53. Do most women prefer men with well-developed muscles to men with well-developed emotions?

_____ 54. Are you generally indifferent to the kind of place in which you live?

_____ 55. Do you consider it a waste of money to buy flowers for yourself or for others?

_____ 56. When you see an art object you like, do you pass it up if the cost would mean cutting back on your food budget?

_____ 57. Do you think it pretentious and extravagant to have an elegant dinner when alone or with members of your immediate family?

_____ 58. Are you often bored?

_____ 59. Do Sundays depress you?

_____ 60. Do you frequently feel nervous?

_____ 61. Do you dislike the work you do to earn a living?

_____ 62. Do you think a carefree hippie lifestyle would have no delights for you?

_____ 63. Do you watch TV selectively rather than simply to kill time?

_____ 64. Have you read any good books recently?

_____ 65. Do you often daydream?

_____ 66. Do you like to fondle pets?

_____ 67. Do you like many different forms and styles of art?

_____ 68. Do you enjoy watching an attractive person of the opposite sex?

_____ 69. Can you describe how your date or mate looked the last time you went out together?

_____ 70. Do you find it easy to talk to new acquaintances?

_____ 71. Do you communicate with others through touch as well as through words?

_____ 72. Do you enjoy pleasing members of your family?

____ 73. Do you avoid joining clubs or organizations?

____ 74. Do you worry more about how you present yourself to prospective dates than about how you treat them?

____ 75. Are you afraid that if people knew you too well they wouldn't like you?

____ 76. Do you fall in love at first sight?

____ 77. Do you always fall in love with someone who reminds you of your parent of the opposite sex?

____ 78. Do you think love is all you presently need to be happy?

____ 79. Do you feel a sense of rejection if a person you love tries to preserve his or her independence?

____ 80. Can you accept your loved one's anger and still believe in his or her love?

____ 81. Can you express your innermost thoughts and feelings to the person you love?

____ 82. Do you talk over disagreements with your partner rather than silently worry about them?

____ 83. Can you easily accept the fact that your partner has loved others before you and not worry about how you compare with them?

____ 84. Can you accept a partner's disinterest in sex without feeling rejected?

____ 85. Can you accept occasional sessions of unsatisfactory sex without blaming yourself or your partner?

____ 86. Should unmarried adolescents be denied contraceptives?

____ 87. Do you believe that even for adults in private, there are some sexual acts that should remain illegal?

____ 88. Do you think that hippie communes and Israeli kibbutzim have nothing useful to teach the average American?

____ 89. Should a couple put up with an unhappy marriage for the sake of their children?

____ 90. Do you think that mate swappers necessarily have unhappy marriages?

____ 91. Should older men and women be content not to have sex?

____ 92. Do you believe that pornography contributes to sex crimes?

____ 93. Is sexual abstinence beneficial to a person's health, strength, wisdom, or character?

____ 94. Can a truly loving wife or husband sometimes be sexually unreceptive?

____ 95. Can intercourse during a woman's menstrual period be as appealing or as appropriate as at any other time?

____ 96. Should a woman concentrate on her own sensual pleasure during intercourse rather than pretend enjoyment to increase her partner's pleasure?

____ 97. Can a man's effort to bring his partner to orgasm reduce his own pleasure?

____ 98. Should fun and sensual pleasure be the principal goals in sexual relations?

____ 99. Is pressure to perform well a common cause of sexual incapacity?

____100. Is sexual intercourse for you an uninhibited romp rather than a demonstration of your sexual ability?

Scoring:

Questions	1–18,	count your minuses
Questions	19–47,	count your pluses
Questions	48–61,	count your minuses
Questions	63–72,	count your pluses
Questions	73–79,	count your minuses
Questions	80–85,	count your pluses
Questions	86–93,	count your minuses
Questions	94–100,	count your pluses
		TOTAL

TOTAL – 1/2(number of zero answers) = **Corrected Total** _____

Corrected Total Score less than 30. You have a shell like a tortoise and tend to draw your head in at the first sign of psychological danger. Probably life handed you some bad blows when you were too young to fight back, so you've erected strong defenses against the kind of intimacy that could leave you vulnerable to ego injury.

Corrected Total Score between 30 and 60. You are about average which shows you have potential. You've erected some strong defenses, but you've matured enough, and have had enough good experiences, that you're willing to take a few chances with other human beings, confident that you'll survive regardless.

Corrected Total Score over 60. This means you possess the self-confidence and sense of security not only to run the risks of intimacy but to enjoy it. This could be a little discomforting to another person who doesn't have your capacity or potential for interpersonal relationships, but you're definitely ahead in the game and you can make the right person extremely happy just by being yourself.

Corrected Total Score Approaching 100. You are either an intimate Superman/ Superwoman or you are worried too much about giving right answers, which puts you back in the under 30 category.

If it is convenient, try taking it with someone you feel intimate with—afterward compare and discuss your answers. It may indicate how compatible you are, socially or sexually. This is one area of interpersonal relationships in which opposites do not necessarily attract. A person of high intimacy capacity can intimidate someone of low capacity who is fearful to respond. But those of similar capacities will tend to make no excessive demands on each other and, for that reason, will find themselves capable of an increasingly intimate and mutually fulfilling relationship.

REACTIONS: Use the space provided to respond to the following questions.

1. What is your level of intimacy? How will knowing this information enhance your present and/or future relationships?

2. If your partner responded to the questionnaire, how did he/she score? How will that information help the two of you in your relationship? Do you feel it is valuable information?

SECTION IX

MARRIAGE AND FAMILY LIFE

As an institution, marriage is found in virtually every society. Marriage has traditionally served various functions, both personal and social. It provides societies with stable units that help facilitate and perpetuate social norms because children are usually taught social mores and expectations by parents or kinship groups. The family unit has served many roles in our society. The traditional nuclear family, however, is fast becoming a minority family form in contemporary America, giving way to the binuclear family. The exercises in this section present a variety of opportunities to examine your opinions regarding relationships, marriage, family life, and parenting.

Marriage and Family Life exercises include:

76. The Marriage Quiz
77. Are You and Your Partner Suited for a Life Together?
78. Relationship Contract?
79. Sexual Attitudes: Family Tree
80. Day by Day: Relationship Responsibilities
81. To Be or Not To Be Parents
82. Attitudes Toward Timing of Parenthood Scale
83. Parenthood: Making Responsible Decisions
84. Do You Know Your Parents as People?
85. Family Strengths Inventory
86. Marriage Today: Points to Ponder

76 The Marriage Quiz

PURPOSE: This quiz is designed to test your knowledge about the myths and misconceptions of marriage.

DIRECTIONS: For each of the questions in this quiz answer TRUE or FALSE in the space provided. If you have a spouse or friend who would like to respond to the quiz, cover your answers with a sheet of paper.

	Friend	You
1. A husband's marital satisfaction is usually lower if his wife is employed full time than if she is a full-time homemaker.	___	___
2. Today most young, single, never-married people will eventually get married.	___	___
3. In most marriages having a child improves marital satisfaction for both spouses.	___	___
4. The best single predictor of overall marital satisfaction is the quality of a couple's sex life.	___	___
5. The divorce rate in America increased from 1960 to 1980.	___	___
6. A greater percentage of wives are in the work force today than in 1970.	___	___
7. Marital satisfaction for a wife is usually lower if she is employed full time than if she is a full-time homemaker.	___	___
8. If my spouse loves me, he/she should instinctively know what I want and need to be happy.	___	___
9. In a marriage in which the wife is employed full time, the husband usually assumes an equal share of the housekeeping.	___	___
10. For most couples marital satisfaction gradually increases from the first year of marriage through the childbearing years, the teen years, the empty nest period, and retirement.	___	___
11. No matter how I behave, my spouse should love me simply because he/she is my spouse.	___	___
12. One of the most frequent marital problems is poor communication.	___	___
13. Husbands usually make more lifestyle adjustments in marriage than wives.	___	___
14. Couples who cohabited before marriage usually report greater marital satisfaction than couples who did not.	___	___

	Friend	You

15. I can change my spouse by pointing out his/her inadequacies, errors, etc.   _____ _____

16. Couples who marry when one or both partners are under the age of 18 have more chance of eventually divorcing than those who marry when they are older.   _____ _____

17. Either my spouse loves me or does not love me; nothing I do will affect the way my spouse feels about me.   _____ _____

18. The more a spouse discloses positive and negative information to his/her partner, the greater the marital satisfaction of both partners. _____ _____

19. I must feel better about my partner before I can change my behavior toward him/her.   _____ _____

20. Maintaining romantic love is the key to marital happiness over the life span for most couples.   _____ _____

SCORING: The Marriage Quiz consists of fifteen myths about marriage that are false and five facts about marriage that are true and are used as filler items to disguise the nature of the test. To score the Marriage Quiz you should first cross out items 2, 5, 6, 12, and 16 (filler items). Count the remaining number of items marked TRUE (incorrect responses). This is your score. The range of scores for the Marriage Quiz is 0–15.

   Total Score = _____

INTERPRETATION: If you scored between **11–15** you have a high belief in marital myths. A score of **6–10** indicates a moderate belief in marital myths, and a score of **0–5** represents a low belief in marital myths. In general, the higher your score, the greater your belief in marital myths.

Now read the explanation of why each statement is a fact or myth.

Item 1: Myth. A husband's marital satisfaction is usually lower if his wife is employed full time than if she is a full-time homemaker. (False)

   The effect of a wife's full-time employment on a couple's marital satisfaction is affected by such variables as social class, husband's and wife's attitudes and commitment to work, and children. Although early studies showed that wife's employment negatively effected marital satisfaction for the husband or wife more recent research shows there is no consistent or significant difference in the marital satisfaction of husbands or wives based on the employment status of the wife.

Item 2: Fact. Today most young, single, never-married people will eventually get married. (True)

   Throughout the 1970s and 1980s the proportion of the United States adult population marrying at least once varied only slightly between 94 and 96 percent.

Item 3: Myth. In most marriages having a child improves marital satisfaction for both spouses. (False) (See answer to item 10.)

Most studies have shown a decrease in marital satisfaction for one or both spouses when a child is born. Although one study of married women suggested that for lower-class women having a child may increase marital satisfaction, a later study of both husbands and wives in the lower class found that lower-class couples experience similar and sometimes more profound marital adjustment problems than middle- and upper-class couples as a result of a childbearing. A more recent study found that the effect of the birth of a child on marital satisfaction varied by a couple's marital adjustment prior to the birth of the child. "The birth of a child apparently precipitates a higher degree of positive change in the lives of the parents high on marital adjustment than those low on marital adjustment." It appears that happiness in one's marriage helps to accentuate any positive changes and to minimize any negative changes that occur as parents adjust to the birth of a child.

Item 4: Myth. The best single predictor of overall marital satisfaction is the quality of a couple's sex life. (False)

A couple's affective problem-solving ability is consistently the best single predictor to overall marital satisfaction. Next in importance are a couple's common interests and the amount and quality of leisure time together. Satisfaction with sex life usually ranks fourth, and communication is also a key predictor of marital satisfaction. In a study of 75,000 young middle-class women, the majority of them felt that love, respect, and friendship were the most important elements in their marriage. They rated sexual compatibility desirable, but not essential.

Item 5: Fact. The divorce rate in America increased from 1960 to 1980. (True)

In 1960 divorce as a percentage of total marital dissolutions (death or divorce) was 33.2 percent; in 1970 the percentage was 44 percent; in 1979, 53 percent of marriages were ending in divorce rather than death. (U.S. National Center for Health Statistics, 1980).

Item B: Fact. A greater percentage of wives are in the work force today than in 1970. (True)

Between 1970 and the end of 1983, the number of married women in the labor force grew from 18,383,000 to 25,534,000; the percentage of all married women working outside of the home grew from 41 percent in 1970 to nearly 54 percent in 1983 (Bureau of Labor Statistics News, 1983).

Item 7: Myth. Marital satisfaction for a wife is usually lower if she is employed full time than if she is a full-time homemaker. (False) (See answer to item 1.)

Item 8: Myth. If my spouse loves me he/she should instinctively know what I want and need to be happy. (False)

This is called the "ESP myth"—expecting my partner to know instinctively what I want and need. This kind of mind reading is significantly more common among distressed, clinical couples than among happily married, nonclinical couples. In reality a person must communicate his/her wants, needs, and expectations to his/her partner in order to get those needs met.

Item 9: Myth. In a marriage in which the wife is employed full time, the husband usually assumes an equal share of the housekeeping. (False)

In terms of hours spent in household chores, the evidence shows that housework is largely women's work whether or not the wife holds an outside job.

Item 10: Myth. For most couples marital satisfaction gradually increases from the first year of marriage through the childbearing years, the teen years, the empty nest period, and retirement. (False)

There are very few good longitudinal studies of marital adjustment and satisfaction over the family life cycle. Burgess and Wallin's (1953) classic longitudinal study showed a rather consistent and significant decline in marital adjustment from the early to later years of marriage. However, most studies on marital satisfaction over the life cycle use a cross-sectional design and, hence, present methodological problems when trying to arrive at conclusions about developmental change. Nonetheless, many of these studies have consistently shown that marriage tends to become less satisfying over the years as couples move from the preparenthood stage of marriage into the parenthood stages. This period of lower satisfaction is followed by increases in satisfaction after the children grow up and leave home. This pattern suggests a curvilinear ("U"-shaped) relationship between marital satisfaction and the family life cycle.

Item 11: Myth. No matter how I behave, my spouse should love me simply because he/she is my spouse. (False)

A person usually loves his/her spouse because the spouse's behavior meets the person's needs. Assuming someone can love another person simply because he/she exists is unrealistic.

Item 12: Fact. One of the most frequent marital problems is poor communication. (True)

Marriage therapists' reports of the most frequent marital problems they encounter show that lack of communication is one of the most frequently reported marital problems. Burns's (1984) study of 335 divorced and separated men and women showed sexual incompatibility and lack of communication as the two most frequent marital problems.

Item 13: Myth. Husbands usually make more lifestyle adjustments in marriage than wives. (False)

Men tend to be less involved in their marriages than women and are less affected by the different stages of the family life cycle. For example, men's marital satisfaction does not decrease as much as women's during the childbearing and childrearing periods. In general, most studies show that wives make more adjustments to marriage and find marriage more stressful than husbands.

Item 14: Myth. Couples who have cohabitated before marriage usually report greater marital satisfaction than couples who did not. (False)

No significant differences in marital satisfaction have been found between married couples who cohabitated before marriage and those who did not.

Item 15: Myth. I can change my spouse by pointing out his/her inadequacies, errors, etc. (False)

Keeping track of and pointing out a spouse's perceived inadequacies or errors is called "negative tracking." Such behavior is characteristic of unhappy couples and only leads to further dissatisfaction and unhappiness in marriage. Marital therapists often train distressed couples to track each other's positive behaviors as part of marital therapy.

Item 16: Fact. Couples who marry when one or both partners are under the age of 18 have more chance of eventually divorcing than those who marry when they are older. (True)

The divorce rate for teenage marriages is three to four times higher than for later marriages. One reason for this is that many teenagers get married because of pregnancy. Even among those marriages which survive, couples married as teenagers report more tension and higher rates of marital dissatisfaction than those who marry later.

Item 17: Myth. Either my spouse loves me or does not love me; nothing I do will affect the way my spouse feels about me. (False)

Love is not an all-or-nothing phenomenon. On different days a spouse may experience different degrees of love for his/her partner. How much love and satisfaction one feels toward a spouse depends heavily upon the spouse's behavior.

Item 18: Myth. The more a spouse discloses positive and negative information to his/her partner, the greater the marital satisfaction of both partners. (False)

Initial studies of self-disclosure and marital satisfaction showed support for and against the notion that the greater the self-disclosure in marriage, the greater the marital satisfaction. In a summary of the literature on self-disclosure and relationship satisfaction, it has been suggested that there is a curvilinear relationship between self-disclosure and marital satisfaction; that is, both too little and too much self-disclosure can reduce relationship satisfaction. However, a positive correlation (linear relationship) between self-disclosure and and marital adjustment was determined from other studies. More recent research shows that the quality of self-disclosure is an important interacting variable in the relationship between quantity of self-disclosure and marital satisfaction. A positive, linear relationship between self-disclosure and marital satisfaction probably exists only if the self-disclosure is positive rather than negative.

Item 19: Myth. I must feel better about my partner before I can change my behavior toward him/her. (False)

It is common in many marriages for spouses to claim that they cannot change their behavior toward their partner "until they first feel more positive about their partner." However, research does not support this notion that feelings must change before one's behavior can change. Part of being happily married is learning that an individual sometimes must do things he/she would rather not do simply to please one's spouse. Often, the individual will reap the benefits of giving of self—his/her partner will be happier and more giving, too. This can lead to more positive feelings about each other and about the marriage.

Item 20: Myth. Maintaining romantic love is the key to marital happiness over the life span for most couples. (False)

Romantic love is characterized by idealism, high emotionality, strong sexual attraction, and a great need to be with a partner. In contrast, compassionate love is characterized by realism, calm, trust, respect, commitment, and friendship. Most of the research and clinical literature on love and marriage suggests that there is a change in the type of love in marriage from a romantic, passionate love early in marriage to more compassionate love later in marriage. The general belief is that the romantic love that permeates the marital relationship in the early years of marriage gradually fades as the idealization of one's partner fades and disillusionment is bred when a spouse's limitations and faults become apparent. This does not mean romantic love totally disappears or may not reappear later in the marriage. Nonetheless, most couples do not identify romantic love as the kind of love that helps maintain marital satisfaction over the life span. Rather, they identify feelings and behaviors characteristic of compassionate love.

REACTIONS: Use the space provided to respond to the following questions.

1. Do you feel that your score accurately represents your level of understanding about marriage myths? Why or why not?

2. Would your score on this quiz have been different three years ago? Explain.

3. In light of the explanations provided, are there any myths in which you still believe? Which ones and why?

SOURCE: Family Relations, "The Marriage Quiz: College Students' Beliefs in Selected Myths About Marriage," Jeffery H. Larson; 37: 1, 3–11, 1988. Copyright © 1988 by the National Council on Family Relations, 3989 Central Avenue, NE Suite 550, Minneapolis, MN 55421. Reprinted by permission.

77 Are You and Your Partner Suited for a Life Together?

PURPOSE: Most people carry an image in their hearts of the "perfect" marriage—marriage as they would wish it to be. But it can be hard to articulate. It is not always possible to state explicitly what it is you want . . . dream . . . wish . . . especially if you are not really sure yourself. And sometimes, it spoils everything when you have to ask for it.

DIRECTIONS: Below you will find an inventory divided into ten areas. In the blanks provided to the right of each statement, you and your partner should answer either AGREE or DISAGREE or NEUTRAL to each statement.

Communication

	You	Partner
1. Let's share our experiences; ask me what I've been doing and tell me what you've been doing.	_____	_____
2. I'd like to be able to express my feelings without fear of criticism.	_____	_____
3. You shouldn't talk so much.	_____	_____
4. You shouldn't assume what I need without finding out first if you're right.	_____	_____
5. You shouldn't moralize.	_____	_____
6. Never lie to me.	_____	_____
7. I'd like you to guess what I need without having to tell you.	_____	_____
8. I wish you would learn to listen to me.	_____	_____
9. You can yell sometimes.	_____	_____
10. I don't like you to interrupt me.	_____	_____

Decisions

	You	Partner
1. I'd like to be the one who makes the important decisions.	_____	_____
2. Let's talk over everything and always make joint decisions.	_____	_____
3. I am ready to lie, bribe, and blackmail just to get my way.	_____	_____

4. Let's agree in advance who's to make decisions in each area of our lives together.

5. Let's try to persuade each other quietly and rationally.   ___ ___

6. When we disagree on major issues let's turn to somebody more experienced for help.   ___ ___

7. We should try to give in without trying to "get back" at each other.   ___ ___

8. When we disagree, we should flip a coin in order to reach a decision. ___ ___

9. I want you to have the responsibility for making our decisions.   ___ ___

10. In order to stay together, we should agree on everything.   ___ ___

Relatives

1. I'd like to spend more time with my family.   ___ ___

2. I would like our parents to help us out financially.   ___ ___

3. I don't like you to criticize my family.   ___ ___

4. I'd like to live near my parents.   ___ ___

5. You should be nicer to my parents.   ___ ___

6. We should spend our holidays with my family.   ___ ___

7. You consult your parents too frequently.   ___ ___

8. Don't compare me to your mother/father.   ___ ___

9. I'd like your parents not to interfere in our lives.   ___ ___

10. We should consult our parents on important issues.   ___ ___

Roles

1. We should divide chores equally between us.   ___ ___

2. My career should come first.   ___ ___

3. You should plan our social life.   ___ ___

4. You should be the one to invite friends over.   ___ ___

5. You should be responsible for the children's education.   ___ ___

6. I'll be responsible for the yard and garden work.   ___ ___

7. You should be responsible for household repairs.   ___ ___

8. My job is to earn a living for the family.   ___ ___

9. I'll be responsible for decorating our home.   ___ ___

10. We'll share the cooking between us.   ___ ___

Conflicts

1. We should never quarrel. _____ _____
2. You should be the first to make up. _____ _____
3. You should learn to control your emotions. _____ _____
4. I don't like you to run away in the middle of a fight. _____ _____
5. We should always make up before we go to bed. _____ _____
6. During a quarrel, we should be allowed to curse. _____ _____
7. When we argue, we shouldn't bring up grievances from the past. _____ _____
8. It's all right to cry during a quarrel. _____ _____
9. It's all right to yell and let off steam when we argue. _____ _____
10. We should always keep our anger under control. _____ _____

Entertainment

1. We should spend all our free time together. _____ _____
2. We must invite friends over at least once a week. _____ _____
3. We should get out of the house quite often and go to a movie, play, concert, or just out to dinner. _____ _____
4. Once a year we should go on a special vacation together. _____ _____
5. I'd like to have time on my own at least once a week. _____ _____
6. We should take time every day to talk things over and be together. _____ _____
7. You shouldn't spend so much time sleeping when we are together. _____ _____
8. I need to have enough time alone to spend on my hobbies. _____ _____
9. We should have a large circle of friends. _____ _____
10. I want to spend as much time as possible at home. _____ _____

Affection

1. You should often tell me you love me. _____ _____
2. I would like you to hug and caress me a lot. _____ _____
3. It's okay for us to show affection in public. _____ _____
4. I'd like you to give me a gift from time to time, not just on birthdays or anniversaries. _____ _____
5. You should tell me more often that I'm attractive. _____ _____
6. You should always remember my birthday/our anniversary. _____ _____
7. From time to time, I'd like us to act out romantic fantasies together. _____ _____

8. I like it when you dance only with me at parties. ____ ____

9. I like you to baby me from time to time. ____ ____

10. I'd like you to take me in your arms and comfort me when I'm sad. ____ ____

Money

1. We should have separate bank accounts. ____ ____

2. We should plan all our household expenses together. ____ ____

3. You should be responsible for paying monthly bills. ____ ____

4. I'll decide what our expenses should be. ____ ____

5. I don't want to have to report to you every time I spend money. ____ ____

6. We should each have some money for our personal use, to spend any way we choose. ____ ____

7. We should put every spare penny into a savings account. ____ ____

8. We should keep a monthly record of expenses. ____ ____

9. We should make only cash purchases and not buy on credit. ____ ____

10. We should spend our money as we please, enjoying today and not worrying about tomorrow. ____ ____

Sex

1. You should initiate sex. ____ ____

2. You should be able to guess what makes me feel good. ____ ____

3. We should have sex more often. ____ ____

4. We should have sex only when I show signs that I really want it. ____ ____

5. Our sex life should be varied. ____ ____

6. You should not feel rejected or try to make me feel guilty when I'm not in the mood to make love. ____ ____

7. You should never desire anyone else. ____ ____

8. You should feel free to have an affair. ____ ____

9. You should tell me if you have an affair. ____ ____

10. You should be responsible for birth control. ____ ____

Parenthood

Note: If you do not have—or plan to have—children, answer "as if" you do, to questions 5–10.

1. We should have only "planned" children.   ____ ____
2. We should postpone having children until we have established
   our careers and are prepared financially.   ____ ____
3. It's a mother's duty to stay home to bring up the children.   ____ ____
4. We will have no children.   ____ ____
5. We should always keep a united front and never argue in front
   of our children.   ____ ____
6. Our children's needs should always come before our own.   ____ ____
7. Our children should be punished when they are bad.   ____ ____
8. Our children should grow up free from any restrictions.   ____ ____
9. Our children should have everything we could not have as children.   ____ ____
10. Whatever happens, we should stay together for the children's
    sake until they are grown.   ____ ____

SCORING: Now compare your answers. For each "compatible" answer, score 1 point. There are several ways to arrive at a compatible score, so a discussion period aimed at determining compatibility is very important.

For example: You have a compatible answer if you both gave the same answer to a statement such as "Let's talk over everything and always make joint decisions."

However, you also have a compatible answer if one of your answers "Disagrees" to such a statement as "I'd like to be the one to make the important decisions" (this person does not want to make the decisions). Therefore, if the other partner answered "Agree" to the same statement, the one person's objection is compatible with the other's agreement with the statement.

A third example is where both of you have answered "Neutral" to an item; your choice is compatible since the issue is not important to either of you. Even if one of you answered "Neutral" and the other answered either "Agree" or "Disagree," communication about the issue involved may determine whether your attitudes are in conflict. One of you may even change your original choice, if the issue—after discussion—fades (or increases) in importance. Being able to arrive at an answer through this discussion indicates compatibility.

After discussing your answers with your partner, total your "compatibility" answers for each questionnaire. List them here:

Communication   _____

Decisions   _____

Relatives   _____

Roles   _____

Conflicts	_____
Entertainment	_____
Affection	_____
Money	_____
Sex	_____
Parenthood	_____
TOTAL	_____

Analysis

Score	Compatibility Prognosis
Below 10	You had better part on friendly terms right now (if you haven't already done so while answering the questionnaire). You are not suited for a life together.
11–50	Each one of you is a distinct individual, with different ambitions and goals. However, this does not mean that you cannot live happily together if you do not mistake interference for intimacy. Keep your distinct worlds.
51–90	You are well matched but should reexamine the issues you disagree on. Try to reach a common denominator.
91 and up	You suit each other perfectly, and stand a good chance for a long and happy life together.

REACTIONS: Use the space provided to respond to the following questions.

1. List three or more statements you feel are very important for you and your partner to agree upon. Why are these so important to you? Does your partner feel the same?

2. Based upon the analysis of your score, do you think you and your partner are suited for a life together? Why or why not?

3. List three areas you feel it is okay to disagree upon. Why? Does your partner feel the same? Explain.

SOURCE: Adapted from Ofra Ayalon and Dr. Zev Segal, *Getting Along*. Copyright © 1981 by Family Bazaar Incorporated/Noah Amit. Reprinted with permission of Grosset & Dunlap, Inc.

78 | Relationship Contract

PURPOSE: Prior to making a permanent commitment, some couples are now developing either written or verbal relationship agreements that define specific plans, rules, or philosophies of importance to each partner entering the relationship. The issues most frequently discussed in these agreements are generally key areas of importance to many couples seeking a fulfilling relationship. You should be aware of them, regardless of whether you will ever wish to develop your own contract. The following sample contract is represented for you to consider either individually, to help clarify your own feelings on these issues, or for discussion with a partner or potential partner, to explore mutual attitudes and expectations.

DIRECTIONS: Consider and answer the following questions. What are your feelings on and expectations of the following areas that are applicable either to you individually or to you and your partner?

Surname

1. Will you take your partner's name? Will you keep your own "birth name"? Both partners take a hyphenated name or a new name? Why?

2. If there are children, what will their surname be? Why?

Birth Control (if applicable)

1. What kind is preferable?

2. Often a change in method becomes necessary. What alternatives are then preferable or acceptable?

3. Whose responsibility is birth control? Is it shared?

4. How do you feel about abortion? Partner's rights in choosing abortion vs. not choosing abortion?

Children

1. How do you feel about becoming a parent?

2. How many children, if any, are you considering?

3. How do you feel about adoption?

4. What are your feelings about parental care and daily responsibility for children? Do you expect shared responsibility, or will one parent be the primary caretaker?

Money

1. What are each person's individual spending and consuming styles and preferences? (Do you handle money freely, tightly, or somewhere in between?)

2. How would you expect your partner to handle finances?

3. Will both partners be wage earners? If so, will you expect to pool your income, or each keep a portion of your own salary?

Household Duties

1. What are your feelings about routine household duties—do you expect one person to be primarily responsible for certain duties or do you expect to share housework? In what areas?

2. How might you work out a housework schedule that would adjust to both persons' needs and preferences?

Living Arrangements

1. Where will you live? What is your housing preference?

2. What kind and amount of privacy do you need? Could you adjust to a partner's differing need? How?

3. How do you feel when sharing your personal possessions? Are there any specific things you would rather not share?

4. How would you decide what to do if job offers interfered with each other's careers?

Leisure Time

1. How much time do you expect to spend together?

2. How much time do you expect to spend with friends, family?

3. How will you decide to spend vacation time? Always together? With children? With friends? With family?

Sexual Rights and Other Relationships

1. How free are you and your partner to develop friendships with other people? Of the same gender? Of the other gender?

2. What will you expect to be the extent of those relationships? Will you always expect to include your partner (or be included) in outside friendships?

3. Describe your feelings when you are jealous. Are you able to communicate those feelings? To what extent?

4. Are you expecting to be committed to sexual exclusiveness with your partner?

5. How would you handle an outside sexual relationship or encounter? Would you tell your partner (or want to know if your partner had the outside encounter)?

Personal Values

1. What are your feelings about religion and its practice? If you and your partner disagree in this area, how would you handle your children's religious training?

2. What are your political beliefs? How active or inactive are you politically? What would be your expectations concerning your partner's political attitudes and practices?

3. Where would you like to be in your career ten years from now? Thirty years from now?

4. Where would you like to be emotionally and/or spiritually ten years from now? Thirty years from now?

REACTIONS:

1. What have you learned about yourself (and your partner if applicable) from this exercise?

2. What issues are of greatest importance to you? Are there any areas you feel are not negotiable given the strength of your feelings on those issues?

3. What areas might you and your partner be able to negotiate?

4. If you were involved in a relationship with someone you loved, but any of the above values were different from your own, how would you deal with the situation? What options might you have?

SOURCE: Susan Woods, Department of Health Education, Eastern Illinois University, Charleston, IL, 1983.

79

Sexual Attitudes: Family Tree

PURPOSE: This scale is designed to help you examine your own attitudes toward premarital sexual intercourse, as well as those of your own family members. It is often helpful to understand the attitudes of others as well as your own if you are to consider the influencing factors from the past. These same factors may need to be considered in the future also.

DIRECTIONS: Each individual develops an attitude toward the acceptability of premarital sexual intercourse. Keep in mind that attitudes do not necessarily predict behavior. Look at continuum A labeled MOTHER and circle the number that best describes what you feel is your mother's attitude toward premarital sexual intercourse.

Then write a paragraph explaining factors in her past and present life that resulted in this pattern of attitudes. Do you feel her attitudes have changed over the past five years? If so, how and why? Can you understand her feelings and see her point of view? Why? Can you accept her attitudes as her way of life? Why?

Now look at continuum B labeled FATHER, and circle the number that you feel best describes your father's attitude toward premarital sexual intercourse. Refer back to the above paragraph and respond to each question in regard to your father's attitude.

Continue this process, responding to the same questions (from the above paragraph) for yourself, your future daughter, and your future son.

		With anyone anytime, any group		Acceptable with a casual date		Acceptable for a caring relationship		Only after marriage
MOTHER	A							
		1	2	3	4	5	6	7
FATHER	B							
		1	2	3	4	5	6	7
YOU	C							
		1	2	3	4	5	6	7
DAUGHTER	D							
		1	2	3	4	5	6	7
SON	E							
		1	2	3	4	5	6	7

A. MOTHER:

B. FATHER:

C. YOU:

D. DAUGHTER:

E. SON:

REACTIONS: Use the space provided to respond to the following questions.

1. Is your attitude toward premarital sex different from that of your mother and/or father? Do your parents know how you feel? Why or why not?

2. How does your attitude toward premarital sex compare with the attitudes you hope your future son and/or daughter will have? What will shape the attitudes of your children?

SOURCE: Martin Reed, Department of Health Education, Eastern Illinois University, Charleston, Illinois, 1983.

80

Day by Day: Relationship Responsibilities?

P URPOSE: When married and/or living with someone (of either gender), you may find there are many household duties and day-to-day chores. How these duties are delineated can be negotiated or may be the cause of disagreements. This exercise is designed to help you sort through feelings on these issues and perhaps come to some understanding with your partner.

DIRECTIONS: Respond to the activity list by indicating whose responsibility you think each activity should be. Use the codes for the choices on this scale below and record the code in the blank to the left of each statement. After completing the scale, cover the column with your responses and ask your partner to respond to this exercise.

Your Job = Y   Do Together = DT
Partner's Job = P   Take Turns (alternate) = TT
Both Do (whomever has time) = BD   Not Applicable = NA

You   Partner   Activities

____ ____   1. Choose the apartment/house to rent/buy

____ ____   2. Move to new city/state for job

____ ____   3. Do household repairs

____ ____   4. Choose a new refrigerator

____ ____   5. Mow the lawn

____ ____   6. Do the laundry

____ ____   7. Cook evening dinner

____ ____   8. Clean the house/apartment

____ ____   9. Take out the trash

____ ____   10. Do the dishes

____ ____   11. Iron clothes

____ ____   12. Shop for groceries

____ ____   13. Handle family finances

____ ____   14. Balance the checkbook

____ ____   15. Send the holiday cards

____ ____   16. Negotiate purchase of a car

You	Partner	Activities
____	____	17. Take the car(s) for tune-ups and repairs
____	____	18. Wash and wax the car(s)
____	____	19. Change the baby's diapers
____	____	20. Get up with a child at night
____	____	21. Take child to day care/school
____	____	22. Go to parent-teacher meetings
____	____	23. Take children to appointments
____	____	24. Choose couple/family free time activity
____	____	25. Choose when to have sex.

SCORING: The way you completed this assessment may change in time. It is often a mistake to assume any one roommate or partner will take on any of these responsibilities. These may seem like small duties, but it would be helpful for anyone sharing living space to discuss them. If your roommate or partner completed the assessment, compare your responses and discuss any differences of opinion.

REACTIONS: Use the space provided to respond to the following questions.

1. Which, if any, of these responsibilities do you feel strongly about? Which does your partner feel strongly about?

2. How do you plan to decide/or have you decided who takes which responsibilities in your current relationship? If you do not have such a relationship, how would you decide if you were married?

81 To Be or Not To Be Parents

PURPOSE: Since two people are needed to conceive a child, two people should decide whether and when to conceive. With the advent of more reliable birth control methods, couples may spend years deciding whether or not to become parents. If or when you consider having a child, this exercise provides a chance to examine you and your partner's expectations of parenthood. *Even if you feel parenthood is far in your future,* this will help you determine your current expectations.

DIRECTIONS: On another sheet of paper, you and your partner should independently write a sentence or two in answer to each question. Then *go through what you have written* and indicate, by a check in the proper column, whether each *prediction* would make you pleased, unhappy, or neither if it came true. Pick out which of the areas covered in the questions are most important to you in your decision.

	Pleased	Unhappy	Neither
1. How will having a child affect my partner's and/or my career and/or education?	_____	_____	_____
2. How will a child affect our financial situation now and later?	_____	_____	_____
3. How will the child affect our relationship with each other?	_____	_____	_____
4. How will the child affect our relationship with family and friends?	_____	_____	_____
5. How will the child affect our freedom, privacy, and spontaneity?	_____	_____	_____
6. How will my partner and I deal with the pregnancy and birth?	_____	_____	_____
7. How will each of us deal with supervising, training, and being with a young child (birth to 8 years)?	_____	_____	_____
8. How will we each deal with supervising, training, and being with an older child or teenager?	_____	_____	_____
9. How will we deal with possible problems of health and personality our child could have?	_____	_____	_____
10. How do we feel about bringing up a child in today's world (i.e., what kinds of problems and solutions are there for the child's future world)?	_____	_____	_____

SCORING: Compare answers with your partner. Discussing realistic predictions of parenthood can quell some fears (or bring others to mind) and be a starting point for making a decision.

REACTIONS: Use the space provided to respond to the following questions.

1. Which of the areas covered in the questions are most important to your decision?

2. At this time, do you foresee children in your future? Explain.

SOURCE: Diane Elvenstar, Ph.D., Director, Advancement Associates, Beverly Hills, CA.; author of *Children: To Have or Have Not?* (Harbor Publishing, 1982) and *First Comes Love* (Bobbs-Merrill, 1983).

82 | Attitudes Toward Timing of Parenthood Scale (ATOP)

PURPOSE: This scale is designed to provide some indication of your attitudes toward the timing of being a parent.

DIRECTIONS: Circle the response option which most closely represents your feelings. The options are strongly agree (SA), agree (A), undecided (U), disagree (D), and strongly disagree (SD).

	SD	D	U	A	SA	Final Scoring
1. The best time to begin having children is usually within the first two years of marriage.	1	2	3	4	5	_____
2. It is important for a young couple to enjoy their social life first and to have children later in the marriage.	1	2	3	4	5	_____
3. A marriage relationship is strengthened if children are born in the early years of marriage.	1	2	3	4	5	_____
4. Women are generally happier if they have children early in the marriage.	1	2	3	4	5	_____
5. Men are generally tied closer to the marriage when there are children in the home.	1	2	3	4	5	_____
6. Most young married women lack self-fulfillment until they have a child.	1	2	3	4	5	_____
7. Young couples who do not have children are usually unable to do so.	1	2	3	4	5	_____
8. Married couples who have mature love for each other will be eager to have a child as soon as possible.	1	2	3	4	5	_____
9. Couples who do not have children cannot share in the major interests of their friends who are parents, and are therefore left out of most social circles.	1	2	3	4	5	_____

10. Children enjoy their parents more when the
    parents are nearer their own age; therefore, parents
    should have children while they are still young.   1   2   3   4   5   _____

11. In general, research indicates that the majority of
    couples approaching parenthood for the first time
    have had little or no previous child care experience
    beyond sporadic baby-sitting, a course in child
    psychology, or occasional care of younger siblings.
    Considering your own background preparation
    for parenthood, would you judge that you are
    well prepared for the parenting experience?   1   2   3   4   5   _____

SCORING: Response options favoring early parenthood receive the highest score (5 points), and those that favor delayed parenthood receive the lowest score (1 point). The range of possible scores is from 10 to 50. Item number 2 is reverse-scored, so if you chose option 4, change it to 2 (or vice versa); if you chose option 5, change it to 1 (or vice versa). Then sum the value of the options you selected for all items to compute your total score.

INTERPRETATION: For items 1–10, scores ranging from **10 to 18** strongly favor delayed parenthood. A score of **19 to 25** moderately favors delayed parenthood. Scores ranging from **26 to 34** moderately favor early parenthood and a score of **35 to 50** strongly favors early parenthood. Research studies at midwestern universities determined 21 as the total mean score for females.

REACTIONS: Use the space provided to respond to the following questions.

1. Do you feel your score accurately represents your attitudes toward the timing of parenthood? Why or why not?

2. If you are not yet married, project into the future and decide how your score would be different five years from now. Explain.

3. If you have children, would your score on this assessment have been different before your children were born? Explain why or why not?

SOURCE: "Attitudes Toward Timing of Parenthood Scale (ATOP)" by P. K. Knaub, D. B. Ebersol, and J. H. Voss, Sex Roles, vol. 9, 1983, p. 358, Plenum Publishing Corp. Used with permission.

83 | Parenthood: Making Responsible Decisions

PURPOSE: Many of the situations that occur daily as part of the regular routine of living can be the cause of parent-child conflict. Each conflict can be a source of irritation to both the child and the parent. But the amount of friction may be greater than necessary. Parents can prevent undue tensions by developing certain anticipatory skills to reduce the chance of entangled problems growing out of these annoying situations.

DIRECTIONS: Three potential or actual problems are listed below. You are asked to formulate an effective method of action to head off a larger problem. This "head them off at the pass" approach is often referred to as "anticipatory decision making." It is based on a philosophy that encourages responsible action by all family members to meet each member's needs. Think of it as a commonsense approach to parenting by *planning ahead*.

1. Situation: Ten-year-old child regularly comes to the dinner table with dirty hands.

   Your feelings: (How would you feel as the parent?)

   Child's feelings: (Describe the child's attitude toward the situation.)

   Goal: (What would you as the parent want to accomplish?)

   Undesirable action: (What action or actions if taken would probably turn the situation into an entangled problem?)

   Desirable action: (What anticipatory decision-making behavior could you use to prevent further problems from developing, and that meets each person's needs?)

2. Situation: Twelve-year-old watches too much television.

   Your feelings:

   Child's feelings:

   Goal:

   Undesirable action:

   Desirable action:

3. Situation: Sixteen-year-old repeatedly stays out beyond curfew on school nights.

   Your feelings:

   Child's feelings:

   Goal:

   Undesirable action:

   Desirable action:

REACTIONS: Use the space provided to respond to the following questions.

1. Do you feel this method of "anticipatory decision making" is helpful in dealing with potential conflict? Why or why not?

2. Have you ever had a chance to practice this with your own child or niece or nephew? How well did it work?

SOURCE: Adapted from "Communications and Parenting Skills: Parent Workbook," by Dr. Judith Frankel D'Augelli, Clinical and Consulting Psychologist and Joan M. Weener, M.S., 1023 Torrey Lane, Boalsburg, PA 16801.

84

Do You Know Your Parents as People?

PURPOSE: Your parents have shared their house and their lives with you for a good number of years. You leave the homestead (if you have) and the time you now share may have evolved into touching base only on holidays, birthdays, times of crisis, or times of celebration. For a short time you feel close to your family again, but soon it is time to leave. Next time you are home try something new. Find out what your parents are like as people. There is a good chance you could develop a new perspective and a better understanding of these two important people.

DIRECTIONS: Respond to the following questions as best you can. On your next visit home, have your parents respond to the same questions and compare your answers. This exercise should stimulate new conversations and give you new insight into your parents as people.

The Early Years

1. What was you mother's/father's nickname?

   Your response: Parents' response:

   Mother _____   Mother _____

   Father _____   Father _____

2. What did your mother/father want to be when she/he grew up?

   Your response: Parents' response:

   Mother _____   Mother _____

   Father _____   Father _____

3. Who was the childhood heroine/hero of your mother/father?

   Your response: Parents' response:

   Mother _____   Mother _____

   Father _____   Father _____

4. If your mother/father ran away from home as a child, where did she/he go?

Your response: Parents' response:

Mother _____   Mother _____

Father _____   Father _____

5. What did your mother/father and her/his mother/father argue about most?

Your response: Parents' response:

Mother _____   Mother _____

Father _____   Father

6. What kind of men/women would your mother/father have dated in high school?

Your response: Parents' response:

Mother _____   Mother _____

Father _____   Father _____

7. If a bully had hit your mother/father on the school playground, what would she/he have done?

Your response: Parents' response:

Mother _____   Mother _____

Father _____   Father

8. Of what childhood accomplishment is your mother/father most proud?

Your response: Parents' response:

Mother _____   Mother _____

Father _____   Father

9. When your mother/father left school to support herself/himself, what was her/his first job?

Your response: Parents' response:

Mother _____   Mother _____

Father _____   Father _____

10. What is your mother's/father's strongest personal memory of World War II, the Korean War, the Vietnam War, or the Gulf War (whichever is applicable)?

Your response: Parents' response:

Mother _____   Mother _____

Father _____   Father _____

What Suits Their Fancy?

11. What is your mother's/father's favorite food?

Your response: Parents' response:

Mother _____   Mother _____

Father _____   Father _____

12. What was a big disappointment in your mother's/father's life?

Your response: Parents' response:

Mother _____   Mother _____

Father _____   Father _____

13. What is your mother's/father's most vivid family memory of the year you were ten?

Your response: Parents' response:

Mother _____   Mother _____

Father _____   Father

14. What musical recording artist would your mother/father prefer to listen to?

Your response: Parents' response:

Mother _____   Mother _____

Father _____   _____Father

15. What is your mother's and father's "song"?

Your response: Parents' response:

Mother _____   Mother _____

Father _____   _____Father

16. If your mother/father was offered a drink at a party, what would she/he order?

   Your response: Parents' response:

   Mother _____   Mother _____

   Father _____   Father

17. If your parents won $100,000, what would they do with the money?

   Your response: Parents' response:

   Mother _____   Mother _____

   Father _____   Father _____

18. If your mother/father were to visit another country, which one would she/he choose?

   Your response: Parents' response:

   Mother _____   Mother _____

   Father _____   Father _____

19. Do you know what can capture your mother's/father's emotions, and make her/him feel misty?

   Your response: Parents' response:

   Mother _____   Mother _____

   Father _____   Father _____

20. If your mother/father could start over in life, what career would she/he pursue?

   Your response: Parents' response:

   Mother _____   Mother _____

   Father _____   Father _____

Days of Courtship and Marriage

21. Where did you parents go on their first date?

   Your response: Parents' response:

   Mother _____   Mother _____

   Father _____   Father _____

22. How did your parents first meet each other?

Your response: Parents' response:

Mother _____   Mother _____

Father _____   Father _____

23. Where and how did your father propose to your mother?

Your response: Parents' response:

Mother _____   Mother _____

Father _____   Father _____

24. What year and where did your parents get married?

Your response: Parents' response:

Mother _____   Mother _____

Father _____   Father _____

25. Did your mother and father like each other when they first met?

Your response: Parents' response:

Mother _____   Mother _____

Father _____   Father _____

26. How long did your parents know each other before they were married?

Your response: Parents' response:

Mother _____   Mother _____

Father _____   Father _____

27. Where did your parents spend their honeymoon?

Your response: Parents' response:

Mother _____   Mother _____

Father _____   Father _____

28. What is your mother's favorite gift from your father in all the years they have been married (and vice versa)?

Your response: Parents' response:

Mother _____   Mother _____

Father _____   Father _____

29. What does your mother wear to please your father (and vice versa)?

Your response: Parents' response:

Mother _____   Mother _____

Father _____   Father _____

30. Which years of marriage does your mother/father remember most fondly?

Your response: Parents' response:

Mother _____   Mother _____

Father _____   Father _____

Point of View: What They Believe In

31. How would your mother/father react to a parking ticket she/he did not deserve?

Your response: Parents' response:

Mother _____   Mother _____

Father _____   Father _____

32. Does your mother/father support Proposition 13?

Your response: Parents' response:

Mother _____   Mother _____

Father _____   Father _____

33. If you and your partner had an abortion, how would your mother/father react?

Your response: Parents' response:

Mother _____   Mother _____

Father _____   Father _____

34. Does your mother/father support the ratification of ERA?

Your response: Parents' response:

Mother _____   Mother _____

Father _____   Father _____

35. What luxury item is most important for your mother/father to have in the family budget?

Your response: Parents' response:

Mother _____   Mother _____

Father _____   Father _____

36. What political or prominent figure, either past or present, does your mother/father most identify with?

Your response: Parents' response:

Mother _____   Mother _____

Father _____   Father _____

37. If you told your mother/father you were moving in with your boyfriend/girlfriend, how would she/he react?

Your response: Parents' response:

Mother _____   Mother _____

Father _____   Father _____

38. How would your mother/father react to overt homosexual behavior?

Your response: Parents' response:

Mother _____   Mother _____

Father _____   Father _____

39. Would you say that your mother's/father's outlook on life is primarily optimistic or pessimistic?

Your response: Parents' response:

Mother _____   Mother _____

Father _____   Father _____

40. What do your mother/father plan to be doing twenty years from now?

Your response: Parents' response:

Mother _____   Mother _____

Father _____   Father _____

SCORING: Give yourself a point for each similar answer you have for each parent. The most points you could possibly have would be 80.

60 and over: You and your parents must talk together quite a bit. That's great. When you are miles away, the communication may be more difficult—but keep it going.

45–59: You may not take enough time to talk with your parents about themselves. When you do take the time to talk, you may be amazed at how much more you learn. In addition, you will understand better why your parents think as they do.

30–44: You are all adults now, so try talking with your parents about themselves. Perhaps you have considered them in the role of "mom" and "dad" for too long. Or perhaps you have been separated from them or one parent at a young age and never really had a chance to get to know them. These questions provide an opportunity for you to open the lines of communication with some nonthreatening topics. You have to take it from here!

REACTION: Use the space provided to respond to the following questions.

1. Did you learn some things about your parents that you did not know before? Explain.

2. Were you comfortable doing this exercise with your parents? Explain. Were your parents comfortable doing this exercise? Explain.

85 | Family Strengths Inventory

PURPOSE: This inventory is designed to assess your family strengths.

DIRECTIONS: To assess your family (choose either the family you grew up in or the family you have formed as an adult), circle the number that best reflects how your family rates on each strength. A "1" represents the lowest rating and a "5" represents the highest.

	Low Rating				High Rating
1. Spending time together and doing things with other.	1	2	3	4	5
2. Commitment to each other	1	2	3	4	5
3. Good communication (talking with each other often, listening well, sharing feelings with each other)	1	2	3	4	5
4. Dealing with crises in a positive manner	1	2	3	4	5
5. Expressing appreciation to each other	1	2	3	4	5
6. Spiritual wellness	1	2	3	4	5
7. Closeness of relationship between spouses	1	2	3	4	5
8. Closeness of relationship between parents and children	1	2	3	4	5
9. Happiness of relationship between spouses	1	2	3	4	5
10. Happiness of relationship between parents and children	1	2	3	4	5
11. Extent to which spouses make each other feel good about themselves (self-confident, worthy, competent, and happy)	1	2	3	4	5
12. Extent to which parents help children feel good about themselves	1	2	3	4	5

SCORING: Add up the numbers you have circled for questions 1–12 to obtain your total score. Place your total score in the space provided.

Total score = _____

INTERPRETATION: A score **below 39** indicates below-average family strengths. Scores between **39 and 52** are in the average range. Scores **above 53** indicate a strong family. Low scores on individual items identify areas that families can profitably spend time on. High scores are worthy of celebration but shouldn't lead to complacency. Like gardens, families need loving care to remain strong.

REACTIONS: Use the space provided to respond to the following questions

1. Were you comfortable completing this inventory? Why or why not?

2. Does this inventory highlight anything you would like to change regarding the family you grew up in or the family your have now? If so what would you change and what steps would you take to make these changes.

86 Marriage Today: Points to Ponder

PURPOSE: As a young adult in the process of dating or perhaps involved in a long-term relationship, it is helpful to take a closer look at what it takes to make a relationship work. Even though not everyone gets married, we all have married friends who at one time or another ask our advice. Perhaps the questions in this exercise will provide some food for thought.

DIRECTIONS: Use the space provided to respond to each question. You may want to ask your significant other, friend, or another family member to respond to the questions on a separate sheet of paper.

1. What do you feel are the most important considerations in choosing a marriage partner?

2. What do you think constitutes or would constitute a successful marriage for you?

3. There is a controversy over the fact that dating may be nothing more than a social arrangement and is not for the purpose of selecting a mate. State and defend your position on this issue.

4. Discuss your views on the role of the engagement period. How long do you think this period should be? Why?

5. How important is "revealing all" to one's potential spouse? Should one's background be an "open book"? Why or why not?

6. How would you counsel a person who has stated he/she wants to break an engagement but don't want to "hurt" the other person?

7. Because we consider marriage a private affair, why would an individual hesitate to marry someone of widely different characteristics just to please society?

8. How important is good communication in marriage? Explain.

9. Why is individual privacy an important aspect to consider in making marriage successful?

10. Should husbands and wives be allowed their secrets or nights out? Why or why not?

11. In what way do children complicate marital adjustment?

REACTIONS: If your partner responded to the questions, share your answers to the questions one at a time and discuss.

1. Are there any differences in responses that cause concern? If so, why?

2. Were these questions helpful to you in clarifying your own opinion on these issues? Explain.

SECTION X | HOMOSEXUALITY

*I*n our society we tend to make clear-cut distinctions between homosexuality and hetero-sexuality. However, the distinction is not quite that precise. A relatively small percentage of people consider themselves to be exclusively homosexual; a greater percentage think of themselves as exclusively heterosexual. These groups represent the opposite ends of a broad spectrum. Individuals between the ends of the spectrum exhibit varying mixtures of preference and sexual experience, which may evolve over time. Keep in mind that sexual orientation is only one aspect of a person's life. The exercises in this section are designed for you to examine some of your feelings toward homosexuality.

The Homosexuality exercises include:

87. Homosexual Comfort/Discomfort Scale
88. Fairweather Johnson or Still Friends?
89. Issues in Human Sexuality: Homosexual School Teachers
90. Issues in Human Sexuality: Homosexuals in the Military

87 | Homosexual Comfort/Discomfort Scale

PURPOSE: This questionnaire is designed to measure the way you feel about working or associating with gay men and/or lesbian women.

DIRECTIONS: Consider each item as carefully and accurately as you can, then place the number indicating your feeling next to each item.

Strongly Agree	Agree	No Opinion	Disagree	Strongly Disagree
1	2	3	4	5

_____ 1. I would feel comfortable working closely with a gay man.

_____ 2. I would enjoy attending social functions where lesbians and gay men were present.

_____ 3. I would feel uncomfortable if I learned that my neighbor was a homosexual.

_____ 4. If a member of my gender made a sexual advance toward me, I would feel angry.

_____ 5. I would feel comfortable knowing that I was attractive to members of my gender.

_____ 6. I would feel uncomfortable being seen in a bar for gay people.

_____ 7. I would feel comfortable if a member of my gender made an advance toward me.

_____ 8. I would be comfortable if I found myself attracted to a member of my gender.

_____ 9. I would feel disappointed if I learned that my child was homosexual.

_____ 10. I would feel nervous being in a group of homosexual people.

_____ 11. I would feel comfortable knowing that a member of my clergy was homosexual.

_____ 12. I would be upset if I learned that my brother or sister was homosexual.

_____ 13. I would feel that I had failed as a parent if I learned that my child was gay or lesbian.

_____ 14. If I saw two men holding hands in public, I would feel disgusted.

_____ 15. If a member of my gender made an advance toward me, I would feel offended.

____ 16. I would feel comfortable if I learned that my daughter's teacher was a lesbian.

____ 17. I would feel uncomfortable if I learned that my spouse or partner was attracted to members of his or her gender.

____ 18. I would feel at ease talking with a homosexual person at a party.

____ 19. I would feel uncomfortable if I learned that my boss was a homosexual.

____ 20. It would not bother me to walk through a predominantly gay section of town.

____ 21. It would disturb me to find out that my physician was homosexual.

____ 22. I would feel comfortable if I learned that my best friend of my gender was homosexual.

____ 23. If a member of my gender made an advance toward me, I would feel flattered.

____ 24. I would feel uncomfortable knowing that my son's male teacher was homosexual.

____ 25. I would feel comfortable working closely with a lesbian.

SCORING: For the following items you must first reverse the scoring of items 3, 4, 6, 9, 10, 12, 13, 14, 15, 17, 19, 21, 24. To do so, change the number you wrote for the item as follows:

>   Change a   1 to a 5
>   2 to a 4
>   3 remains the same
>   4 to a 2
>   5 to a 1

When you have written in these new numbers and crossed out the old numbers, add up your total number of points. From this total score subtract 25.

This is your score: _____.

The scale measures the degree to which you have dread or discomfort of being in close quarters with homosexual persons. The minimum score is 25 and represents the least amount of dread and discomfort. The maximum score is 100 and represents the greatest amount of dread and discomfort. On studies with this instrument, the average score of college students is 53. In the college students studied, 4 percent have a score of 25 or less; 7 percent have a score of 75 or more; and 55 percent have a score greater than 50. In general, a score of 0 to 25 is highly nonhomophobic; **26 to 50** is moderately nonhomophobic; **51 to 75** is moderately homophobic; and **75 to 100** is highly homophobic.

REACTIONS: Use the space provided to respond to the following questions.

1. Mark your score on the scale below with an "X".

25————————————————50————————————————-75————————————————-100

Explain what your score means to you.

2. Would your score on this assessment have been different five years ago? Explain.

3. Are you comfortable with your attitude in regard to homosexuality or would you like to change your attitude? Explain.

SOURCE: "A Strategy for the Measurement of Homophobia," *Journal of Homosexuality*. © 1980, by permission of The Haworth Press, Inc. All rights reserved.

88 Fairweather Johnson or Still Friends?

PURPOSE: This exercise is designed for you to examine how you would (or did) respond to a friend of the same gender who has just "come out" and wants you to know that she/he is gay.

DIRECTIONS: Read carefully the paragraph below. Use the space provided to respond to the following questions.

It's Saturday afternoon, you're hanging out, and a knock comes upon your door. You open up, and at your doorstep is a very close friend. After warm greetings you grab a snack and drinks. The conversation is filled with catching up on what you both have been doing and the latest on mutual friends. The conversation turns serious and your friend of the same gender informs you that she/he is gay.

1. What is your immediate reaction?

2. What questions would you have for your friend?

3. What concerns, if any, would you have about the opinions of other people who may find out that your friend is gay?

4. Would it be easier to deal with this situation if your friend was the opposite gender as opposed to a friend of the same gender? Explain your feelings here.

5. What would you predict will happen (if anything) to your friendship in the future?

6. What other concerns would you have with regard to your friend's future and his/her relationship with family and other friends?

89 Issues in Human Sexuality: Homosexual School Teachers

Should homosexuals be employed as school teachers?

DIRECTIONS: Read each paragraph below carefully, making sure you clearly understand both sides of the issue before you write your reactions.

Some people believe that homosexuals should not be employed as school teachers. They argue that because children are in their formative years, they are impressionable and are likely to be influenced to be homosexual. Even if they don't become homosexuals per se, these children may be influenced to experiment with homosexual activities that are illegal or are viewed as immoral. Because adults in positions of authority serve as role models for children, these people argue that homosexuals should be denied employment in jobs where they are in charge of children or youth.

Others find these arguments absurd. They contend that there is no evidence that a teacher's sexual preference has any impact on students. Most homosexual teachers are not likely to make their sexual preferences known, because a person's sexuality is not an appropriate topic for classroom discussion. Further, there have always been homosexual teachers; they simply didn't make the fact known. Most sex researchers believe that an individual's sexual orientation is developed by age four or five. Therefore, children are in no danger from well-adjusted teachers of either sexual persuasion. Only teachers with psychological problems might have an adverse effect.

REACTIONS: With which side do you agree? Explain your feelings.

SOURCE: George B. Dintiman and Jerrold S. Greenberg, *Health Through Discovery,* © 1983, Addison-Wesley Publishing Co., Inc., Reading, MA, p. 306. Reprinted with permission.

90 : Issues in Human Sexuality: Homosexual's in the Military

Should homosexuals be allowed to serve in the military?

DIRECTIONS: Read each paragraph below carefully, making sure you clearly understand both sides of the issue before you write your reactions.

Some people believe that homosexuals (gay men and lesbian women) should not be allowed to serve in the military. Problems with living in close quarters, training for important missions, going to war in combat situations, and esprit de corps have all been suggested by those opposed to homosexuals in the military. The fear of same sex relationships at the unit level and managing the "fall out" from relationship problems are also concerns of those opposed to gay men and lesbian women serving in the military. Those opposed to homosexuals serving in the military also usually feel this is not a lifestyle to be accepted.

Some people believe homosexuals should be allowed to serve in the military. They contend there is no evidence that homosexuals would have any impact on a military unit functioning effectively. Gay men and lesbian women do not make their sexual orientation an issue in the military just as heterosexual men and women should not make sexual orientation an issue. Heterosexual relationships in the military have the same potential for problems; however, it should not be an issue for either. Moreover, for years gay men and lesbian women (who have been in the closet) have been model military employees with excellent service records.

REACTIONS: With which side do you agree? Explain why you agree with a particular side and add to the rationale.

VARIATIONS IN SEXUAL BEHAVIOR

A typical sexual behavior refers to a variety of sexual activities that in their fully developed form are statistically uncommon in the general population. Such behaviors exist in many gradations, ranging from mild, infrequently expressed tendencies to full-blown, regularly manifested behaviors. The exercises in this section are designed for you to examine a variety of variant or atypical behaviors that exist, to some degree in modern society.

The Variations in Sexual Behavior exercises include:

91. Sexuality-Related Practices and the Law
92. Point of View: Variant Sexual Behavior

91 Sexuality-Related Practices and the Law

PURPOSE: To date there has been a significant amount of controversy in the United States with regard to sexual behavior. Our present laws pertaining to sexuality deal not only with rapists and child molesters, but also with the private practices of married and nonmarried couples. In most states approximately 95 percent of all married men and the majority of married women have experienced orgasm in an illegal manner. Perhaps some of our existing laws need to be reevaluated and changed. This exercise is designed to help you and a partner/friend express and examine your attitudes toward our existing laws.

DIRECTIONS: Respond to each of the sexuality-related practices below by using the scale provided. Use the first column of blanks for your own responses. Then cover your responses and have your partner or friend use the second column to respond to each statement.

A = Should be prohibited by law
B = Should be regulated by law
C = Should be regulated by informal nonlegal measures
D = Should be a matter of private decision

You   Friend

____ ____ 1. Rape

____ ____ 2. Child molestation

____ ____ 3. Divorce

____ ____ 4. Artificial insemination

____ ____ 5. Female sterilization

____ ____ 6. Male sterilization

____ ____ 7. In vitro fertilization

____ ____ 8. Circumcision

____ ____ 9. Publication of adult pornographic material

____ ____ 10. Display of adult pornographic material

____ ____ 11. Sexuality education in elementary school

____ ____ 12. Sexuality education in middle school

You   Friend

____ ____ 13. Sexuality education in high school

____ ____ 14. Dissemination of contraceptive information

____ ____ 15. Dissemination of contraceptive devices

____ ____ 16. Bisexual behavior

____ ____ 17. Homosexual behavior

____ ____ 18. Heterosexual behavior

____ ____ 19. Nonmarital cohabitation

____ ____ 20. Female prostitution

____ ____ 21. Male prostitution

____ ____ 22. Fellatio

____ ____ 23. Cunnilingus

____ ____ 24. Exhibitionism

____ ____ 25. Anal intercourse

____ ____ 26. Adultery

____ ____ 27. Polygamy

____ ____ 28. Sexual nuisance via phone calls/letters

____ ____ 29. Topless public nudity

____ ____ 30. Total public nudity

____ ____ 31. Sex change operations

____ ____ 32. Sperm banks

____ ____ 33. Surrogate parenting

____ ____ 34. Abortion as a result of rape

____ ____ 35. Abortion as a result of incest

____ ____ 36. Abortion

____ ____ 37. Group sex

____ ____ 38. Public display of affection

____ ____ 39. Sexual intercourse in public

____ ____ 40. Group marriage

____ ____ 41. Open marriage

____ ____ 42. Chorionic villus sampling

____ ____ 43. Amniocentesis

____ ____ 44. Publication of child pornographic material

____ ____ 45. Display of child pornographic material

____ ____ 46. Abortion counseling

REACTIONS: Use the space provided to respond to the following questions.

1. Do you feel that your responses to these sexuality-related practices are similar to most people your age? Explain.

2. Which of these sexuality-related practices do you strongly support. Explain why.

3. For which of the sexuality-related practices were your responses different from those of your partner? Do these differences create any problems in your relationship?

92 Point of View: Variant Sexual Behavior

PURPOSE: Looking back on human history, especially sexual behaviors, it is evident that modes of sexual behaviors are as varied as individuals themselves. Over the years sexual behaviors have been labeled according to their acceptance or nonacceptance with regard to social, religious, and cultural modes. Some of these sexual behaviors are considered criminal acts even though they are practiced by a relatively high percentage of people. This exercise is designed for you to examine and express your attitude toward a variety of sexual behaviors.

DIRECTIONS: Respond to each item by placing a check mark in one of the four boxes that best represents your attitude toward each sexual behavior described. Then place a check mark in one of the five boxes that best represents what you feel should be the legal sanctions with regard to each sexual behavior.

Legend: Attitudes
- ER = Erotic
- AC = Acceptable
- AB = Abnormal
- ED = Emotionally Disturbed

Legal Sanctions
- RL = Repeal laws regulating sexual behavior
- DC = Decriminalize, require therapy not prison
- UN = Undecided
- MS = Misdemeanor, short-term sentence
- FL = Felony, long-term sentence

Behavior	Attitudes					Legal Sanctions				
	ER	AC	AB	ED		RL	DC	UN	MS	FL
SADISM: sexual gratification from inflicting pain (physical or psychological) on others										
MASOCHISM: sexual gratification from inflicting pain (physical or psychological) on self										
FETISHISM: sexual gratification achieved by means of an inanimate object, or part of the human body, bearing sexual symbolism for the individual										
ANALISM: sexual pleasure from stimulation of the anus										
KLISMAPHILIA: erotic pleasure from receiving enemas										
COPROLALIA: sexual pleasure from using so-called filthy language										

Legend: Attitudes   Legal Sanctions

ER = Erotic   RL = Repeal laws regulating sexual behavior
AC = Acceptable   DC = Decriminalize, require therapy not prison
AB = Abnormal   UN = Undecided
ED = Emotionally   MS = Misdemeanor, short-term sentence
     Disturbed   FL = Felony, long-term sentence

Behavior	Attitudes					Legal Sanctions				
	ER	AC	AB	ED		RL	DC	UN	MS	FL
FROTTAGE: sexual pleasure from rubbing or pressing against a desired person										
GERONTOSEXUALITY: a young person having distinct sexual interest preference for an elderly person										
UROPHILIA: sexual arousal from contact with urine										
AUTOSEXUALITY: solitary sexual behavior as in masturbation										
GROUP SEXUALITY: sexual relations between three or more people										
ACROTOMOPHILIA: being sexually aroused by a partner who is an amputee										
NARRATOPHILIA: need to listen to erotic narratives in order to achieve sexual arousal										
PROSTITUTION: engaging in sexual relations for payment										
MATE SWAPPING: sexual exchange of partners among two or more married couples										
SOMNOPHILIA: being dependent on the fantasy or actuality of intruding on and fondling a sleeping stranger for sexual arousal										
MYSOPHILIA: sexually turned on by something soiled or filthy such as underwear or used menstrual pads										
VOYEURISM: sexual gratification by observing others in the nude without their consent										
BESTIALITY (ZOOPHILIA): sexual contact between animals and humans										
NECROPHILIA: sexual gratification by viewing or having intercourse with a corpse										
INCEST: sexual interactions between close relatives other than husband and wife										

Legend: Attitudes   Legal Sanctions

      ER = Erotic   RL = Repeal laws regulating sexual behavior

      AC = Acceptable   DC = Decriminalize, require therapy not prison

      AB = Abnormal   UN = Undecided

      ED = Emotionally   MS = Misdemeanor, short-term sentence

           Disturbed   FL = Felony, long-term sentence

Behavior	Attitudes					Legal Sanctions				
	ER	AC	AB	ED		RL	DC	UN	MS	FL
TROILISM: two people engaging in sexual activities while a third observes										
ASPHYXIOPHILIA: employing partial asphyxiation, as by hanging in order to achieve or maintain sexual arousal or to facilitate or enhance orgasm (usually an adolescent male)										
PEDOPHILIA: sexual contact between a child and an adult										
COPROPHILIA: sexual gratification associated with the act of defecation or contact with feces										
PICTOPHILIA: being dependent on sexy pictures for sexual response										
TRANSVESTISM: sexual gratification by dressing in the garments of the opposite sex										
URETHRALISM: sexual pleasure from stimulation of the urethra by some object										
APOTEMNOPHILIA: being sexually excited by the fantasy or reality of being an amputee										

REACTIONS: Use the space provided to respond to the following questions.

1. Which of the atypical sexual behaviors in this exercise do you find to be the most unacceptable? Why?

2. Do you think that social and cultural conditions contribute to the much higher incidence of atypical sexual behavior among men than women? Explain.

3. What kinds of laws about prostitution make sense to you? How do you justify this point of view?

SECTION
XII

SEXUALITY, ETHICS, AND THE LAW

Throughout most of Western history, laws regulating sexual conduct were taken for granted. Sexual legislation is quite ancient, dating back certainly to the time of the Old Testament. Since that time, in countries where the Judeo-Christian tradition is influential, attempts to regulate morals have been the rule. Today we are likely to regard sex as a private matter that very much affects society and therefore is a fit subject for law. Most societies regulate sexual behavior, both by custom and by law. The exercises in this section offer some good perspective on some of the legal aspects of human sexuality in our culture.

The Sexuality, Ethics and the Law exercises include:

93

Love and the Law: Test Your Knowledge

PURPOSE: The past generation has seen fast-moving and remarkable changes in sex laws. The number of laws regulating sexual behavior is considerable. This exercise is designed to test your knowledge on some of these basic laws pertaining to sexuality.

DIRECTIONS: Read each question carefully and mark in the space provided YES or NO.

_____ 1. Doug and Karen live together. After the birth of their daughter (she was unplanned), Doug decides he wants out of the relationship. Is he responsible for paying child support?

_____ 2. Aubrie's career as a lawyer is very promising—until she met Tom, the owner of his own construction company and father of a four-year-old boy from a previous marriage. After several months of dating, Aubrie decides to move in with Tom, who then pressures her into giving up her practice and staying home with his son. Two years later, the relationship ends, and Aubrie, out of the work force for so long, has trouble restarting her career. Is Tom at all responsible for supporting her?

_____ 3. No-fault divorce has become one of the biggest legal trends of the 1980s. Is it allowed in every state?

_____ 4. Your Aunt Charlotte has passed away, leaving you with an $8,000 inheritance. You plan to use the money toward the purchase of a new car, but your husband wants to spend it on fixing up the house. Legally, he insists, nothing can be done with the money until you both come to an agreement. Is he correct?

_____ 5. Is polygamy—being married to more than one person at a time—prohibited by any federal statutes?

_____ 6. Rich, a history professor, earned his doctorate while married to Marla for seven years. Marla not only helped pay for his education but covered most of the household expenses. The two filed for divorce only after Rich earned his degree and began a faculty position. Is Marla entitled to compensation?

_____ 7. Wendy, a college sophomore, goes out on a date with Mark, a junior. At the end of their evening, Mark forces Wendy to have sex. Can Wendy charge him with rape?

_____ 8. Is homosexuality illegal in some states?

_____ 9. Fred and Carole have been married for eighteen months. Now Fred is filing for divorce because Carole refuses to have sex. Does Fred have a case?

_____ 10. For ten years Chester, a meek, shy man, has been physically abused by his wife Bertha. Can Chester get a restraining order against Bertha?

_____ 11. Before the wedding ceremony, Peter assured Kathy that he wanted to have children. After they married, Peter changed his mind, and Kathy called for an annulment. Is Kathy entitled?

_____ 12. Are there any states in which men are not allowed to sell their sperm?

_____ 13. During a very bitter divorce, Matthew learns that he is not the biological father of his four-year-old daughter. He petitions the court for visitation rights nonetheless. Does he have any chance of receiving them?

SCORING: The correct answers are:

1. Yes. In all cases, the main concern of the court is the welfare of the child, usually best cared for with support from the father.

2. No. Without a written agreement or witnesses to an oral pact, a man is not responsible for supporting a woman he lived with once the relationship is terminated, even if she gave up her career for him.

3. Yes. No-fault divorce, when neither party is held responsible for the breakup of the marriage, exists in some form in every state.

4. No. Gifts and inheritances, if not put into a marital fund, such as a joint bank account or investment, belong solely to the recipient. Go ahead and get the car.

5. No. At the present time, no federal statutes prohibit polygamy. It is, however, barred in every state.

6. Some states are beginning to consider professional degrees or licenses as marital property; however, this is far from being a given. Marla should consult a legal counselor; since Rich got his doctorate during their marriage and Marla's support helped make it possible, she could very well receive monetary compensation.

7. Yes, and unfortunately, cases like this are not rare. Recent studies of university students regarding date rape have suggested that approximately one in eight females have been raped and that about 90 percent of date rapes go unreported.

8. Yes. The Supreme Court on June 30, 1986, ruled that the right to have homosexual relations is not guaranteed by the Constitution, which means states can legislate against it. Homosexual sodomy is now illegal in about twenty-five states.

9. Yes. Denying your spouse sex without good cause, referred to as "constructive abandonment" in some states, is grounds for divorce if continued for over a year.

10. Yes. Approximately 95 percent of domestic-abuse victims are women; however, men are still eligible for orders of protection.

11. Yes, if Kathy can prove that Peter intended to deceive her. If he has had a genuine change of heart, which does not warrant an annulment, the marriage will have to be dissolved by divorce.

12. No. A man can sell his sperm in all fifty states.

13. Yes. Matthew may become what is known as an equitable parent, provided he meets three criteria: He and the child must both acknowledge the relationship, he must want parental rights, and he must agree to pay child support.

REACTIONS: Use the space provided to respond to the following questions.

1. What aspects of human sexuality do you think it is reasonable for the law to regulate?

2. If you were a state legislator, what kinds of laws would you favor regarding AIDS?

3. If you were a state legislator, what kinds of laws would you favor regarding surrogate parenting?

4. Do you think that it is too easy to get married? Do you think it is too easy to get divorced? Explain.

94 | Sexual Ethics Checklist

Purpose: This inventory is designed to give you some indication of your level of sexual ethics.

Directions: Answer (**True** or **False**) in the space provided for the following questions on sexual ethics and behavior. Questions noted with "M&F" are for both males and females to answer. Questions with only "M" or only "F" are only for males and females, respectively.

M&F_____ 1. I would tell a potential sex partner if I had been exposed to a sexually transmitted disease.

M&F_____ 2. If I were in a steady dating relationship and had sexual intercourse with someone else one time only, I would still tell my steady about it.

M&F_____ 3. If I heard that a single woman with whom I work was very upset over finding she was pregnant, I would refrain from telling any of my friends at work.

M&F_____ 4. If I were dating a person who had told me clearly and emphatically that he/she did not want to have intercourse, and we both became intoxicated and the person agreed to have sex, I would go ahead.

F_____ 5. If I were a female who was crazy about a guy I was dating, and unexpectedly had a chance to have intercourse with him, I would tell him I was on the pill even if I was not. Of course I'd get on it the next day for sure.

M_____ 6. If I knew my male friend was very pushy with women, and he asked me to set it up to leave him alone with a female friend of mine who did not know him, I would refuse to participate.

M&F_____ 7. If I was in a group that was laughing at a movie that made light of rape or a rape attempt, I would tell them I didn't like to see rape be made a joke of like that.

M&F _____ 8. If my friends pressured me to brag about someone I had dated—whether we had done anything sexual or not—I would refuse to talk about private things with them.

M&F_____ 9. If I were sexually involved with someone and I did not believe in abortion as a choice, I wouldn't bring up the subject for fear that I might lose the other person.

M ____ 10. If the guys had drilled a hole into the women's locker room wall and I knew the women being viewed would feel terribly violated if they knew, I would refuse to participate.

M&F ____ 11. If a potential sex partner asked me what kinds of sexual risks I had taken in my life, I would tell the truth.

M&F ____ 12. If I were in the heat of passion with someone who was saying "No" and I thought of some line I could say to get the other person to go ahead, I probably would.

SCORING: The most ethical answers would probably be **True** to 1, 2, 3, 6, 7, 8, 10, and 11; and *False* to 4, 5, 9, and 12.

INTERPRETATION: But surprise! Your answers may not have much meaning. Why not? Because people tend to answer questions the way they think they *should* rather than responding the way they *would* in the real pressure situations of life. It sounds good to say we wouldn't do anything unethical. But it requires character to follow up. It requires a constant ability to put ourselves in another's place.

REACTIONS: Use the space provided to respond to the following questions.

1. Are there any questions (1–12) where you disagree with the scoring? Why or why not?

2. How do you think your partner or best friend would score on this inventory? Explain. If you do not know, discuss these statements with your partner or friend and then explain what you learned.

95 | Children and Sex Offenders

PURPOSE: You may have warned your children or other children you know about strangers, in hopes that keeping them away from strangers and odd people will keep them safe. However, only 10 to 15 percent of the offenders of children are strangers. Most commonly, sexual assaults on children are by someone known to them who takes advantage of the child's trust. Telling them only about strangers leaves them much more vulnerable than they need to be. The following inventory brings to light a few characteristics of potential sexual offenders.

DIRECTIONS: If you know someone who you suspect could be a sexual offender, you may want to ask yourself the following questions about him or her. Respond with a YES or NO in the blank following each question for questions in Part I, numbers 1 through 7. Then respond to the questions for Part II in the space provided.

PART I

1. Does he/she repeatedly tickle, pat, and attempt physical contact that is not wanted by a child?
2. Does he/she relate to a child in a sexual manner, flirting or carrying on with comments about a child being a "real charmer" or a "knock-out"? _____
3. Does the child indicate discomfort with someone or try to avoid him/her? _____
4. Was he/she abused as a child? _____
5. Does he/she batter his/her spouse or abuse his/her children? _____
6. Does he/she choose children as companions and enjoy the position of power the age advantage gives him/her?
7. Does he/she consistently entice children to his/her house? _____

PART II

1. In what way can you encourage your children to say "no" or resist advances that a friend, relative, or stranger makes?

2. What should you do when a child tells you he/she has been assaulted?

SCORING:

PART I:

If you responded YES to any of the seven questions, you may want to look further into the relationship between the person and child you have in mind. One or two positive responses are not sufficient to accuse a person of being a sexual offender; however, there may be sufficient cause to be more aware of what is happening in the relationship.

PART II:

1. One way to prepare a child to resist is to give some simple examples of what might happen and then sample responses. You can encourage your children to say "no" by noticing and acting on a child's discomfort.

2. The best response is to go slowly, not ask for too much too quickly and to keep the focus on the child's needs. Reassure the child that you will protect and support him/ her. Tell him/her you are glad that he/she told you. When he/she first starts talking about the assault, he/she can be helped by gentle questions. Can you tell me what happened? Use your own words—it's okay to go slowly. Don't pressure the child to talk. Ask questions that help the child give information back to you. Tell your child you believe what he/she has told you.

REACTIONS: Use the space provided to respond to the following questions.

1. Did you have a particular person in mind as you responded to questions in Part I? As a result of your responses to the questions, are you concerned? If so, what do you plan to do?

2. List some other effective means of communicating with children to prevent possible sexual abuse.

SOURCE Caren Adams and Jennifer Fay, *No More Secrets: Protecting Your Child From Sexual Assault.* © 1981 By Caren Adams and Jennifer Fay. Reproduced for Valois and Kammermann with permission from Impact Publishers, Inc., P.O. Box 1984, San Luis Obispo, CA 93406. Further reproduction prohibited.

96 | Was That Sexual Abuse?

PURPOSE: Recognizing past sexual abuse is an important step in sexual healing. It helps people make a connection between sexual issues or problems and their original source. For many survivors, acknowledging sexual abuse is a difficult step. Someone may recall memories that leave them uncomfortable but hesitate to label those experiences as abuse. Sexual abuse can happen to men and women.

DIRECTIONS: To help you understand the meaning of sexual abuse, and to identify whether you have been sexually abused, consider these four questions. Respond YES or NO in the space provided.

_____ 1. Were you unable to give your full consent to the sexual activity (intimidated, under the influence of alcohol or other drugs, asleep, not mentally alert, a child)?

_____ 2. Did the sexual activity involve the betrayal of a trusted relationship (relative, teacher, religious leader, therapist, employer or babysitter)?

_____ 3. Was the sexual activity characterized by force or violence? Or threat of force or violence?

_____ 4. Do you feel that you were abused (physically or mentally)?

SCORING: If you answered YES to any of the above questions, you have been sexually abused. How you have dealt with it depends upon your strength, tolerance level, and support systems. If you have been abused—no matter how bad your experience was compared with others'—your sexuality has been tainted by the experience. The harm done to you is real and it matters.

Know Your Sexual Rights

These rights protect and enable each of us to develop positive sexuality.

1. The right to develop healthy attitudes about sex
2. The right to sexual privacy
3. The right to protection from bodily harassment and harm
4. The right to say no to sexual behavior

5. The right to control touch and sexual contact

6. The right to stop sexual arousal that feels inappropriate or uncomfortable

7. The right to develop our sexuality according to our sexual preferences and orientation

8. The right to enjoy healthy sexual pleasure and satisfaction

Perpetrators of sexual abuse can confuse their victims about many of these rights. And although offenders may try to convince themselves and their victims otherwise, sexual abuse does not occur by accident. Abusers either intentionally harm or take actions that they know could cause harm. Either way, they rob victims of their sexual rights.

Recognizing that an experience was in fact sexual abuse can be difficult, but denying it also takes great mental energy. When you acknowledge sexual abuse, you allow yourself to recognize the catastrophe of sexual abuse as part of your life history. You take back power and can begin to mend the hurts of the past. Then, when you share the experience of your abuse with others, you can do it with your chin held high. *You are no longer a victim. You are a survivor, on your way to becoming a thriver.*

1. If you have responded YES to any of the above questions, how has the experience affected your sexuality? If not you, is there someone close to you who has experienced sexual abuse? How has it affected that person's sexuality?

2. Briefly explain how you or your friend have learned to deal with the emotions and memories of the experience?

97 | Is It Sexual Harassment?

PURPOSE: The statements in this inventory are designed to test your knowledge of sexual harassment in an educational setting or in the workforce.

DIRECTIONS: Read each of the following statements and indicate in the blank provided whether it is TRUE or FALSE. Then ask a friend of the opposite gender, or if you have a job ask your boss, if he/she would respond to the statements. Compare your responses and read the explanations.

	You	Friend
1. Sexual harassment issues concern only women in the workforce.	____	____
2. Staring at another employee is not sexual harassment.	____	____
3. Most claims of sexual harassment involve requests for sexual favors in exchange for something else.	____	____
4. Policies involving sexual harassment must include all employees at all levels of the organization.	____	____
5. A sexually explicit picture or cartoon hanging over an employee's workstation may be sexual harassment.	____	____
6. Sexual harassment includes unwanted behavior directed from one person to another.	____	____
7. Sexual harassment includes an unwanted behavior that is sexual or related to the gender of the person.	____	____
8. Sexual harassment often occurs in a situation where one person has power over another.	____	____
9. The courts look at sexual harassment from the view of the person who is accused.	____	____
10. For sexual harassment to occur there must be a victim or victims.	____	____
11. One type of sexual harassment is when there is a hostile environment in the workplace or an educational setting.	____	____
12. Sexual jokes, innuendos, and sexually explicit language may be considered sexual harassment.	____	____
13. A hug or a kiss on the cheek may be considered sexual harassment.	____	____
14. Picking lint off someone's clothes or rubbing someone's shoulder can be considered sexual harassment.	____	____

15. "Accidental" repeated touching may be considered sexual harassment. _____ _____

16. If a sexual behavior or one related to gender is repeated and pervasive, it may then be considered a problem. _____ _____

17. When supervisors make light of sexual harassment incidents, the issues usually resolve themselves. _____ _____

18. Adults in consensual relationships cannot later charge sexual harassment. _____ _____

19. Sexual harassment complaints should be filed with the appropriate authority at the time the incidents occur. _____ _____

20. If an employee is found guilty of sexual harassment, the employer can be held liable. _____ _____

SCORING:

1. FALSE. Sexual harassment issues concern both men and women in the workforce or any other setting. Sexual harassment most often occurs between men and women, but also occurs between persons of the same gender. The greatest number of sexual harassment cases are filed with a man sexually harassing a woman.

2. FALSE. Staring at another employee may be considered sexual harassment if it is an unwanted persistent behavior and it is done in a sexual manner or related to the gender of the other person. This is especially true if the victim feels the other person has power or authority over them.

3. FALSE. Most court claims of sexual harassment filed are not concerning requests for sexual favors in exchange for something else. The greatest number of sexual harassment cases filed at this time involve claims of a hostile work environment, meaning that someone's behavior has substantially interfered with a person's education or employment.

4. TRUE. Policies regarding sexual harassment must include all levels of employees in the workplace, persons in an educational setting or any other setting. No one should be exempt from the policy, including executive and administrative personnel.

5. TRUE. A sexually explicit picture or cartoon at an employee's workstation may be considered sexual harassment since it creates an "intimidating or offensive" educational or work environment.

6. TRUE. There are three elements that define sexual harassment. Unwanted sexual behavior or unwelcome sexual behavior directed at another person is one of these elements.

7. TRUE. A second element used to define sexual harassment is an unwanted behavior that is sexual or related to the gender of the person.

8. TRUE. This is the third element of sexual harassment. The unwanted behavior occurs in the context of a relationship where one person has formal or informal power over the other.

9. FALSE. Sexual harassment is always viewed by the courts from the victim's perspective. If the victim feels the behavior is sexual or related to gender and unwelcome it may be considered sexual harassment.

10. TRUE. One or more persons must feel there has been unwanted sexual or gender-based behavior from a person who has power over them. There is no victim and therefore no sexual harassment unless someone feels the behavior is unwelcome and sexual in nature or is related to gender.

11. TRUE. One type of sexual harassment is when a hostile work environment exists. The behavior is sexual harassment when it has either the purpose or effect of "substantially interfering" with a person's education or employment or the behavior creates an "intimidating, hostile, or offensive" educational or work environment.

12. TRUE. Persistent sexual jokes, innuendos, and sexually explicit language are types of behavior that can be considered sexual harassment by creating a hostile environment for an individual or group of individuals.

13. TRUE. A simple hug or a kiss may be considered sexual harassment if these behaviors are persistent and unwanted by the victim.

14. TRUE. Picking lint off someone's clothes or rubbing someone's shoulders are potentially sexual harassment. They are considered sexual harassment if they are unwanted by the victim and continuing behaviors. Touching an employee or anyone in a subordinate position is a potential problem.

15. TRUE. The courts view unwanted sexual behavior from the victim's perspective. Therefore, although the accused may claim the behavior is accidental, if the unwanted behavior is sexual in nature and continues it may be considered sexual behavior.

16. TRUE. A behavior that is sexual in nature or related to gender and involves one person who has power over another may be considered sexual harassment. This is one of the elements definitive of sexual harassment.

17. FALSE. If a complaint of sexual harassment is made, a supervisor should document and investigate the situation. Complaints of sexual harassment do not resolve themselves or go away.

18. FALSE. One of the persons involved in a consensual relationship may feel at some time that he/she has been sexually harassed by the other person in the relationship. If this is true, the consensual relationship does not prohibit the victim from claiming sexual harassment. Consensual relationships where one person has authority or power over another are potential problems. These consensual relationships often result in claims of sexual harassment. The person in the power position is normally held liable.

19. TRUE. Complaints of sexual harassment should be filed with the appropriate authority within an organization at the time they occur. By documenting the incident when it happens, there is more information to prove or disprove a claim. Plus, claims of sexual harassment will not just "go away."

20. TRUE. If an employee is found guilty of sexually harassing another employee, the employer can be held liable for allowing the harassment to occur. Therefore, it is in the best interest of every business or educational institution to have a complete Sexual Harassment policy in place and make certain all employees and executives understand the definition of sexual harassment.

INTERPRETATION: Count your total number of correct responses and write it in the space below.

Total Correct Responses = _____

If you had **15 or more correct** responses you have a good understanding of the issues of sexual harassment. A score of **7–14** correct responses indicates you know something about sexual harassment, but need to do some reading to better understand the issue. A score of **6 or fewer** correct responses indicates you have a lot to learn about sexual harassment. Since this is an issue that effects both men and women you need to learn more about what sexual harassment is and what to do in case it happens.

REACTIONS: Use the space provided to respond to the following questions.

1. Have you ever been sexually harassed by a person having formal or informal power or authority over you? Explain the situation. How old were you and how did you handle it at the time? If it were to happen now, explain how would you handle it differently.

2. Have you or your friend (who also responded to this inventory) ever behaved in a manner or said something that could be construed as sexual harassment by another person? If so, explain what both of you would do differently today.

98 | Sexual Decisions: Sexual Assault

PURPOSE: Is a man ever justified in using force in order to have sexual relations with a woman? Most teenagers report that there is no circumstance in which force is ever justified in sexual relations between men and women. When examining a number of situations describing encounters between men and women, however, researchers have found a willingness among both sexes to justify male force. The following situations and questions are designed to explore your feelings and attitudes toward the use of varying degrees of male force in a variety of situations.

DIRECTIONS: Read and respond to the following descriptions by answering the questions following each situation.

Situation 1

A married mother of three children parks her car and walks toward the door of a suburban home where her women's club is meeting. As she nears the door, a man grabs her around the neck from behind, dragging her quickly to nearby bushes. While turning her around he hits her across the face, leaving her unconscious. She awakens dazed, bleeding, and in pain following the rape and assault.

1. What do you feel about the man in this situation? Why?

2. What do you feel about the woman in this situation? Why?

3. In your opinion, have any aspects of the woman's behavior contributed to the assault? Why or why not?

4. Was the man's use of force in any way justified in this description? Why or why not?

Situation 2

Jill and Ron have been dating for several months, engaging in petting, although they agreed to wait for sexual intercourse until "they know each other better." Following a party at Ron's apartment, they began petting after the other people had left. When Jill said they should stop and that she had to leave for home, Ron became angry, held Jill down, and had intercourse with her despite her protests. Jill was stunned and angry, but she felt little would be gained by reporting the assault.

1. What do you feel about the man in this situation? Why?

2. What do you feel about the woman in this situation? Why?

3. In your opinion, have any aspects of her behavior contributed to the assault? Why or why not?

4. Was the use of force in any way justified in this situation? Why or why not?

SOURCE: Susan Woods, Department of Health Education, Eastern Illinois University, Charleston, IL, 1983.

99 | Rape: Fact or Myth?

Purpose: While all aspects of rape are not yet understood, there are many misconceptions that can be dispelled. Respond to these questions to test your knowledge.

DIRECTIONS: Read each statement and decide whether it is TRUE or FALSE. Indicate your response in the column to the right. Then ask a friend of the opposite sex to respond in the other column. Compare your responses.

	You	Friend
1. Rape is an act of passion; the rapist is sexually aroused and out of control.	___	___
2. Seductive clothing that women wear today provokes many rapes.	___	___
3. The majority of rapes are committed by a male stranger against a female.	___	___
4. A rapist is mentally ill.	___	___
5. Rape victims are young, single, beautiful women.	___	___
6. Children are usually raped by strangers.	___	___
7. Most rapes occur on the streets or in alleys.	___	___
8. Rapists are young, unmarried men.	___	___
9. A person who resists a rapist will be killed.	___	___
10. Rape is usually a planned act.	___	___
11. People cannot be raped against their will.	___	___
12. Most rapes are interracial.	___	___
13. The majority of rapes occur at night.	___	___
14. Among your mother, sister, wife/girlfriend, one of the four will probably be raped in her lifetime.	___	___
15. Having sex with a person who has passed out does not count as rape.	___	___
16. A man cannot be raped.	___	___
17. A person who is raped often causes the rape by retreating from an agreement to have sex.	___	___

18. A person who goes to another person's home on a first
    date implies he/she is willing to have sex.   _____ _____

19. Women say "no" when they mean "yes."   _____ _____

20. If a couple has ever had consensual sex before, forced intercourse
    between them later is not considered rape.   _____ _____

21. There is a fine line between seduction and rape; a person can't
    always be expected to know where one ends and the other begins.   _____ _____

22. Many people who report rape are lying because they are angry
    and want to get back at the person they accuse.   _____ _____

SCORING: Now compare your friend's responses to yours. The only statements that are TRUE are numbers 10 and 14. All the remaining statements are FALSE. Read the following brief explanations for each question.

1. FALSE. Sexual assault is primarily an act of violence and aggression. The majority of offenders use some form of overt violence or force.

2. FALSE. Rape is not sexually motivated. Regardless of whether a woman wears "sexy" clothing, the chances of being assaulted are not increased or decreased. Regardless of what a person wears, no one has the right to assault another person.

3. FALSE. In over half the sexual assault cases, the victim and offender know each other in some way. Eighty to 90 percent of college students who are raped are raped by a date or acquaintance. Yet over half of the reported rapes occur among strangers.

4. FALSE. Rapists come from all socioeconomic backgrounds. Most men convicted of rape are considered normal—not sexual perverts or psychotic. The only difference is they tend to be more violent, aggressive, and need to totally dominate the actions of women.

5. FALSE. There is no typical rape victim. Victims are poor and rich, healthy and handi-capped, babies and 96 years old, married and single, from all races and socioeconomic groups. Homosexual men also find themselves as victims of rape.

6. FALSE. The majority of sexual assaults of children are by someone the child knows. A sig-nificant percentage of assaults are by relatives.

7. FALSE. One-third to one-half of all rapes occur in the victim's home.

8. FALSE. Over half of all convicted rapists are married and have children.

9. FALSE. A small percentage of rapes end in murder, although rapists threaten to kill the victim. The decision to resist an attacker must be left to the individual and based upon the situation.

10. TRUE. Studies show that more than 80 percent of all rapes were planned in advance. Often it is the intent to rape that is planned but not the specific victim. Only 16 percent were spontaneous rapes where the rapist had no prior intent to commit rape.

11. FALSE. People often resist rape; however, they are overpowered or their life is threatened by a gun or knife. In addition, rapists sometimes threaten to harm children. The clothing and shoes women typically wear inhibit efforts to fight or run.

12. FALSE. Most rapes are within the same race since people usually stay within their own neighborhoods.

13. FALSE. The incidence of rape is spread evenly throughout the daylight and evening hours.

14. TRUE. One of eight women will be raped during her years in college. One in four have been raped since the age of 14.

15. FALSE. In most states, rape is defined as sex without consent. A person who is unconscious due to alcohol or drugs or any other cause is unable to give consent.

16. FALSE. While the raping of men by women can happen, it is not often reported. Sex researchers have found that the human male can function sexually against his own wishes in a variety of severe emotional states. The reported incidence of a heterosexual man raping a homosexual man is higher.

17. FALSE. The person who is raped does not cause the rape. Rape is an act of violence and is motivated by aggression, immature sexual behavior, or impulse at the moment.

18. FALSE. This behavior does not imply consensual sex.

19. FALSE. This is an old myth. When a woman says "no" to sex, her partner should respect her wishes. Unfortunately some rapists think women want to be coerced into sexual activity.

20. FALSE. Previous consensual sex does not give anyone the right to force intercourse at a later time. While many states have a marital rape exemption, these laws have recently been contested.

21. FALSE. A very small percentage of reported rapes are false accusations since very few women wish to undergo the difficulties to prosecute for rape. To the contrary, it is estimated that a large number of actual rapes go unreported.

INTERPRETATION: Count the number of correct responses.

Total Correct = _____

If you had **15 or more** correct responses you have a good understanding of rape. A score of **8–14** correct responses indicate that you have a fair knowledge of rape, but you should seek additional information. A score of **7 or fewer** correct responses represents a low level of knowledge concerning rape. In light of the number of rapes that occur each year, it would be helpful for you to learn more about rape and precautions for you and loved ones to avoid rape.

REACTIONS: Use the space provided to respond to the following questions.

1. After reviewing these myths, what can you do to protect yourself from date rape?

2. What can you do to protect others you know from rape?

3. What would you do if you were raped by a friend? By a relative? By a stranger?

4. What would you do if your partner or a friend were raped? How would you feel?

100 | What Happens After Someone Is Raped?

PURPOSE: After a rape has occurred, victims are often not certain what to do or where to go for assistance. The following exercise is designed to test your knowledge and to offer helpful ideas in the unfortunate event that a rape occurs to you or someone you know.

DIRECTIONS: Respond to each question by writing a YES or NO in the blank to the right of the question.

Yes   No

1. Are you required to contact the police after a sexual assault occurs? _____ _____

2. Is it important to seek medical attention immediately after a sexual assault? _____ _____

3. Should you clean yourself up (i.e., shower, brush your teeth, wash hands) before seeking medical treatment? _____ _____

4. Can you seek treatment at a private physician's office? _____ _____

If you go to a hospital for treatment, the following examination is performed:

- Your body will be examined and treated for any physical injuries.

- Women are given a pelvic exam and their genitals examined to check for injuries and collect fluids.

- Men are given a general exam of their genitals and anal region to check for injuries and collect fluids.

- A rape kit is used during the exam to collect specific physical evidence (sperm samples, pubic hair, clothing fibers, saliva samples, and noticeable bruises and marks).

- STD tests are conducted to determine if you have any sexually transmitted diseases prior to the rape. Follow-up exams and testing will be conducted to determine if you contracted any STDs from the assault.

- An HIV antibody test will be conducted. A follow-up test will be conducted to determine if you contracted HIV from the assault.

- A pregnancy test will be given to determine if you were pregnant prior to the assault. If there is any chance you could become pregnant from the assault, a doctor may prescribe the "morning after pill" or hormone injections.

5. Do you have to receive these previously mentioned treatments?   _____ _____

6. Is a rape kit important if the assailant is to be prosecuted?   _____ _____

7. If you go to a hospital for treatment are the police automatically notified?   _____ _____

8. Can anyone obtain your medical records from the hospital?   _____ _____

9. Are you obligated to prosecute the assailant if the police are notified of the sexual assault?   _____ _____

10. Does contacting the police mean the sexual assault will be made public information?   _____ _____

11. Do you have to testify in front of a judge and/or jury to prosecute the assailant?   _____ _____

12. Does a verdict of not guilty mean the rape did not occur?   _____ _____

SCORING: The correct responses and brief explanations are listed below. Compare your responses to those listed below.

1. NO. It is your right and your decision whether or not to contact the police. However, contacting the police is an important step to take if you wish to consider prosecuting the assailant and to document the prevalence of rape in your community. At the same time, you may wish to contact your local rape crisis center. Trained volunteers and professionals can help you and explain procedures.

2. YES. The physical exam that is performed at the same time the rape kit is used is important to assess any injuries and conduct testing for sexually transmitted diseases or pregnancy. The rape kit itself (if properly handled) provides evidence of the rape that is legally admissible in court.

3. NO. Rape victims are asked *not* to brush their teeth, wash their hands, shower, urinate, defecate, douche, or change their clothes prior to seeking medical help. These actions can destroy evidence vital to the prosecution of the assailant.

4. YES. A physician's office has the advantage of being more private than an emergency room. However, most emergency rooms have the advantage of being specially equipped to collect evidence from sexual assault survivors using the rape kit.

5. NO. You make the decision whether or not to receive medical treatment or have tests conducted. A written statement must also be signed by you before the HIV antibody test is performed.

6. YES. It is almost impossible to prosecute the assailant without the information gained from the rape kit. Having a rape kit does not mean that charges have to be filed. It simply makes more options available when the decision of whether or not to prosecute the assailant has to be made.

7. YES. Hospitals are required to notify the police of any sexual assaults. However, hospitals are not required to report the survivor's name unless prior consent by the survivor has been granted.

8. NO. Without your approval, no medical records can be accessed. Your personal physician can receive your records if you, and only you, ask for them to be released. The police and family members may not see your records unless prior consent has been given (an exception to this is if your medical records are subpoenaed into court).

9. NO. Contacting the police leaves your legal options open. You are under not obligation to pursue prosecution of the assailant.

10. YES. The police will make the information to the case available. But, they DO NOT release your name unless a court case is brought against the assailant.

11. YES. In most cases the survivor does have to testify in front of a judge and/or jury. In some cases the judge will allow a video taping of the survivor containing both prosecuting and defense questions to be admitted.

12. NO. Unfortunately our justice system is not perfect and it is important for you to remember that a verdict of not guilty does not mean that the rape did not occur. It is also important for you to remember that a verdict of not guilty does not mean that you are responsible in any way for what happened to you.

NOTE: The procedures discussed in the above statements may vary from state to state. You may want to learn if these procedures are the same in your state of residence.

INTERPRETATION: Count the total number of correct responses.

Total Number Correct = _____

If you answered **9 or more** of the questions correctly, you have a good knowledge of what to expect and what to do following a sexual assault. If you answered **5–6** questions correctly, you have some knowledge about what to do after sexual assault, but you may find it helpful to learn more. If you had **fewer than 5** correct responses, you need to learn more about what to do after sexual assault so that you can be of assistance to friends or others to whom this may happen.

REACTIONS: Write your responses to following questions in the space provided.

1. If you or someone close to you were raped, what would you do in the first few hours after the sexual assault? What new information did this give you that you did not know previously?

2. Do these medical and legal considerations that arise immediately after the assault differ in your state of residence? If no, what new things did you learn? If there are some differences in your state, explain the differences.

SOURCE: Gregory Thatcher, MSPH, and Sandra K. Kammermann, MS, EdS, Schools of Public Health and Medicine, University of South Carolina. Copyright © 1996 by Valois, Kammermann & Associates. All rights reserved. Used with permission of authors.

101 Coercive Sex Choices

Sexual coercion places both men and women in "victim" roles, although women are victimized more often.

The development of effective strategies to deal with the problem of coercive sex requires changing the traditional gender role socialization that makes females vulnerable to sexual abuse and pushes males into the "victimizer" role. Decisions to make such changes are usually based upon our values and attitudes toward the use of power and influence.

PURPOSE: The exercise that follows is designed to assist you in clarifying your choices about ways to deal with the problem of coercive sex.

DIRECTIONS: Write in the feelings and behaviors you would most likely experience or engage in for each of the first eight questions. In question 9, check the appropriate box to identify your choice.

1. If you were witnessing a rape of a stranger in a public place (e.g., bus depot) . . .
   a. How would you feel?

   b. What would you do?

2. If your spouse were the victim of a forceable rape . . .
   a. How would you feel?

   b. What would you do?

3. If you learned that a child in your neighborhood was being subjected to an incestuous relationship with his or her parent . . .

   a. How would you feel?

   b. What would you do?

4. If you learned that two of your children (e.g., son and daughter) were involved in brother-sister incest . . .

   a. How would you feel?

   b. What would you do?

5. If you learned that your spouse was asked to participate in sexual activity with his or her boss in order to keep a job or get a promotion . . .

   a. How would you feel?

   b. What would you do?

6. If you were applying for a position of employment that you wanted very badly and the prospective employer made it clear that hiring depended on your sexual "availability" and he requested a "sample" as a sign of "good faith" . . .

   a. How would you feel?

   b. What would you do?

7. If you were constantly stared at, touched, and visually and verbally "raped," and generally taken advantage of at work . . .

   a. How would you feel?

   b. What would you do?

8. If you were invited to a private showing of sexually explicit movies at a neighbor's home and realized that the films you were viewing were of young children engaged in sexual activity . . .

   a. How would you feel?

   b. What would you do?

9. If a referendum appeared on the ballot in your state to require mandatory sentence for coercive sexual behavior, how would you vote on the following? Place a check mark in the appropriate space.

	Sentence		
Coercive Sex	Long Term	Short Term	None
Forcible rape			
Statutory rape			
Parent-child incest			
Sibling incest			
Sexual harassment at work			

SCORING: Responses to this inventory would be very specific to each individual. Taking a closer look at these issues and discussing them with significant others may help you clarify your feelings with regard to coercive sex.

REACTIONS: Use the space provided to respond to the following questions.

1. About which type of coercive sex are you most concerned? Why?

2. What can you as an individual do to prevent any type of coercive sex?

102 | Cyberromance: Real Infidelity or Just Mousing Around?

PURPOSE: This exercise is designed to explore your feelings about Internet electronic mail relationships. In essence, what is real infidelity in cyberspace? You be the judge.

DIRECTIONS: Read the following scenario carefully and respond to the questions that follow.

Consider for just a few minutes, a rendezvous in cyberspace, computer to computer. Many times people start out playing around only to be surprised they're in this a lot more deeply than they thought. They find themselves rushing when they get home to see if there's e-mail. It becomes a red-hot extramarital affair, conducted entirely through e-mail. The intensity of Internet messages escalates quickly to hearts that thump and hands that move to various pulsating portions of human anatomy. This is not fiction. "Infidelity" is rampant on the Internet and on-line services according to experts. And now the legal fallout has reached the courtroom.

Cyberromance Leads to Divorce Suit

> In what is being called a first case of its kind, a New Jersey husband is suing his wife for divorce, claiming she committed adultery during dozens of sexually explicit exchanges on America Online. The two "cyberlovers" never met, although they planned to.

Reactions: Use the space provided to respond to the following questions.

1. Do you think a cyberromance is grounds for divorce? Why or why not?

2. Can a computer affair actually be considered infidelity? Why or why not?

3. How long would a cyberromance have to last before you could classify it as infidelity? Explain.

4. With the convenience of the Internet do you think a cyberaffair could be as time consuming and/or disruptive as a regular affair? Explain.

5. If a cyberaffair doesn't include physical sex between two people can it really be considered an affair? Explain.

6. If a person uses self-stimulation to orgasm, would that constitute a "sexual affair"?

7. Do you think that there are any positive aspects with regard to cyberaffairs? Explain?

INTERPRETATION:

Divorce Attorneys: They are almost unanimous in saying that they would not call computer liaisons infidelity. Legally they say, "you can't prove adultery unless there is actual sex."

Sex Therapists: Would suggest that a cyberspace attachment strong enough to be considered an affair need not include sexual contact between two people. A computer affair moves to the level of an emotional affair when it includes:

- Intimacy: You're more intimate in your cyber relationship than in your primary relationship.
- Secrecy: Your mate doesn't know how deeply you're involved.
- Sexual Chemistry: There is a sexual tension, even if it isn't acted upon.

XIII | SEXUALLY TRANSMITTED DISEASES

I n the United States, there is an increasing incidence of sexually transmitted diseases. However, public understanding of STDs, particularly of preventive measures, has not shown a comparable increase. Combined efforts to curtail the spread of STDs including education, offering free medical care, and requiring physicians to report all cases of venereal disease have not been successful. To combat this public health problem, more emphasis needs to be placed on prophylactic measures. There are a variety of potentially valuable preventive measures that concerned individuals and couples can take. The exercises in this section offer an opportunity to examine some of the realities of sexually transmitted diseases and measures to prevent their spread.

The Sexually Transmitted Disease exercises include:

103. STD Knowledge, Attitude, and Behavior Quiz
104. Behavioral Risks for HIV: How Do They Rate?
105. Facts and Misconceptions About HIV and AIDS
106. Communicating About HIV and AIDS
107. Sex, Drugs, and STDs
108. AIDS: A Family Affair

103

STD Knowledge, Attitude, and Behavior Quiz

PURPOSE: STD is an acronym for Sexually Transmitted Disease. These diseases are communicable and represent a serious health hazard. Each person would be wise to take stock of his or her knowledge and behavior concerning STDs. Since the STDs represent an intimately personal health issue affecting the entire community, your decision to help control this problem is crucial. This quiz, therefore, is an exercise which will help you identify what you know, feel, and do about the STDs.

DIRECTIONS: The quiz consists of three parts: (1) knowledge, (2) attitudes and intentions, and (3) behavior. Answer each part as honestly as you can.

PART 1: Knowledge

1. Which of the following is probably *most effective* for the prevention of sexually transmitted disease in women:

   a. Use a vaginal spray regularly.

   b. Use a medicated douche regularly, especially after intercourse.

   c. Limit the number of sexual contacts.

   d. Wash the vulva with soap and warm water during bath or shower.

2. Changes in methods of choice in birth control practice has been credited with part of the rise in STD rates. Which of the following is thought to be most responsible for this?

   a. Use of IUDs which may be expelled

   b. The use of the "pill" by so many women

   c. A marked reduction in the use of condoms by males

   d. The use of spermicidal jellies and foams

3. In the United States, the *most common* STD is:

   a. Syphilis

   b. Herpes genitalis

   c. Nongonococcal urethritis

   d. Gonorrhea

4. Which of the following is characteristic of the initial phase of syphilis?

   a. Penile discharge in men; no symptoms in women

   b. A skin rash all over the body

   c. A chancre at the site where the organism enters the body

   d. Painful blisterlike lesions on the genitals

5. The second stage of syphilis is characterized by:

   a. Painful, blisterlike lesions on the genitals

   b. A skin rash

   c. High fever, genital inflammation, and night sweats

   d. No observable symptoms

6. The probability of successful treatment of syphilis depends mostly on:

   a. The stage of the disease in which treatment is started

   b. Where the symptoms appear on the body

   c. How badly the person from whom you caught the disease was infected

   d. The type of medicine purchased at the drug store

7. The medical term for a yeast infection is:

   a. Trichomoniasis

   b. Gardnerella vaginalis

   c. Candidiasis

   d. Chlamydial infection

8. The incubation period (that is, time between infection and appearance of symptoms) in persons with symptomatic syphilis is about:

   a. Three to four days

   b. Twenty-five days

   c. Ten to ninety days

   d. Three to four weeks

9. Which of the following statements concerning common vaginal infections is *false?*

   a. They are more common than gonorrhea or syphilis.

   b. The vaginal environment is typically alkaline in nature.

   c. The lactobacilli usually help maintain a healthy vaginal environment.

   d. Antibiotic therapy may increase the likelihood of vaginal infection.

10. Which of the following statements concerning trichomoniasis is true?

    a. Both men and woman may carry this infection, but men often have no symptoms.

    b. The most common symptom in women is a watery gray discharge that smells like burning rubber.

    c. Treatment consists of vaginal suppositories such as nystatin.

    d. There are no long-term effects of trichomonal infection.

11. Which of the following is a symptom of candidiasis?

    a. A thin, gray discharge with a flour paste consistency

    b. A frothy, yellow or white discharge with a bad odor

    c. A white, clumpy discharge that resembles cottage cheese

    d. Painful, blisterlike bumps on the labia

12. _____ is a bacterial microorganism now recognized as the cause of a diverse group of genital infections.

    a. Chlamydia trachomatis

    b. Candida albicans

    c. Trichomonas vaginalis

    d. Gardnerella vaginalis

13. The Human Papilloma Virus is most closely associated with:

    a. Female sterility

    b. Endometriosis

    c. Cervical cancer

    d. Pelvic inflammatory disease

14. _____ typically occurs when chlamydial or other infectious organisms spread from the cervix upward, infecting the lining of the uterus, fallopian tubes, possibly the ovaries, and other adjacent abdominal structures.

    a. Nongonococcal urethritis

    b. Conjunctivitis

    c. Prodromal keratitis

    d. Pelvic inflammatory disease

15. _____ and _____ in men are commonly caused by chlamydial infections.

    a. Nongonococcal urethritis; lymphogranuloma venereum

    b. Viral hepatitis; epididymitis

    c. Nongonococcal urethritis; epididymitis

    d. Trichomoniasis; epididymitis

16. The diagnosis of nongonococcal urethritis includes which of the following?

    a. Appearance of discharge

    b. Pain on urination

    c. History of sexual exposure

    d. All of the above

17. There is a marked tendency for a_____ infection to coexist with other STDs.

    a. Chlamydial

    b. Trichomoniasis

    c. Candidiasis

    d. Syphilitic

18. Ectopic pregnancy, sterility, and arthritic pain in the joints are some of the more severe consequences of _____ when it is left untreated in women.

    a. Herpes

    b. Viral hepatitis

    c. Trichomoniasis

    d. Gonorrhea

19. Which of the following STDs can infect the throat and the anus as well as the genitals?

    a. Gonorrhea

    b. Gardnerella vaginalis

    c. Scabies

    d. Candidiasis

20. The most common symptom(s) of gonorrhea in men is/are:

    a. Bad-smelling, cloudy penile discharge and burning sensations during urination

    b. White, cheesy penile discharge and ticklish sensation during urination

    c. Inflammation of the penile glans and foreskin

    d. Thick, greenish penile discharge

21. What is the percentage of women infected with gonorrhea who will not notice any discomfort or symptoms of this disease?

    a. About 10 percent

    b. Between 10 and 25 percent

    c. Between 20 to 40 percent

    d. Between 50 and 80 percent

22. One week after sexual contact with a new partner, Gary experiences burning during urination and a cloudy discharge from penis. Assuming he does *not* have NGU, the suspected disease would *most likely be:*
    a. Gardnerella vaginalis
    b. Syphilis
    c. Shingellosis
    d. Gonorrhea

23. Although _____ is the common treatment for gonorrhea, it is not effective against _____. It is important that a laboratory diagnosis is made prior to treatment.
    a. penicillin; NGU
    b. tetracycline; herpes
    c. erythromycin; scabies
    d. doxycycline; PID

24. Which of the following statements concerning pubic lice *is false?*
    a. They may be found in the armpits or scalp.
    b. They may be found in the pubic hair.
    c. They may be transmitted nonsexually.
    d. They are treated with tetracycline.

25. The primary symptom of pubic lice is:
    a. Tiny red spots on the genitals
    b. Smooth, rounded, waxy-looking bumps on the genitals that are painless
    c. Itching in the pubic area
    d. Genital chancres that itch

26. _____ is usually manifested as cold sores on the mouth or lips, and _____ generally as lesions on and around the genital areas.
    a. HSV 1; HSV 2
    b. HSV 2; HSV 1
    c. HIV 1; HIV 2
    d. HIV 2; HIV 1

27. When is a person who has herpes contagious?
    a. When the person experiences prodromal symptoms
    b. When the papules develop into blisters
    c. During asymptomatic periods
    d. All of the above

28. It is recommended that a woman abstain from coitus after a herpes outbreak until what point?

    a. When the blister begins to form a crust

    b. When the sores on the labia have completely healed

    c. Ten days after the sores on the labia have completely healed

    d. One month after the scores on the labia have completely healed

29. Which of the following is *not* one of the factors that may trigger a herpes outbreak?

    a. A diet high in complex carbohydrates

    b. Emotional stress

    c. Sunburn

    d. Being overtired

30. Herpes genitalis makes a woman more susceptible to:

    a. Diabetes

    b. Cervical cancer

    c. Cirrhosis of the liver

    d. Influenza

31. Which of the following statements concerning viral hepatitis is *true?*

    a. There are six major types of viral hepatitis.

    b. Non-Álnon-B type is sexually transmitted, while type B is probably not.

    c. Treatment consists of bed rest and adequate fluid intake.

    d. All of the above.

32. A symptom of viral hepatitis is:

    a. High fever

    b. Yellowing of the whites of the eyes

    c. Diarrhea

    d. All of the above

33. An STD that is not curable at the present time is:

    a. Gonorrhea

    b. Genital herpes

    c. Chlamydial infections

    d. Trichomoniasis

34. Which of the following statements concerning genital warts is *true?*
    a. The incubation period is seven to ten days.
    b. Some warts progress to cancerous states in men and women.
    c. The incidence of genital warts has gradually been decreasing.
    d. All of the above.

35. In most, but not all cases, an individual will develop antibodies to HIV within _____ of being infected.
    a. one month
    b. three months
    c. six months
    d. one year

36. Which of the following conditions may act in conjunction with HIV to produce AIDS?
    a. Herpes
    b. Gonorrhea
    c. Chancroid
    d. All of the above

37. Which of the following blood tests is *most commonly* used to detect the presence of antibodies to HIV?
    a. Western blot
    b. HIV-CDC
    c. HIV ELISA
    d. HSV screen

38. The average incubation period for full blown AIDS is estimated to range between:
    a. Six months and one year
    b. One and five years
    c. Eight and eleven years
    d. Twelve and fifteen years

39. Which of the following statements *is false?*
    a. Studies of high-risk gay men have shown that fear of AIDS has resulted in a significant reduction in the number of their sexual partners.
    b. Studies of high-risk gay men have shown that fear of AIDS has resulted in significant numbers of men entering into monogamous relationships.
    c. Surveys of high school and college-age students have indicated that fear of AIDS has resulted in significant changes in sexual behavior.
    d. All of the above

40. Which of the following statements concerning transmission of HIV is *false?*

    a. The risk of transmitting the virus via tears and vaginal secretions is increasing.

    b. There is no evidence that the virus can be transmitted by casual contact.

    c. There is no danger of being infected as the result of donating blood.

    d. All of the above

41. Although there is no cure for AIDS, a variety of drugs, which are still experimental, have been found to slow the deterioration of the immune system. The most effective of these drugs is:

    a. Azidothymidine

    b. Zovirax

    c. Videx

    d. Acyclovir

42. Most of the pathogens that cause STDs are alike in that they:

    a. Thrive in the moist genital membranes

    b. Thrive in dark, warm, moist body surfaces

    c. Thrive in light, cold, dry areas of the body

    d. Usually cause PID if not treated

43. _____ is characterized by diarrhea, fever, and inflammation of the large intestines. It may be transmitted by contact with infected feces or by oral stimulation of the anal area.

    a. Lymphogranuloma venereum

    b. Chancroid

    c. Shingellosis

    d. Molluscum contagiosum

44. _____ is a disease caused by a pox virus that produces small, painless lesions that are shiny and waxy on top. They may be removed by squeezing out the center core.

    a. Molluscum contagiosum

    b. Shingellosis

    c. Chancroid

    d. Scabies

45. Which of the following is *not true* concerning the difficulties in controlling STDs?

   a. Success depends upon early detection and treatment of all infected persons and their sexual contacts.

   b. Public funds to assist medical authorities in searching out and treating infectious contacts have increased greatly and now are more than adequate for the need.

   c. It is difficult to legislate effectively against human behavior leading to the spread of STDs.

   d. There is a natural reluctance in both adults and teenagers to divulge the source of their contacts or even to seek treatment.

   e. Often a patient will have two or more concurrent STDs.

PART II. *Attitudes and Intentions*

Read each statement below and circle your response. Use this key:

SA = Strongly Agree	AS = Agree Somewhat	U = Undecided	DS = Disagree Somewhat	SD = Strongly Disagree

1. Being responsible sexually is one of the best ways to reduce the risk of getting STDs.   SA A U D SD

2. Getting treated early by a doctor is the key to preventing the harmful effects of STDs.   SA A U D SD

3. A person with an STD has an obligation to inform his/her sex partner that she/he might be infected with an STD.   SA A U D SD

4. The best way to get a sex partner to a doctor is to take him or her to a clinic yourself.   SA A U D SD

5. Making sex behavior changes is necessary once an STD has been diagnosed.   SA A U D SD

6. If I were to have sex, the chance of getting an STD would make me cautious about sex with more than one person.   SA A U D SD

7. I would feel uncomfortable doing things before and after sex to keep from getting an STD.   SA A U D SD

8. It would be an insult if a sex partner suggested we use a condom to prevent STD infection.   SA A U D SD

9. I would be embarrassed to discuss STD with my partner.   SA A U D SD

10. If I had an STD I would help the student health service and public health people to find my sex contacts.   SA A U D SD

11. I will limit my sex partners to only one because of the risk of getting an STD.   SA A U D SD

12. I will avoid genital contact anytime I think there is a chance of getting an STD.   SA A U D SD

13. I would not stop from having sex with the thought
of getting an STD.   SA   A   U   D   SD

14. If I were having sex with multiple partners, I would have
regular STD checkups.   SA   A   U   D   SD

15. For me sexual abstinence is the best way to avoid getting
an STD.   SA   A   U   D   SD

PART III. Behavior

Circle all that apply to each question.

1. Your lover informs you that he/she has gonorrhea. What do you do?

   a. Become furiously angry

   b. End the relationship

   c. Thank the person for his/her honesty

   d. Talk about real issues facing the relationship

   e. Experience shock

   f. Seek diagnosis and treatment

   g. Other: _____

2. Given your choice, if you thought you had gonorrhea, where would you go for treatment?

   a. Personal physician

   b. Emergency room at hospital

   c. Public health clinic

   d. Free medical clinic

   e. Drug store

   f. School nurse

   g. Other: _____

3. A free STD clinic is being proposed for your neighborhood. Both residents and nonresidents will be eligible for diagnosis and treatment. At the City Council meeting you will most likely take the position of:

   a. We need one.

   b. Put it someplace else.

   c. Leave treating STD to hospitals and private doctors.

   d. Acceptable if limited to residents over 18.

   e. Would not bother to take a position.

   f. We need one, but not for free—charge fees.

   g. Other: _____

4. Not knowing your sexual partner, you would insist on:
   a. Contraception before STD prevention
   b. STD prevention before contraception
   c. Both contraception and STD prevention
   d. The male using a condom
   e. Only vaginal sexual intercourse (i.e., no oral or anal intercourse)
   f. A physical examination of his/her sexual organs prior to sex
   g. Other: _____

5. Besides your lover, which of the following persons would you tell about your STD treatment?
   a. Mother and father
   b. Priest, minister, or rabbi
   c. Brother or sister
   d. Friend
   e. No one ever
   f. New partner
   g. Other: _____

6. Today you have been treated for gonorrhea; what do you do now?
   a. Tell your lover.
   b. Have sex with someone new.
   c. Abstain from sex until after three separate culture tests are negative.
   d. Leave the clinic never to return.
   e. Tell your lover after having sexual intercourse.
   f. Don't know what to do.
   g. Other: _____

7. You have discovered crabs on your pubic hair. Now what?
   a. Wash all bathroom toilets.
   b. Seek diagnosis and appropriate prescription.
   c. Purposely infect victims.
   d. Do nothing but scratch.
   e. Do not wear clothing that has been worn within twenty-four hours.
   f. Warn all possible contacts.
   g. Other: _____

8. You have herpes genitalis for which there is no foolproof treatment. What will you tell your partner?

   a. The condom should be used until children are desired.

   b. Both you and partner should accept equal exposure.

   c. Nothing.

   d. The disease will go away by itself like a cold sore.

   e. It's too late to worry.

   f. Other: _____

9. A suggestion for symptom relief from herpes is to:

   a. Drink large quantities of cranberry juice.

   b. Wash frequently, and dry the genital area with a blow dryer.

   c. Take frequent hot baths for 30-45 minutes.

   d. Keep Vaseline or other lubricant on the affected area at all times.

   e. Consume moderate quantities of lemon-lime soda drinks.

   f. Keep a water-based lubricant on the affected area at night.

   g. Other: _____

10. Which of the following is the *best* description of a "short-arm inspection"?

   a. Discreetly examining your partner's genitals prior to genital sexual contact.

   b. "Milking" the penis for a suspicious discharge

   c. Examining the vulva for the presence of an unusual discharge, unpleasant odor, sores, blisters, etc.

   d. Gently "rolling the testicles" of your partner between your index finger and your forearm for an existing STD

   e. Examining the anal canal of a potential sex partner for abrasions prior to intercourse

   f. Carefully squeezing the labia minora while inspecting for uncommon vaginal discharge

   g. Other: _____

11. What is suggested as the single most important AIDS prevention message to convey to people?

   a. Wear latex condoms before engaging in genital sex with a partner.

   b. Wear a full-body, natural-membrane condom before engaging in genital sex with a partner.

   c. Get to know prospective sexual partners for several months before engaging in genital sex.

   d. Discreetly inspect your partner's genitals before engaging in genital sex.

   e. Select a sexual partner only after knowing his/her religious preference.

   f. Combine latex condoms and contraceptive cream for maximum protection.

   g. Other: _____

12. Janet experiences recurrent herpes outbreaks fairly frequently. Which of the following suggestions would be least helpful to her in minimizing the incidence of future outbreaks?
   a. Avoid acidic foods.
   b. Get plenty of rest.
   c. Wear nylon underwear.
   d. Learn relaxation techniques.
   e. Drink adequate quantities of cranberry juice.
   f. Utilize a sauna or hot tub facility as often as possible.
   g. Other: _____

13. A suggestion to minimize the possibility of contracting a sexually transmitted disease is to:
   a. Use spermicidal foam, cream, or jelly.
   b. Inspect your partner's genitals.
   c. Use a latex condom.
   d. Conduct a monthly short arm inspection.
   e. Use a water-based lubricating jelly during intercourse.
   f. Avoid acidic foods during menstruation.
   g. Other: _____

14. Knowing what you do about STDs, will you:
   a. Continue to have multiple sex partners at random
   b. Be selective in your partners
   c. Reduce your sexual activities to a few partners
   d. Maintain a monogamous relationship
   e. Only have sex for reproductive purposes
   f. Abstain
   g. Other: _____

15. Learning more about STDs will continue to have an effect upon your behavior. How so?
   a. To be more open about STD-related problems with a lover
   b. To not be promiscuous
   c. To use a condom at all times
   d. It will not have an effect
   e. Will continue the pick-up scene no matter what
   f. To help others learn
   g. Other: _____

SCORING: In this quiz you have discovered new observations about yourself in regard to STD. Since this quiz does not cover more than an ice cube on the top of the iceberg, you should refer to your text and other materials for a complete STD discussion. In North America, sexually transmitted diseases which are prevalent include: AIDS, chlamydia, viral hepatitis, gonorrhea, syphilis, nongonococcal urethritis, vaginitis, urinary tract infections, chancroid, venereal warts, herpes genitalia, and crabs, among others.

PART I: *Knowledge* — The correct answers are:

1. c	13. c	24. d	35. b
2. c	14. d	25. c	36. d
3. d	15. c	26. a	37. c
4. c	16. d	27. d	38. c
5. b	17. a	28. c	39. c
6. a	18. d	29. a	40. a
7. c	19. a	30. b	41. a
8. c	20. a	31. c	42. a
9. b	21. d	32. d	43. c
10. a	22. d	33. b	44. a
11. b	23. a	34. b	45. b
12. a			

SCORING: Total your number of correct answers and place your score in the space provided. If you scored **between 36 and 45** you have a very good general knowledge of sexually transmitted diseases. A score **between 24 and 35** would indicates a good working knowledge of STDs. If you scored **between 12 and 23** you have only a fair knowledge base and you might want to increase your understanding of sexually transmitted diseases. A score **between 1 and 11** is poor and a course in human sexuality or some advanced reading on STDs would be in order.

Part I Total Score: _____

PART II: *Attitudes and Intentions*

SCORING: Use the key below to score your responses. Calculate your total score and place it in the space provided.

For items: 1–6, 10–12, 14, 15

Strongly Agree = 1 point
Agree = 2 points
Undecided = 3 points
Disagree = 4 points
Strongly Disagree = 5 points

For items: 7–9, 13

Strongly Agree = 5 points
Agree = 4 points
Undecided = 3 points
Disagree = 2 points
Strongly Disagree = 1 point

PART II **Total Score:** _____

INTERPRETATION: The range of scores on this scale is 15–75. If you scored between 15 and 34 you could consider your attitudes and intentions to be low risk for STDs. A score of 35 to 55 would represent a moderate level of risk, and if you scored between 55 and 75 your attitudes and intentions would indicate high-risk behavior that can spread sexually transmitted disease.

PART III: *Behavior*

SCORING: Some of the answers are better than others from a personal and public health perspective. So, while there are not correct answers in the sense of right and wrong, the list below identifies the preferred behavior.

1. c, d, f	5. none	9. b	13. a, b, c
2. c, d	6. a, c	10. b	14. none
3. a, f	7. b, e, f	11. c	15. a, f
4. c, d, f	8. b, d	12. c	

REACTIONS: Use the space provided to respond to the following questions.

1. Were you surprised by any of your answers or any of these items? Explain.

2. Do you think STDs are prevalent on your campus? Explain.

3. Do you think the U.S. Public Health Service has done a good job in controlling the spread of sexually transmitted disease? Explain.

4. Currently, which STDs are on the rise? Why? Explain.

104 | Behavioral Risks for HIV: How Do They Rate?

It is not who you are that places you at risk for HIV infection; rather, it is the risk you assume regarding a range of behaviors. Different behaviors have different degrees of risk.

PURPOSE: This exercise is designed to examine various behaviors and subsequently determine what level of risk they involve with regard to HIV infection.

DIRECTIONS: Read each of the behavioral statements below and rank each one in the space provided as NO, LOW, MODERATE, or HIGH risk for HIV infection. Place your answer in the space provided at the right of each statement.

1. Penile-vaginal intercourse with a latex condom correctly used and spermicidal foam that kills HIV, and withdrawing prior to ejaculation _____

2. Mutual masturbation with ejaculation on, not inside, partner _____

3. Fellatio without a latex condom, putting the head of the penis inside the mouth and withdrawing prior to ejaculation _____

4. Use of sex toys (not disinfected between uses) by more than one partner, without using a latex condom _____

5. Intercourse between the thighs _____

6. Anal intercourse with a latex condom correctly used with a lubricant that contains spermicide that kills HIV, and withdrawing prior to ejaculation _____

7. Mutual masturbation with internal touching using finger cots or latex condoms _____

8. Penile-vaginal intercourse using spermicidal foam but without a latex condom, and withdrawing prior to ejaculation _____

9. Body rubbing _____

10. Cunnilingus (oral sex on a woman) _____

11. Deep wet kissing (French kissing) _____

12. Penile-vaginal intercourse with internal ejaculation with a latex condom correctly used and with spermicidal foam that kills HIV _____

13. Use of sex toys (dildos, etc.) that have been properly sterilized between uses and are not shared by partners, along with latex condoms _____

14. Penile-vaginal intercourse with internal ejaculation using a latex condom correctly but with no spermicidal foam   _____

15. Penile-vaginal intercourse without spermicidal foam and without a latex condom and withdrawing prior to ejaculation   _____

16. Mutual masturbation with only external touching   _____

17. Hugging/massage/dry kissing   _____

18. Anal intercourse with internal ejaculation with a latex condom correctly used with spermicide that kills HIV   _____

19. Masturbating alone   _____

20. Brachiovaginal activities (vaginal fisting)   _____

21. Anal intercourse without a latex condom, withdrawing prior to ejaculation   _____

22. Fellatio (oral sex on man) without a latex condom, but never putting the head of the penis inside mouth   _____

23. Masturbating alongside another person but not touching one another   _____

24. Penile-vaginal intercourse with internal ejaculation without a latex condom but with spermicidal foam   _____

25. Brachioproctic activities (anal fisting)   _____

26. Fellatio to ejaculation with a condom   _____

27. Fellatio without a latex condom with ejaculation in mouth   _____

28. Penile-vaginal intercourse with internal ejaculation without a latex condom and without any other form of barrier contraception   _____

29. Anal intercourse with internal ejaculation without a latex condom   _____

30. Abstinence   _____

Answer/Explanation Key:

1. *Penile-vaginal intercourse with a latex condom correctly used and spermicidal foam that kills HIV, and withdrawing prior to ejaculation.* **LOW RISK** — In this situation the condom could break, and pre-ejaculate fluids possibly containing HIV could be deposited in the vaginal canal. If the spermicidal foam is not inserted properly and sufficient in amount to kill any HIV present then there is a low possibility that infection could occur.

2. *Mutual masturbation with ejaculation on, not inside, partner.* **LOW RISK** — The virus that causes AIDS cannot live outside the body. Caution must be exercised as not to ejaculate on or near skin that is not "intact" (an open cut or sore).

3. *Fellatio without a latex condom, putting the head of the penis inside the mouth and withdrawing prior to ejaculation.* **MODERATE RISK** — In this situation, an oral sore or abrasion in the buccal cavity or gums of the mouth could come in contact with pre-ejaculate fluid with some concentration of HIV.

4. *Use of sex toys (not disinfected between uses) by more than one partner, without a latex condom.* **HIGH RISK** — Sex toys can pass HIV from one partner to another if they have not been disinfected.

5. *Intercourse between the thighs.* **LOW RISK** — The virus that causes AIDS cannot live outside the body. Be sure to keep ejaculate away from any skin that is not "intact" (open sore or cut on the thighs, legs, or any other part of the body).

6. *Anal intercourse with a latex condom correctly used with a lubricant that contains spermicide that kills HIV, and withdrawing prior to ejaculation.* **MODERATE RISK** — The mucous membranes of the anal canal are thin and abrasions may occur with anal intercourse even with a lubricant that kills HIV. Condom slippage/breakage are also possibilities. Keep in mind that the anal canal has no natural lubrication. Correct use of latex condoms is important here.

7. *Mutual masturbation with internal touching using finger cots or latex condoms.* **LOW RISK** — Internal touching would constitute a low risk here. There is the possibility of condom or cot breakage or slippage and some body fluid coming in contact with skin that is not "intact."

8. *Penile-vaginal intercourse using spermicidal foam but without a latex condom, withdrawing prior to ejaculation.* **HIGH RISK** — Vaginal intercourse without a latex condom combined with withdrawal is high risk unless you are sure your partner is HIV negative and free of other STDs. Spermicide is effective but not 100 percent used alone. Combination of foam and latex condoms is recommended for protection against all STDs including HIV.

9. *Body rubbing.* **NO RISK** — Avoid contact between two sources of skin that are not "intact" (open sores, cuts, or abrasions).

10. *Cunnilingus (oral sex on a woman).* **LOW RISK** — HIV concentrations in saliva have been documented as too weak to cause infection. However, vaginal secretions can harbor the virus. Oral health of the partner is (cuts in the mouth or bleeding gums) important here.

11. *Deep wet kissing (French kissing).* **NO RISK** — Scientific findings suggest that HIV concentration in saliva is too weak to cause infection.

12. *Penile-vaginal intercourse with internal ejaculation with a latex condom correctly used and with spermicidal foam that kills HIV.* **MODERATE RISK** — Condom use if correct is reliable. Moderate risk involves condom slippage or breakage even with spermicide as a back-up protection.

13. *Use of sex toys (dildos, etc.) that have been properly sterilized between uses and are not shared by partners, along with latex condoms.* **NO RISK** — No exchange of body fluids and disinfectant kills any HIV that might be present.

14. *Penile-vaginal intercourse with internal ejaculation using a latex condom correctly but with no spermicidal foam.* **MODERATE RISK** — Condom slippage and/or breakage along with no spermicide leads to moderate risk here.

15. *Penile-vaginal intercourse without spermicidal foam and without a latex condom and withdrawing prior to ejaculation.* **HIGH RISK** — Vaginal intercourse with no barrier or chemical contraception is high risk for HIV if you do not know for sure that your partner is HIV negative. Pre-ejaculate fluid may contain HIV and may cause infection.

16. *Mutual masturbation with only external touching.* **LOW RISK** — Mutual masturbation may involve an exchange of body fluids with external touching. Caution here in not letting body fluids come in contact with any skin that is not "intact."

17. *Hugging/massage/dry kissing.* **NO RISK.**

18. *Anal intercourse with internal ejaculation with a latex condom correctly used with spermicide that kills HIV.* **MODERATE RISK** — Correct condom use with spermicide that kills HIV makes this risk moderate. Anal intercourse is still risky and condom use and spermicide are highly recommended if you choose to engage in this risk behavior. It should be noted here that spermicide use is rare in this situation according to national self-report studies of sexually active people.

19. *Masturbating alone.* **NO RISK.**

20. *Brachiovaginal activities (vaginal fisting).* **MODERATE RISK** — Fisting can cause irritation to the vaginal canal leading to abrasions and increased opportunity for HIV to pass from an open cut or sore on the hand or arm. Risk is relative here in view of the person delivering the fist into vagina (open cuts on fingers, hand, or lower arm) and the person receiving the fist into her vagina (vaginal irritation, menstrual fluids, sores, or cuts).

21. *Anal intercourse without a latex condom, withdrawing prior to ejaculation.* **HIGH RISK** — Anal intercourse is the highest risk behavior. The anal canal was not designed for intercourse and the mucous membranes are thin and easily irritated. Nonlatex condom use is not recommended. Pre-ejaculate fluids with HIV could pass to the blood stream via abrasions in the anal canal.

22. *Fellatio (oral sex on man) without a latex condom, but never putting the head of the penis inside the mouth.* **LOW RISK** — Not putting the head of the penis in the mouth classifies this behavior as low risk. The general rule of thumb according to HIV/AIDS prevention and education experts is, "if it's wet and not yours use latex."

23. *Masturbating alongside another person but not touching one another.* **NO RISK.**

24. *Penile-vaginal intercourse with internal ejaculation without a latex condom but with spermicidal foam.* **HIGH RISK** — Vaginal intercourse without a latex condom is a high-risk behavior even with spermicidal foam if you are not 100 percent sure your partner is HIV negative. Spermicidal foam, if inserted properly, sits near the cervix and would not completely protect the vaginal canal. Vaginal irritation with bleeding could occur, menstrual fluids could pass the virus before the spermicide could kill all of the HIV.

25. *Brachioproctic activities (anal fisting).* **MODERATE RISK** — The mucous membranes of the anal canal are thin and irritation can lead to abrasions enabling HIV to pass to the

bloodstream from an open sore or cut on the fist or arm. Risk is relative here to the person doing the fisting and the person receiving the fisting.

26. *Fellatio to ejaculation with a condom.* **LOW RISK** — The possibility of condom tearing or breaking makes this situation a low risk.

27. *Fellatio without a latex condom with ejaculation in mouth.* **MODERATE RISK** — Non-condom use and the possibility of oral cuts or abrasions for passage of HIV constitutes moderate risk in this situation.

28. *Penile-vaginal intercourse with internal ejaculation without a latex condom and without any other form of barrier contraception.* **HIGH RISK** — This behavior offers no chemical or barrier protection from HIV infection. It is high risk and should be avoided unless you are in a long-term monogamous relationship and your partner is HIV negative.

29. *Anal intercourse with internal ejaculation without a latex condom.* **HIGH RISK** — This behavior offers no chemical or physical barrier against the virus that causes AIDS. Anal intercourse is the highest risk behavior for HIV infection. The anal canal was not designed for intercourse and the mucous membranes are thin, susceptible to irritation, and a subsequent mode of infection.

30. *Abstinence.* **NO RISK** — Best protection against HIV and other STDs.

IMPORTANT NOTE: The behaviors presented in this exercise are seldom mutually exclusive and subject to classification of risk. The behaviors that put people at risk for HIV are similar to those for risk of other STDs. With regard to latex condom using the C&C rule is most imperative: Correctly & Consistently.

REACTIONS: Please use the space provided to respond to the following questions.

1. Were you surprised by any of the answers? Explain why or why not?

2. If you could change any current policy or legislation regarding HIV/AIDS what would you change? Explain why?

105 | Facts and Misconceptions about HIV and AIDS

Health experts have stated that there are two major problems with the AIDS epidemic. First is the fatal virus itself and second is the lack of knowledge about HIV and the misconceptions people have regarding AIDS.

PURPOSE: This exercise is designed to help you determine some facts from fallacies about HIV and AIDS.

DIRECTIONS: Read each statement carefully and respond in the space provided deciding whether it is a MYTH or a FACT.

1. You can tell when people are HIV infected because they look unhealthy. _____

2. The human immune system usually protects you from disease. _____

3. HIV is spread through the sharing of IV needles or syringes and through sexual intercourse with a person who is infected with HIV. _____

4. People get HIV because they are gay. _____

5. You cannot become HIV infected by donating blood. _____

6. HIV is not transmitted by casual everyday contact such as hugging, sharing bathrooms, and clothing. _____

7. A blood test exists that can determine whether or not you will contract AIDS. _____

8. If a woman has sexual intercourse with just one man, her child cannot be born HIV infected. _____

9. People with AIDS or people infected with HIV should be quarantined. _____

10. A man cannot become HIV infected if he has sexual intercourse only with women. _____

11. Blood, vaginal secretions, and semen pass HIV from one person to another. _____

12. Any person who has sexual intercourse can become infected with HIV. _____

13. HIV can be spread by sneezing and coughing. _____

14. Even with medical technology, there is no cure for AIDS. _____

15. It is somewhat uncommon for a woman to get HIV/AIDS.   _____

16. Keeping a bandage over open sores and cuts can be a protection against HIV/AIDS.   _____

17. You can get HIV by kissing someone infected with HIV.   _____

18. Most common symptom of HIV infection is . . . nothing.   _____

19. It is best to be tested for HIV infection at 3 months and then again at 6 months after possible exposure.   _____

20. There is such thing as "safe sex."   _____

21. As a result of HIV/AIDS education, over 70 percent of unmarried American couples now use condoms.   _____

22. People increase their risk of HIV infection ten times if they do NOT use a condom when having intercourse with a person whose HIV status they do not know.   _____

23. In heterosexual intercourse with an HIV-infected partner, women are at greater risk of becoming infected than men.   _____

24. People without any symptoms of illness may carry and transmit HIV to a sex partner.   _____

25. People who have one sexually transmitted disease are at higher risk than those who do not, of contracting a second STD, including HIV.   _____

26. Many men who have had sexual experiences with other men don't describe themselves as "gay."   _____

27. Anal intercourse puts a person at risk for HIV infection only when it occurs between males.   _____

28. As a result of the AIDS epidemic, the number of unmarried people having sexual intercourse has decreased significantly in the last five years.   _____

29. Almost everyone who contracts HIV gets ill with full-blown AIDS within one year.   _____

30. Some experts believe that the only positive outcome of the AIDS epidemic may be to improve the quality of people's sex lives.   _____

Answer/Explanation Key:

1. MISCONCEPTION — People infected with HIV may look healthy and may stay healthy; however, they are able to transmit HIV every time they have unprotected sexual intercourse or share IV drug needles or syringes. You cannot tell by looking at someone whether or not they have been infected with HIV. Many infected persons do not know they are infected.

2. FACT — One function of the immune system is to fight germs that enter the body. With HIV infection or AIDS, the immune system can break down until it is no longer able to fight off what are known as "opportunistic infections." Opportunistic infections are infections that would normally not occur if the immune system were healthy and working.

3. FACT — In addition to being transmitted through sexual intercourse and the sharing of IV drug needles or syringes, the virus can also be passed from an infected mother to her unborn child. Before a blood test was developed, there was also the risk of contracting the virus through contaminated blood used during transfusions; however, there is now very little risk of this in the United States, because all blood supplies are now screened and any contaminated blood is discarded.

4. MISCONCEPTION — HIV is transmitted primarily through sexual intercourse and IV drug use, including steroids. Therefore, anyone is able to acquire the virus. AIDS is not just a disease of homosexual men. HIV is found in heterosexuals, people of all races and colors, men, women, and children. People become HIV infected because of what they do, not who they are. Homosexual and bisexual men have become HIV infected by having sexual intercourse with infected partners, a high-risk behavior.

5. FACT — Only disposable needles are used at blood collection centers. These needles are never reused. Therefore, there is no risk in donating blood.

6. FACT — The human immunodeficiency virus (HIV) does not live or grow in the environment. It cannot be transmitted through casual, everyday contact. There have been no reported cases of transmission through such activities as sneezing, coughing, eating in restaurants, swimming in swimming pools, or using toilets.

7. MISCONCEPTION — The blood test technique called the ELISA can detect the presence of antibody to HIV in people who look and feel well. A positive test result does not mean that a person has AIDS or will get AIDS in the near future. It means that the person became infected at some time with HIV and might infect others with whom he or she has sex or shares needles or syringes. The test is not a diagnosis of AIDS.

8. MISCONCEPTION — If the man is infected, the mother may be infected by him, and the baby by her.

9. MISCONCEPTION — Since HIV is not transmitted by casual contact — that is, through nonsexual, day-to-day interaction — there is no need to keep people with AIDS (or people who are infected with HIV) separate from the rest of the population.

10. MISCONCEPTION — Women who are infected with HIV can transmit the virus to their male sexual partners.

11. FACT — HIV is transmitted primarily through sexual intercourse and IV drug abuse. Infected semen and vaginal secretions can transmit HIV from one person to another during sexual intercourse, and infected blood can be injected from one person to another during IV drug abuse.

12. FACT — Men and women, heterosexual or homosexual, can get HIV infection if they do not take such precautions as abstaining from IV drug abuse; having sexual intercourse only within marriage or a long-term, mutually faithful relationship when it is known that both partners are not infected; or practicing protected sex (using latex condoms and spermicides together) or abstaining from sexual intercourse.

13. MISCONCEPTION — HIV is a very fragile virus. It cannot be transmitted through sneezing or coughing. There have been no reported cases of transmission through such activities as sneezing or coughing.

14. FACT — AIDS is a worldwide disease and medical researchers all over the world are searching for a cure. Unfortunately, a cure or a vaccine is probably many years away. Prevention is the only way to protect yourself against HIV infection.

15. MISCONCEPTION — Initially, there were very few cases of HIV infection in the female population. But because of bisexual and heterosexual intercourse (vaginal, anal, oral) as well as intravenous (IV) drug use with infected individuals, the number of women infected with HIV is ever increasing. The vaginal mucous membrane is particularly vulnerable to injury. Aggressive cervical cancer, pelvic inflammatory disease, yeast infections, pulmonary tuberculosis, and recurrent bacterial pneumonia are the most common symptoms in women infected with HIV.

16. FACT — Keeping a bandage over open sores or cuts can be a form of protection against HIV infection. Any protective covering over an open sore or cut can help protect against infection from many organisms, including HIV.

17. MISCONCEPTION — Getting HIV/AIDS from kissing a person with HIV is a misconception. To date, scientists tell us that the concentration of HIV in saliva, tears, and urine is so small that is unlikely that these fluids can transfer the virus to another person. A recent study by the U.S. Centers for Disease Control & Prevention found that HIV may not even be present in perspiration (sweat). **Please note: If there is blood in any of these fluids, the risk then becomes high.**

18. FACT — The most common symptom of HIV infection is nothing. Most people infected with HIV will show no symptoms for many years. At that time the disease is only detectable via blood tests—Elisa and the Western Blot—that detect antibodies to HIV until the advanced stages (prior to AIDS): fever, tiredness, enlargement of lymph nodes, loss of appetite, 10- to 15-pound weight loss and a yeast infection of the mouth.

19. FACT — It is best to be tested for HIV infection 3 to 6 months after possible exposure. Someone can carry the virus that causes AIDS from 6 to 12 weeks but still escape detection in a blood test. The longest time in CDC records is 14 weeks. This is why the U.S. Centers for Disease Control and Prevention recommends being tested 3 months and then again 6 months after exposure.

20. FACT — There is such a thing as "safe sex." The safest course is abstinence. Hugging, kissing, and body rubbing are relatively safe alternatives. When one is mature enough to engage in sexual behavior the safest option at that time is to have sex with only one, mutually faithful, uninfected partner. Both people must also avoid other risky behaviors. Anything else should be considered "risk reduction," or the more popular term "safer sex," because even latex condoms cannot eliminate all risk, although studies suggest that they are highly effective when used consistently and correctly. If you are entering into a monogamous sexual relationship, you should still protect yourself—during every act of lovemaking (at least for 6 months and then only until both partners have tested negative for HIV).

21. MISCONCEPTION — During the past five years, the number of unmarried sexual active couples using condoms has increased from approximately 12 to 16 percent.

22. FACT — Assuming that condoms are 90 percent effective, medical researchers estimate that people reduce their probability of becoming infected with HIV ten times with the use of condoms. However, condoms may be more or less effective than this estimate.

23. FACT — Studies note that the concentration of HIV is higher in semen than in vaginal secretions, and that abrasions or cuts occur more often inside the vaginal canal than on the penis. Also, semen remains inside the vagina without exposure to the air which kills the virus. Therefore, transmission of HIV is more efficient from man to woman than woman to man.

24. FACT — The average incubation time for HIV, from infection to diagnosis of full-blown AIDS, is now 8 years. During much of this time a person may have no symptoms. Yet, very soon after infection a person can infect others. In fact, in the weeks and even months following infection, a test for HIV may not detect the presence of the virus because antibodies have not been formed.

25. FACT — There is increasing evidence that people who have one STD are at higher than average risk for a second infection. This may be related to: (1) lifestyle; (2) that fact that open sores in the genital area, common symptoms of many STDs including herpes, syphilis, and genital warts, provide an easy access for other infections; and (3) decreased effectiveness of the person's immune system.

26. FACT — Both the man himself and a potential partner need to evaluate the risk of being infected in terms of whether he has had sex with another man, not in terms of whether he identifies himself as gay (homosexual). Since HIV infection may be widespread in a particular gay community, any male who has had or will have sex with another man must consider himself at some level of risk and act accordingly.

27. MISCONCEPTION — It is incorrect to assume that anal intercourse occurs only among gay men. Some heterosexual couples, in particular, teenage girls in satisfying boyfriends (and to remain vaginal virgins) also have anal intercourse and since the mucous membranes of the rectum are thin, they are particularly vulnerable to injury whether the receiving partner is male or female. In addition, blood vessels close to the surface provide easy access of infection to the bloodstream. Many health experts believe that anal intercourse is too dangerous and should be avoided completely. Others recommend auspiciously knowledgeable use of latex condoms.

28. MISCONCEPTION — The percentage of unmarried women who have had intercourse rose from about 70 percent in 1991 to 75 percent in 1996.

29. MISCONCEPTION — Most people infected with HIV will not develop full-blown AIDS for approximately 10 years or more. The time between becoming infecting with HIV and becoming ill with AIDS-related illnesses is called an incubation period. Incubation usually lasts a minimum of 2 years. About one-half of HIV-infected people will develop AIDS 7 to 10 years after becoming infected with the virus that causes AIDS. The maximum incubation is still unknown.

30. FACT — The risks associated with AIDS have led many couples to develop a longer, possibly deeper, relationship before initiating sexual activity, in particular sexual intercourse. Safer sex also requires care in the selection of a partner and effective communication between partners, both of whom have the potential for enhancing lovemaking.

(For further clarification on HIV and AIDS refer to any current human sexuality text or another reliable source of information).

REACTIONS: Use the space provided to respond to the following questions.

1. Why do you think the spread of AIDS continues to be a problem despite all the current available medical technology?

2. Currently, what is the best hope for curtailing the spread of AIDS? Explain.

106 | Communicating About HIV and AIDS

P URPOSE: Choosing the "right" language on an interpersonal, moral, and political basis is important as we deal effectively with the HIV/AIDS epidemic.

DIRECTIONS: Listed below are several incorrect or inappropriate terms with regard to communicating about HIV/AIDS. Read each term and then write the correct terminology in the space provided.

1. INSTEAD OF: USE:
   "AIDS patients"
   _____

2. INSTEAD OF: USE:
   "victims"
   _____

3. INSTEAD OF: USE:
   "dying from AIDS"
   _____

4. INSTEAD OF"   USE:
   "innocent"
   _____

5. INSTEAD OF: USE:
   "high-risk group"
   _____

APPROPRIATE RESPONSES AND RATIONALE: The following are offered as appropriate responses and rationale for the incorrect or inappropriate responses in the exercise.

1. USE: "people with AIDS" or "people living with AIDS"

   Rationale: "Patients" tends to imply that people living with AIDS are sick 100 percent of the time, which is typically not the case. In addition it tends to detract from hope that people with AIDS and their families and friends work hard to foster and express on a consistent basis.

2. **USE: "people with AIDS"**

   Rationale: Using "victims" tends to deny people living with AIDS dignity and hope. "Victims" or "victim" also implies that they are passive about their health and well-being.

3. **USE: "living with AIDS"**

   Rationale: People with HIV/AIDS are living longer today and have better potential for more meaningful lives, which makes "dying from" less likely to be true at any given time. Also, "dying from" tends to remove the aspect of hope.

4. **USE: nonjudgmental, specific wording**

   Rationale: Passing judgment on people as innocent or guilty of their own illness tends to discourage behaviors such as testing for infection, prevention of infection, and compassionate quality care, all of which are critical if we are to combat this epidemic and, as a society, promote dignity and value for every life.

5. **USE: "high-risk behavior"**

   Rationale: No group is predisposed to HIV infection and should not be stereotyped as such. HIV is an equal opportunity infection; it does not discriminate according to gender, age, race, sexual orientation, religion, or socioeconomic status. It is what people DO (their behavior), not who they ARE, that places them at risk for HIV infection.

Try to avoid the following HIV/AIDS communication faux pas:

1. To say or write "HIV Virus" is incorrect terminology. It implies Human Immunodeficiency Virus Virus. It would be more appropriate to say a person is "infected with HIV" or that they are "infected with HIV, the virus which causes AIDS."

2. "HIV" and "AIDS" are both acronyms for health/medical terminology: Human Immunodeficiency Virus, and Acquired Immune Deficiency Syndrome. You should always capitalize all the letters in "HIV" and AIDS."

REACTIONS: Now use the space below to respond to the following questions

1. Which of the incorrect or inappropriate terms associated with AIDS or HIV have you used? Explain the situation.

2. Do you understand why the alternate terminology given is more appropriate? Why or why not?

107

Sex, Drugs, and STDs?

Purpose: A variety of STDs are in epidemic stages in communities across the country. Risk-taking behavior is believed to be a significant contributor to this problem. This exercise is designed to explore the relationship between drug use and STDs, including HIV.

Directions: Read the problem situation below carefully making sure you understand the dilemma before you respond to the questions that follow.

Julie and Richard have been dating for about three months. Julie is a college freshman who has had sexual intercourse with her boyfriend Richard a few times. Before they started having intercourse, they talked about their past sexual and drug-use experiences. Julie was a virgin who had never used drugs, and Richard said the same. Just recently, Julie found out from several reliable sources that Richard lied to her. Not only was he sexually active for some time before he knew her, but he also used drugs (Julie doesn't know what kind of drugs he used).

1. What do you feel is the problem in this situation?

2. What feelings would you expect the people involved in this situation to have?

3. What possible solutions to this problem would you suggest?

4. Appraise and select the best solution to this problem and explain why you feel it is the best solution.

108

AIDS: A Family Affair

PURPOSE: The human immunodeficiency virus has touched every aspect of human life including the family. This exercise is designed to help you examine the impact that HIV can have on family members and how families might go about dealing with the problem of an HIV-infected family member.

DIRECTIONS: Read the problem situation below carefully, making sure you have a grasp of the family and social dynamics before you respond to the questions that follow.

Kevin has an older brother, Don, who has just been diagnosed with AIDS. As it turns out, Don is gay, but no one in the family had known that until now. At the present, Kevin's family is so distraught by the news that Don is gay and that he has AIDS that they are reacting by having nothing to do with him. They do not visit him, they do not call him, he is not even a topic of conversation in this family. Kevin is perplexed and feels caught in the middle of this family affair. Kevin loves his brother and wants to help and support him.

1. What do you feel is the problem in this situation?

2. What do you think are the important facts in this situation?

3. What feelings would you expect the people involved in this situation to have?

4. What possible solutions to this problem would you suggest?

5. Appraise and select the best solution to this problem and explain why you feel it is the best solution.

SECTION XIV | SEXUALITY EDUCATION

Children, adolescents, and adults are curious about sex and sexuality. This is perfectly normal and good and it motivates them to learn. The only problem is that people in our society often do not know what to do about sexuality education. Most children and adolescents receive their sexuality education from their peers, not from their parents; as a result, those who argue for sex education in the home rather than in the school are not being realistic. Most Americans do favor sexuality education in the school, including education about AIDS. Also, the presumed negative effects of sexuality education are not substantiated by research efforts. The exercises in this section are designed to help you examine some of your feelings about sexuality education.

The Sexuality Education exercises include:

109. Are You Approachable?
110. Sexual Messages and the Media: You Be the Judge
111. Sexuality Education for Children: Points to Ponder
112. Issues in Human Sexuality: Pregnant Valedictorian
113. Sexuality Education in the Schools

109 | Are You Approachable?

PURPOSE: As an adult you will be asked questions about sex and sexuality. In society today children are constantly bombarded with messages about sex—some positive and some negative. You will need to help your children and perhaps children from other families sort out the knowledge and form their opinions as they assimilate all the information they receive.

DIRECTIONS: Respond to each of the following questions as a responsible adult. You may wish to discuss these situations with your partner or friend.

1. Your six-year-old niece stops at the racks of condoms in the pharmacy, picks up a box of condoms, and asks, "What is this?"

2. Your eight-year-old nephew is watching television and sees a commercial for prevention of AIDS. He then asks, "What is AIDS?" and "How do you get it?"

3. You feel it is time to talk with your eleven-year-old daughter about menstruation, responsible sexual behavior, and relationships. How do you approach the subject to make it a comfortable experience for you both? What are the important concepts for you to get across?

4. You feel it is time to talk with your twelve-year-old son about responsible sexual behavior, wet dreams, and relationships. How do you approach the subject to make it a comfortable experience for you both? What are the concepts you want to get across?

110

Sexual Messages and the Media: You Be the Judge

PURPOSE: This exercise is designed for you to evaluate a television program or a movie for its sexual content.

DIRECTIONS: During a single program or film, check any of the following that occur. Use the space provided and make a check mark (✔) for each time an incident or image is portrayed or each time a particular behavior, comment, or attitude is projected. If there is laughter in the movie directed toward any of your observations ignore this and mark it appropriately.

Name of Show or Movie _____

Date of Viewing _____

_____ 1. One gender dominates over the other (the use of power).

_____ 2. Hostility is shown to characters by calling names of insulting the opposite gender.

_____ 3. Characters lie to their spouses/significant partner about sex.

_____ 4. Characters lie to get sex from someone.

_____ 5. One person deceives a sex partner.

_____ 6. Characters play head games or manipulate partners in love relationships.

_____ 7. Jokes or put-downs are made regarding commitment in relationships (jokes about bad relationships or marriages).

_____ 8. Couple has sexual intercourse with no mention of contraception.

_____ 9. Couple has sexual intercourse without any mention of risk for sexually transmitted disease.

_____ 10. Women or men make uninvited comments regarding the secondary sex characteristics (breasts, etc.) of another person.

_____ 11. Characters publicly put down the sexual abilities of another person.

_____ 12. Characters project a titillating attitude about sex (making sexual implications out of incidents that are really not sexual) or they laugh about double meaning words that could be interpreted as sexual.

_____ 13. Character laughs at serious sexual problems (situation comedies that joke about unwed parenthood, disease, prostitution, or deception, etc.).

_____ 14. An employer or fellow employee makes sexual remarks to another employee, or engages in more serious sexual harassment.

_____ 15. Women or men are consistently portrayed as stupid.

_____ 16. Males are portrayed as insensitive.

_____ 17. Characters are engaged in sexual aggression or violence irrelevant to the plot (ranging from insults to rape).

_____ 18. Males are portrayed as more interested in sexual conquests than in the woman's feelings.

_____ 19. Women are portrayed as weak or frightened.

_____ 20. Women are depicted as not really minding sexual coercion or as liking it.

_____ 21. Rape is attempted (even if it began as mutual affection or lovemaking).

_____ 22. A completed rape is shown.

_____ 23. Program or film implies the rape myth that women are always interested in sex.

_____ 24. Program or film implies the rape myth that men cannot help but be sex-driven.

_____ 25. Program or film projects any other form of sexual aggression or exploitation.

REACTIONS: Use the space provided to respond to the following questions.

1. Briefly discuss the two most prevalent negative sexual images or concepts portrayed in the program of movie that you watched.

2. From your response above (question 1) were either of these themes necessary in reaching the plot of the program or movie? Explain why or why not.

3. Would you allow your 12-year-old daughter to view this program or movie? Why or why not?

4. Would you allow your 12-year-old son to view this program or movie? Why or why not?

111

Sexuality Education for Children: Points to Ponder

PURPOSE: Today, as for many years, the debate continues regarding what is appropriate sexuality education for children. Perhaps you have opinions on this issue and perhaps your opinions are still forming. Use these questions to help you in the decision-making process.

DIRECTIONS: Use the space provided to respond to the questions. After responding, you may find it helpful to discuss these issues with others (i.e., teachers, partners, teenagers, family members).

1. What sources are available today to children for gaining sex information?

- Which sources do you think are most often the primary sources?

- How much confidence do you place on each source to be able to give complete and accurate information correlated with the current needs of children?

2. How do you see your role as a parent in the sex education of your children?

- When would you begin to introduce each area of sex education?

3. Describe reactions of some parents to sexuality education which could have a negative effect on the child's acceptance of his/her sexuality.

• How would you rectify the situation(s) mentioned above? Explain.

4. How is sexuality education best accomplished in the home?

5. What areas of sexuality education should not be discussed in the family setting? Why?

112 | Issues in Human Sexuality: Pregnant Valedictorian

S hould a pregnant teenager give a valedictory address?

DIRECTIONS: Read each paragraph below carefully, making sure you clearly understand the issue before you write your reactions.

The top student at Jack Yates High School in Houston, Texas, who had a child and was pregnant at the time, delivered the valedictory speech, despite previous doubts by school officials allowing her to do so.

"You and I are special," Carrie Mae Dixon told 400 classmates during her commencement ceremonies held at Texas Southern University. "We made many sacrifices, and some of us even went against the odds."

Miss Dixon, at age 18, became the center of controversy in April of her senior year when an article about her for the school paper was killed by Principal Chester Smith. The article detailed Miss Dixon's first pregnancy and how she was shuffled among relatives after her mother died and her stepfather deserted her and eight siblings. Smith said the school newspaper article was too personal.

Miss Dixon said she doubted school officials would allow her to give the valedictory address since she was pregnant a second time. However, school officials later stated that there was no policy preventing her from giving her speech.

Miss Dixon plans to attend the University of Houston and has $17,500 in scholarships. She and her 20-month-old daughter are living with her boyfriend's family.

REACTIONS: Use the space provided to respond to the following questions.

1. Should the school district have allowed Ms. Dixon to give the valedictory address? Explain.

2. Do you feel that there are other options available to recognize the talents and achievements of Miss Dixon? Explain.

3. If you were the school superintendent what would you have done in this situation? Explain.

113

Sexuality Education In the Schools

PURPOSE: Various studies have documented that the majority of parents and community leaders are in favor of sexuality education in the schools. However, school-based sexuality education continues to be an issue. This exercise is designed to provoke some thought regarding your opinions about various aspects of sexuality education for school-aged children and adolescents.

DIRECTIONS: Read each of the following questions carefully. Then respond to each question without consulting any of your friends, roommates, or printed material.

1. What is your definition of sexuality education?

2. What are some of the arguments against sexuality education in the schools?

3. What are some of the reasons for sexuality education in the schools?

4. What should be the objectives of a sexuality education program in the schools?

5. Should sexuality education be a part of the experience of all school-aged children? Explain why.

6. What do you feel is the responsibility of the home, church/synagogue, and the school, respectively, for sexuality education?

7. At what age should sexuality education begin? Why?

8. What topics do you think should always be included in a sexuality eduction program?

9. Should contraception be taught as a component of a sexuality education program in the schools? Explain.

10. Should the topic of homosexuality be discussed in school-based sexuality education? Explain.

11. Do you think there are any topics that should never be discussed in a school-based sexuality education program?

12. Describe the best person to teach sexuality education in the schools.

APPENDIXES

Inventory for Self-Evaluation

The questions in this inventory can be used in a variety of ways. You can simply think about them, write down your own responses, and reflect on them privately at a later time; you can share your responses with an intimate partner who also writes out her or his responses; or you can do likewise with a small group of friends. If you choose to exchange responses within a small group, do not sign the response sheets; shuffle them, distribute them randomly, and have the group discuss the variety of responses. Then each person is free from the pressure to identify her or his personal written response.

1. **Health status.** Are you at a level of physical fitness that feels good for you? Zestful sexmaking requires energy and endurance, as well as erotic enthusiasm. Adequate nutrition and regular exercise can make a direct contribution to less stressful and more enjoyable erotic pleasuring. Hartman and Fithian have documented in their clinic that joggers and others in fit condition have "easy orgasms"—less physiologically stressful though no less intense and enjoyable subjectively. If you experience painful intercourse, be sure to have a medical examination, for that may indicate a biological or psychological cause.

Are you aware of your emotions, feelings, moods? Sometimes we go through the motions of working at intercourse or some other sexual activity without really being there; thus the body is not properly responsive. There is no need to be puzzled about occasional or periodic nonresponsiveness. There is usually a good reason for it if we can get in touch with ourselves.

Do you take drugs or medications or have an illness that can hinder your optimum sexual functioning? Diabetes mellitus, for example, is the most frequent medical reason for impotence and can cause impaired orgasm in the female. If you are having orgasm difficulties and are not diabetic, check to see whether there is a history of diabetes in your family. If there is, consult your physician. Certain types of drugs—antihypertensives for high blood pressure, antabuse for alcohol abuse, some antidepressants and antipsychotic agents—or high doses of certain other drugs, such as those used to relieve anxiety (Valium, Librium, meprobamate), can cause orgasm problems. Cigarette smoking has been found to decrease sexual desire and capacity. Even oral contraceptives may decrease sexual interest for some women. If you suspect that a drug regimen is causing undesirable changes in your sexual responsibility, bring it to the attention of your health practitioner so that alternatives or lower dosages may be considered. It is unwise to make a unilateral decision to discontinue medication—the consequence could be far graver than a disruption of your sexual response pattern.

2. **Body image.** Have you made peace with your own body? Can you stand in front of that mirror—maybe with a sexmaking friend—and touch every touchable part of you while saying out loud what is delightful, charming, nice about that part? Look, naked, into a full-

length mirror, smile and say to yourself, "Hi, you lovely body!" Your body is lovely—it probably treats you better than you treat it! Except for those who suffer the genuine torment of believing they should have the body of the other sex, many people create endless but needless misery for themselves by disliking or being ashamed of their own bodies. Don't be one of them—alter what is possible for the sake of good health; aim for reasonable weight and fitness. And fall in love with yourself. Everybody has a body—like yours.

3. **Self-pleasuring patterns.** How do you feel about touching your own body? Can you enjoy self-pleasuring without feeling guilty or self-indulgent? It is your right to be appreciative of your body and its marvels of sensuality. The benefits of self-pleasuring are many. Never, ever will you be without warm, loving hands to soothe you or delight you—with or without a vibrator, feathers, a powder puff, oils and creams, rubber, leather—whatever turns you on. If you do not have hands or movable hands, try any method you can imagine to stimulate yourself wherever it feels best. If guilt is too high a price for masturbation, give other parts of your body sensual affection. A foot massage, for example, or a knee massage—wherever you carry tension or feel weary. Take the time to lower the lights, put on your favorite music, burn some good incense, and explore your own body.

4. **Sexual fantasies.** Could you write out or relate one of your favorite erotic fantasies? Or would you be "too embarrassed"? Do you give yourself permission to be flooded with sensual images and imagine what, for you, are arousing, erotic behaviors? A great deal of sexual activity goes on in our minds. Much of it is ordinary and realizable: a special partner, new and different partners, a familiar partner with exciting, new activities; group sex with loving friends; elements of water, sand, grass, sun; romantic places and spaces; a sexual modality other than your usual—be it homosexual, heterosexual, or bisexual. You may find yourself experiencing your fantasies in reality if you ask yourself what is keeping you from doing so.

5. **Sexual values.** What do you deeply believe and value about your sexuality? Do you have a system of sexual values with which you are comfortable? Are your sexual values consistent with your desires and with your actual behavior? Sex in fantasy or erotica is always easy because it doesn't involve encounters with real persons in actual situations. But getting involved with live bodies may mean getting involved with conflicting value systems. Making intelligent and satisfying choices is sometimes quite difficult. Clair Wooster and Robert Meyners urge people to write out their personal sexual creeds. In an open, sharing manner, they offer a statement of their sexual values for the sake of dialogue. They believe:

> . . . in a sexual style that makes sex an integral part of the entire range of human values; in expressive sex; in touch; in relational sex; in sexual communication; in independence; in freedom with commitment; in trust; in equality; in values as possibilities we may allow to happen (rather than norms we must live up to); in consent; in the privacy of sex; in the search for morality that will replace the ethics of procreation with sexual styles that are responsible to the human ecosystem.

And they conclude their creed with this affirmation:

> We believe that the sanctity of human life endorses the value of sex for its own sake. Sex is not only a means to other values such as intimacy and security, family or children. It is an amazing joy in and of itself. We celebrate sex as a quality of experience which transcends the pettiness of daily existence!*

It is not important that you agree with any of the above principles, for the point of writing out your own "sexual creed" is to articulate your sexual values for the present time in your life. You have the right to assume responsibility for the quality and direction of your own sexual life.

6. **Gender preferences.** Where on the gender preference chart do you place yourself now? How do you feel about where you are now? Where would you like to be on the scale five years from now? If sexmaking or sensual pleasuring with a partner has no interest for you, perhaps you haven't recognized your preferences. Although there is considerable attention in the media to heterosexual and homosexual issues, there is scant attention to bisexual and asexual concerns. But, whatever your preferences, seek assistance or support, if you need it, so you can be free to be you.

7. **Sexual expectations.** What do you expect in a "typical" sexual encounter? Are your expectations reality-oriented? Or do you expect "too much" too quickly? Young people often expect that each sexual encounter will be fabulous. But it requires time to learn what the other needs and desires and to express one's own needs and desires; expectations may not be similar. There is a tendency to rate the performance and to be blamed or to label oneself as a sexual failure. The worst that should happen, however, is that potential sexmakers chalk it up to experience and have a few chuckles.

8. **Contraceptive use.** If you and your partner do not choose pregnancy, can you plan ahead for sexmaking and use your chosen contraceptive method effectively? If you are a woman relying on a diaphragm-spermicide method, will you be assertive about taking time to put it in? If you are a man relying on the condom-foam combined method, are you relaxed and confident enough about your own "masculinity" not to panic if you lose your erection while putting on the condom? Certain conception control methods involve shared responsibility. Even when only one partner is using contraception, effective use of the method may require the support and cooperation of the other person. Better yet, the mechanics of applying conception control devices—to yourself or to your partner—can be handled erotically, enhancing pleasure rather than detracting from it. If neither partner has a reliable contraceptive method, a little imagination can lead to satisfying nonintercourse methods of sexual pleasuring.

9. **Sexually transmitted diseases.** Are you knowledgeable about the symptoms of sexually transmitted diseases? Can you recognize them in yourself? In a partner? Are you willing to take the responsibility for talking about the possibility of STDs—yours or your partner's—before sexmaking with a new partner? Can you openly suggest and use measures to minimize risks

---

*From Robert Meyners and Claire Wooster, *Sexual Style, Facing and Making Choices about Sex* (New York: Harcourt Brace Jovanovich, 1979), pp. 171–175. Reprinted by permission.

if you and your partner decide to go ahead with sexmaking? People of any gender preference should inform themselves about the possibility of contracting or spreading sexually transmitted diseases. There are alarming increases in the incidence of many kinds of diseases spread by sexmaking. Measures such as careful genital washing and use of a condom and spermicide help prevent spread of diseases between an infected person and an uninfected partner. If you do contract some kind of sexually transmitted disease, early treatment and informing your sex partner(s) is critical to your health and theirs.

10. **Partner pleasuring.** If you have an ongoing relationship, how satisfied are you with its overall quality? Do you like your partner? Do you accept or receive pleasure as well as give it—not necessarily during the same episode of pleasuring? Are either of you spectators of your own performances? In other words, do you view your sexual behavior as an audience might view a sporting event, or are you so involved you don't have time to be a spectator to your own sexmaking? In the ebb and flow of relationships, there are times of tension or hurt feelings; but such experiences need not be reflected in your sexmaking. Begin by telling your partner what you particularly like to do to your partner and what you like to have done to you by your partner. Express any dislikes about your sexual exchanges in a constructive way and listen to your partner's likes and dislikes. Both of you will begin to feel you're getting enough touching, cuddling, and romantic affection.

11. **Communication level.** What sex language turns you on? Turns you off? Is there anything about your sexual self that you fear to reveal? Can you tell what about your sexual identity you most enjoy? Least enjoy? Something has been assumed all along that cannot be taken for granted—namely, the necessity to acquire sexual communication skills to deal with all of the previous factors. You need to update your factual knowledge, be willing to experiment with sex language, and have the ability to be vulnerable—to self-disclose and try new forms of risk taking. It is a complicated, upsetting, anxious, humorous, joyful enterprise.

By reflecting on the above eleven items in the Inventory for Sexual Self-Evaluation, you can begin to assess the quality of your own sexual health and to sort out and assign priorities to those areas where you choose to seek improvement or enrichment.

REACTIONS: Use this space to write down any thoughts or feelings you might have from taking this inventory.

SOURCE: Adapted from G. D. Nass, R. W. Libby, and M. P. Fisher, *Sexual Choices.* Copyright © 1981 by Wadsworth, Inc. Reprinted by permission of the publisher, Wadsworth Health Sciences Division, Monterey, CA.

: **The Yellow Pages for Your Sexuality**

This section is designed as a resource list for those who wish to pursue additional information, a service, a sexuality related issue or problem or an advanced degree in human sexuality. (Please note: Address and phone number changes are a possibility.)

HEALTH SERVICE INFORMATION AND REFERRALS FOR REPRODUCTIVE HEALTH AND SEXUALLY TRANSMITTED INFECTIONS

Access to Voluntary and Safe Contraception
79 Madison Avenue, 7th Floor
New York, NY 10016
(212) 561-8000

Advocates for Youth
1025 Vermont Avenue NW, Suite 200
Washington, DC 20005
(202) 347-5700

American Cancer Society
2200 Lake Blvd, Suite A Atlanta City Unit
Atlanta, GA 30319
(404) 841-0700

American College of Nurse-Midwives
1522 K Street NW, Suite 1120
Washington, DC 20005

American Fertility Society
1608 13th Avenue South, Suite 10
Birmingham, AL 35205

American Foundation for the Prevention of Venereal Disease, Inc.
799 Broadway, Suite 638
New York, NY 10003
(212) 759-2069

American Society for Psychoprophylaxis in Obstetrics
1200 19th Street NW, Suite 300
Washington, DC 20036
1-800-368-4404 or (202) 857-1128

Association for Family Living
32 West Randolph Street
Chicago, IL 60601

Association for Voluntary Surgical Contraception
122 East 42nd Street
New York, NY 10168

Centers for Disease Control and Prevention
Division of Sexually Transmitted Diseases
1600 Clifton Road
Atlanta, GA 30329
(404) 639-3534

Emory University Planning Program
67 Peach Park Drive NE, Suite 115
Atlanta, GA 30309
(Request that you write for information)

The Herpes Resource Center
260 Sheridan Avenue
Palo Alto, CA 94306
(415) 328-7710

International Cesarian Awareness Network
P.O. Box 152
Syracuse, NY 13210
(315) 424-1942

International Childbirth Education Association
P.O. Box 20048
Minneapolis, MN 55420-0048
(612) 854-8660

La Leche League International, Inc.
1400 N. Meacham
Schaumburg, IL 60173-4840
(847) 519-7730, Fax: (847) 519-7730

Midwives Alliance of North America
30 South Main Street
Concord, NH 03301
(603) 225-9586

National Abortion Rights Action League
1156 15th Street NW, Suite 700
Washington, DC 20005
(202) 828-9300

National Alliance for Optional Parenthood
2010 Massachusetts Avenue NW
Washington, DC 20036

National Association of Parents and Professionals for Safe Alternatives in Childbirth
Route 1, Box 646
Marble Hill, MO 63764
(573) 238-2010

National Clearinghouse for Family Planning Information
P.O. Box 2225
Rockville, MD 20852

National Right to Life Committee, Inc.
419 7th Street NW, Suite 402
Washington, DC, 20004
(202) 626-8800

National Women's Health Network
514 10th Street NW, Suite 400
Washington, DC 20004
(202) 347-1140

The Population Institute
107 2nd Street NE
Washington, DC 20002
(202) 544-3300

Population Information Program
The John Hopkins University
111 Marketplace
Baltimore, MD 21202
(410) 659-6300

PMS ACCESS
P.O. Box 9326
Madison, WI
1-800-222-4PMS

Religious Coalition for Reproductive Choice
1025 Vermont Avenue NW
Washington, DC 20005
(202) 628-7700

Resolve, Inc. (Infertility help)
P.O. Box 474
Belmont, MA 02178
(617) 623-0744

Society for Protection of the Unborn Through Nutrition
17 North Wabash Avenue, Suite 603
Chicago, IL 60602

U.S. Alliance for the Eradication of VD
USEVD/Operation Venus
1213 Clover Street
Philadelphia, PA 19103

HIV/AIDS NATIONAL TELEPHONE HOTLINES AND ORGANIZATIONS

Centers for Desease Control National AIDS Hotline
1-800-342-AIDS (English)
1-800-344-SIDA (Spanish)
1800-AIDS-TTA (Deaf Access)
(919) 361-8425 (Fax)

National AIDS Clearinghouse
1-800-458-5231 (Reference Specialists)

AIDS Clinical Trials Information Services
1-800-874-2572

National Sexually Transmitted Diseases Hotline
1-800-227-8922

American Foundation for AIDS Research (AMFAR)
733 Third Avenue, 12th Floor
New York, NY 10017
1-800-392-6327

Pediatric AIDS Foundation
(310) 395-9051

National Commission on AIDS
1730 K Street NW, Suite 815
Washington, DC 20006
(202) 254-5125

National Task Force on AIDS prevention
631 O'Farrell Street
San Francisco, CA 94109
(415) 749-6700

Project Inform
1965 Market Street, Suite 220
San Fransisco, CA 94103
1-800-822-7422

AIDS Action Foundation
1875 Connecticut Avenue NW, Suite 700
Washington, DC 20009
(202) 986-1300

AIDS Project Los Angeles
6721 Romaine Street
Los Angeles, CA
(213) 962-1600

World Health Organization
525 23rd Street NW
Washington, D.C. 20037
(202) 861-4346

American Association of Physicians for Human Rights
(415) 225-4547

Minority Task Force on AIDS
c/o NY City Council of Churches
(212) 563-8340

National Red Cross
17th & D Streets NW
Washington, DC 20006
(202) 737-8300

U.S. Public Health Service Public Affairs Office
(202) 690-6867

National STD Hotline: Operated by The American Social Health Association
1-800-227-8922
Inquires to:
ATTN: STD Hotline
1382 7th Street
RTP, NC 27709

Childhelp USA Hotline
P.O. Box 630
Los Angeles, CA 90028
1-800-422-4453

ACLU AIDS Project
American Civil Liberties Union
132 West 43rd Street
New York, NY 10036
(212) 944-9800 (ext. 545)

AIDS Action Council
Federation of AIDS-Related Organizations
1875 Connecticut Avenue, NW, Suite 700
Washington, DC 20009
(202) 986-1300

American Foundation for AIDS Research
733 Third Avenue, 12th Floor
New York, NY 10017
(212) 682-7440
1-800-392-6327

National Resource Center on Women and AIDS
200 P Street NW, Suite 508
Washington, DC 20036
(202) 872-1770

Gay Men's Health Crisis
1290 West 20th Street
New York, NY 10017
(212) 807-6655

National AIDS Clearinghouse
Box 6003
Rockville, MD 20849-6003
1-800-458-5231

National Hemophilia Foundation
110 Greene Street
New York, NY 10012
(212) 219-8180

National Lesbian and Gay Health Association
1407 S Street NW
Washington, DC 20009
(202) 939-7880

SUPPORT AGENCIES FOR SEXUAL ABUSE, RAPE, HARASSMENT, AND SOCIAL SUPPORT

(Please refer to the Community Service Numbers in the front of your local telephone directory or the yellow pages for local listings of agencies and support organizations. They can provide immediate help and/or offer assistance in a crisis or emergency situation.)

American Professional Society on the Abuse of Children
332 South Michigan Avenue, Suite 1600
Chicago, IL 60604
(312) 554-0166

Antisocial and Violent Behavior Branch
National Institute of Mental Health
5600 Fishers Lane, Room 18-105
Rockville, MD 20857
(301) 443-3728

Clearinghouse on Child Abuse and Neglect Information
Office of Public Information and Education
P.O. Box 1182
Washington, DC 20013

National Clearinghouse on Domestic Violence
P.O. Box 2309
Rockville, MD 20852

National Rape Information Clearing House
National Center for the Prevention and Control of Rape
5600 Fishers Lane
Rockville, MD 20857

National Resource Center on Child Sexual Abuse
2204 Whitesburg Drive, Suite 200
Huntsville, AL 35801
1-800-543-7006

Incest Recovery Services
P.O. Box 7999
Dallas, TX 75209
(214) 559-2170

Incest Resources, Inc.
c/o Women's Center
46 Pleasant Street
Cambridge, MA 02139
(617) 354-8807

Violence and Traumatic Stress Research Branch
Division of Epidemiology and Research
National Institute of Mental Health
NIH Parklawn Building, Romkm 10C-24
5600 Fishers Lane
Rockville, MD 20857
(301) 443-3728

Working Women's Institute
539 Park Avenue
New York, NY 10021
(212) 838-4420

Transsexual and Transgender Organizations and Support Groups

The American Educational National Transgender Information Services, Inc.
P.O. Box 33724
Decatur, GA 30033
(404) 939-2128, Fax: (404) 939-1770, Computer Data Base Helpline: (404) 939-0244

Bi-Social Center
7136 Matilija Avenue
Van Nuys, CA 91405
(213) 873-3700

Boston Women's Health Collective
240A Elm Street
Somerville, MA 02144
(617) 625-0271

Center for Research and Gay Education in Sexuality (CERES)
San Francisco State University
San Francisco, CA 94132
(415) 338-1137

Ground Zero (Education and Support for Gay, Lesbian, Bisexual, and Transgender Issues)
P.O. Box 1982
Colorado Springs, CO 80901
(719) 635-6086

Harry Benjamin Gender Dysphoria, Association, Inc.
900 Welch Road, Suite 402
Palo Alto, CA 94304
(Request that you write for information.)

Hetrick-Martin Institute for Gay and Lesbian Youth
2 Astor Place
New York, NY 10003
(212) 638-4200

I Seek a Transsexual Female and Intros
6 Firethorne Way
Toms River, NJ 08755
(908) 341-2073

Impotents Anonymous
119 South Ruth Street
Maryville, TN 37801

Impotence Information Center
Department USA
P.O. Box 9
Minneapolis, MN 55440

International Foundation for Gender Education
P.O. Box 367
Wayland, MA 01778-0367
(617) 894-8340

J2CP On-Line Information Services (Transgender Information)
P.O. Box 184
San Juan Capistrano, CA 92693-0184

John Augustus Foundation (JAF) (Transgender and Gender Identity Information)
P.O. Box 82085
Portland, OR 97282-0085
(503) 370-3999

Lambda Legal Defense and Education Fund
666 Broadway
New York, NY 10012

National Androgyny Center
P.O. Box 7429
San Diego, CA 92107

National Coalition for Black Lesbians and Gays
19641 W. Seven Mile Road
Detroit, MI 48219
(313) 537-0484

National Lesbian and Gay Health Association
1407 S Street NW
Washington, DC 20009
(202) 939-7880

National Gay and Lesbian Task Force (NGLTF)
2320 17th Street NW
Washington, DC 20009-2702
(202) 332-6483

National Organization for Changing Men
794 Penn Avenue
Pittsburgh, PA 15221

National Organization for Women
1000 16th Street NW, Suite 700
Washington, DC 20036
(202) 331-0066

National Transsexual-Transvestite Feminization Union (NATTFU)
P.O. Box 297
Peru, IL 61354
(818) 223-6971

Pacific Center for Human Growth (PCHG)
2712 Telegraph Avenue
Berkeley, CA 94705
(510) 548-8283

Parents and Friends of Lesbians and Gays
(Parents Flag)
1101 14th Street NW, Suite 1030
Washington, DC 20005
(202) 638-4200

Renaissance Education Association (REA) (Gender Identity Information)
P.O. Box 60552
King Prussia, PA 19406
(215) 630-1437

Society for the Second Sex, Inc. (Tri-Ess Sorority) (Hetrosexual Cross-dressers Organization)
P.O. Box 194
Tulare, CA 93275
(209) 688-9246

Society for the Study of Alternative Lifestyles
2741 Orangethorpe, Suite A
Fullerton, CA 92633

Women's Center
46 Pleasant Street
Cambridge, MA 02139
(617) 354-8807

JOURNALS AND NEWSLETTERS IN HUMAN SEXUALITY RESEARCH AND EDUCATION

About Women on Campus
National Association for Women in Education
1325 18th Street NW, Suite 210
Washington, DC 20036-6511

Adolescence
Libra Publishers, Inc.
391 Willets Road
Roslyn Heights, NY 11577

AIDS Education and Prevention
Guilford Publications, Inc.
72 Spring Street
New York, NY 10012
1-800-365-7006

Alternative Lifestyles
Human Sciences Press
72 Fifth Avenue
New York, NY 10011

Annals of Sex Research
Juniper Press
P.O. Box 7205
Oakville, Ontario L6J 6L5
Canada

Annual Review of Sex Research
Society for the Scientific Study of Sexuality
P.O. Box 208
Mount Vernon, IA 52314

Archives of Sexual Behavior
Plenum Publishing Corp.
233 Spring Street
New York, NY 10013

Bisexuality: News, Views, and Networking
Gibbon Publications
P.O. Box 20917
Long Beach, CA 90801-3917

British Journal of Sexual Medicine
Medical News Tribune
1 Bedford Street
London WC2E9HD, England

Child and Family
National Commission on Human Life, Reproduction and Rhythm
Box 508
Oak Park, IL. 60303

Contemporary Sexuality
American Association for Sex Educators, Counselors, and Therapists
P.O. Box 238
Mount Vernon, IA 52314-0238

Family Coordinator
National Council on Family Relations
3989 Central Avenue NE, Suite 550
Minneapolis, MO 55421

Family Life Educator
ETR Associates
P.O. Box 1830
Santa Cruz, CA 95060-1830

Family Planning Perspectives
Alan Guttmacher Institute
120 Wall Street, 21st Floor
New York, NY 10005
(212) 248-1111

The Female Patient: Practical Advice for Better Care
P.W. Communications Inc.
515 Madison Avenue
New York, NY 10022

Homosexual Counseling Journal
H.C.C.C., Inc.
30 East 60th Street
New York, NY 10022

Journal of Adolescent Health
Elsevier Science Publishing Company
655 Avenue of the Americans
New York, NY 10010
(212) 633-3806

Journal of Health and Social Behavior
American Sociological Association
1722 N Street NW
Washington, DC 20036

Journal of the History of Sexuality
University of Chicago Press
P.O. Box 37005
Chicago, IL 60637

Journal of Homosexuality, Journal of Gay and Lesbian Psychotherapy, Journal of Psychology and Human Sexuality, Journal of Social Work and Human Sexuality
Haworth Press
10 Alice Street
Binghamton, NY 13904-1580

Journal of School Health
American School Health Association
Box 709
Kent, OH 44240

Journal of Sex Research
Society for the Scientific Study of Sexuality
P.O. Box 208
Mount Vernon, IA 52314

Journal of Sex and Marital Therapy, Journal of Sexual Addiction
Brunner/Mazel, Inc.
19 Union Square West
New York, NY 10003

Journal of Youth and Adolescence
Plenum Press
227 West 17th Street
New York, NY 10011

Medical Aspects of Human Sexuality
Clinical Communications, Inc.
250 East 39th Street
New York, NY 10016

Planned Parenthood Report
Planned Parenthood-World Population
810 Seventh Avenue
New York, NY 10019
(212) 541-7800

Sex Problems Court Digest
Juridical Digests Institute
1860 Broadway, Suite 1401
New York, NY 10023

Sex Roles: A Journal of Research
Plenum Publishing
233 Spring Street
New York, NY 10013

Sexual Behavior
Interpersonal Communications, Inc.
299 Park Avenue
New York, NY 10017

Sexual and Marital Therapy
Carfax Publishing
P.O. Box 2025
Dunnellon, FL. 34430-2025

Sexuality and Disability
Human Sciences Press
233 Spring Street, New York, NY 10013

Sexually Transmitted Diseases
J. B. Lippincott
East Washington Square
Philadelphia, PA 19105

The SIECUS Report
Sex Information and Education Council of the United States
130 West 42nd Street, Suite 450
New York, NY 10036

VD News
American School Health Association
260 Sheridan Avenue
Palo Alto, CA 94306

Women and Health
Haworth Press
10 Alice Street
Binghamton, NY 13904-1580

NATIONAL PROFESSIONAL ASSOCIATIONS AND ORGANIZATIONS

Alan Guttmacher Institute
120 Wall Street, 21st Floor
New York, NY 10005
(212) 248-1111

Alliance of Genetic Support Groups
1001 22nd Street NW, Suite 800
Washington, DC 20037
1-800-336-GENE

American Academy of Pediatrics
1801 Hinman Avenue
Evanston, IL 60204

American Alliance for Health, Physical Education, Recreation, and Dance
1900 Association Drive
Reston, VA 22091
(703) 476-3400

American Association of Marriage and Family Counselors
255 Yale Avenue
Claremont, CA 91711

American Association of Sex Educators, Counselors, and Therapists (AASECT)
P.O. Box 238
Mount Vernon, IA 52314-0238

The American Board of Sexology
1939 18th Street NW, Suite 1166
Washington, DC 20009
(202) 462-2122

American College of Obstetricians and Gynecologists, Resource Center
409 12th Street, SW
Washington, DC 20024-2188
(202) 638-5577

American Institute of Family Relations
5287 Sunset Boulevard
Los Angeles, CA 90027

American Psychological Association Task Force on Psychology, Family Planning and
Population Policy
1200 17th Street NW
Washington, DC 20036
(914) 638-6992

American Public Health Association
1015 15th Street NW
Washington, DC 20005
(202) 789-5600

Association of Sexologists
1523 Franklin Street
San Francisco, CA 94109
(415) 928-1133 Fax: (415) 928-8284

Association for the Study of Abortion, Inc.
120 West 57th Street
New York, NY 10019

Child Study Association of America
50 Madison Avenue
New York, NY 10010
(914) 394-7931

The Coalition on Sexuality and Disability, Inc.
380 Second Avenue, 4th Floor
New York, NY 10010
(212) 242-3900

Family Service Association of America
44 West 23rd Street
New York, NY 10010

Institute for Family Research and Education
760 Ostrum Avenue
Syracuse, NY 13210

Institute for Sex Education
18 South Michigan Avenue
Chicago, IL 60603
(312) 335-9640

Institute for Sex Research, Inc. and Kinsey Institute for Research in Sex, Gender, and Reproduction
Room 313 Morrison Hall
Indiana University
Bloomington, IN 47405
(812) 855-7686

International Academy of Sex Research
c/o Dr. Heino Meyer-Bahlburg
722 West 168th Street
New York, NY 10032

International Society of Psychoneurendocrinology
Department of Psychiatry
Emory University School of Medicine
Atlanta, GA 30322
(318) 675-7876

Masters and Johnson Institute
1 Campbell Plaza, Suite 4B
St. Louis, MO 63139
(314) 781-1112

National Clearinghouse for Human Genetic Diseases
805 15th Street, Suite 500
Washington, DC 20005

National Council on Family Relations
3989 Central Avenue NE, Suite 550
Minneapolis, MN 55421
(612) 781-9331

National Institute of Child Health and Human Development
Office of Information, U.S. Public Health Service
9000 Rockville Pike
Bethesda, MD 20014
(301) 496-5133

National Sex Forum (Please Contact):
The Institute for The Advanced Study of Human Sexuality
1523 Franklin Street
San Francisco, CA 94109
(510) 928-1133 Fax: (415)-928-8284

National Society of Genetic Counselors
Clinical Genetics Center
Children's Hospital of Philadelphia
34th and Civic Central Boulevard
Philadelphia, PA 19104
(212) 596-9802

Planned Parenthood Federation of America
810 Seventh Avenue
New York, NY 10019
(212) 541-7800

Sexuality and Disability Training Center
University Hospital
75 East Newton Street
Boston, MA 02118
(617) 638-7358

Sexuality Information and Education Council of U.S. (SIECUS)
130 West 42nd Street, Suite 350
New York, NY 10036-7802
(212) 819-9770

Society for the Scientific Study of Sexuality
P.O. Box 208
Mount Vernon, IA 52314
(319) 895-8407

EDUCATIONAL OPPORTUNITIES IN HUMAN SEXUALITY

California State University, Northridge
Department of Family Environmental Science
Program: Minor in Human Sexuality
Northridge, CA 91330
(818) 885-4830 or (818) 885-3051

San Francisco State University
Human Sexuality Studies Program
Program: Undergraduate Minor
1600 Holloway Avenue
Department of Psychology
San Francisco, CA 94132

The Institute for the Advanced Study of Human Sexuality

Degrees: Master of Human Sexuality, Doctor of Human Sexuality, Doctor of Education, Doctor of Philosophy. Certificates: Clinical Sexology, Associate in Sex Education/Counseling, Sexological Instructor/Advisor of AIDS/STD Prevention, Erotology, and Sex Offender Evaluation.

1523 Franklin Street
San Fransico, CA 94109
(415) 928-1133

University of Georgia
Department of Psychology
Program: Ph.D. in Experimental Life-Span Development Psychology with specialty in Human Sexual Behavior.
Degree: Ph.D. in Psychology
Department of Psychology
Athens, GA 30602-3013
(706) 542-3084, Fax: (706) 542-3275

Loyola University, Chicago
Department of Psychiatry, Medical School
Program: Loyola Sexual Dysfunction Training Elective
No degree awarded. Certificate of attendance granted.
2160 South First Avenue
Maywood, Illinois 60153
(708) 216-3752, Fax: (708) 216-5383

Indiana University
University Graduate School
Department of Applied Health Science
Program: Ph.D. Minor in Human Sexuality
Bloomington, IN 47405
(812) 855-7974, Fax: (812) 855-3936

University Of Northern Iowa
Program: Family Services: emphasis in human sexuality
Degree: B.A. in Family Services, emphasis in human sexuality
Cedar Falls, IA 50614-0332
(319) 273-2814, Fax: (319) 273-2222

University of Kansas
Department of Psychology
Clinical Psychology, Clinical Child Psychology
Degree: Ph.D.
425W Fraser Hall
Lawerence, KS 66045
(913) 864-4195, Fax: (913)864-5224

John Hopkins University
Program: Post Fellowship in Clincal/Medical Psychology: Sexual Disorders Tract
Certification granted
600 N. Wolfe Street
Division of Medical Psychology
Baltimore, Maryland 21205

Institute for Sex Therapy, Education, and Research
Program: Human Sexuality Home Study Course
Certification granted: APA CE Credits
223 E. State Street, Suite 200
Traverse City, MI 49684
(616) 947-1444, Fax: (616) 947-2444

University of Minnesota
Department of Family Practice and Community Health, Medical School
Program: The Program in Human Sexuality offers a Postdoctoral Fellowship for advanced clinical and research training
Certification granted
1300 South 2nd Street
Minneapolis, MN 55454

University of Minnesota
Department of Sociology
Program/Degree: Specialization in sexuality under a B.A., M.A., Ph.D. degree in Sociology
Minneapolis, MN 55455

University of New Hampshire
Family Research Laboratory
Program: Family Violence Research Fellowship
Annual stipend awarded
Horton SSC, Room 126
Durham, NH 03824
(603) 862-1888, Fax: (603) 862-1122

Hofstra University
Program/ Degree: Master of Arts in Interdisciplinary studies: Emphasis in Sexuality
Counseling; Master of Arts: Marriage and Family Counseling, Certificate in Family
    Counseling
New College
130 Hofstra University
Hempstead, NY 11550-1090

New York University
Department of Health Studies
Program: Graduate Specialization in Human Sexuality
Degree: M.A., Ph.D.
35 West 4th Street, 12th Floor
New York, New York 10003
(212) 998-5793, Fax: (212) 995-4192

University Hospitals of Cleveland
Program: Center for Marital and Sexual Health
Certification of Completion
Three Commerce Park, Suite 350
Beachwood, OH 44122
(216) 831-2900, Fax: (216) 831-4306

University of Pennsylvania
Graduate School of Education
Program: Human Sexuality Education Program
Degree: M.S. in Education—Human Sexuality Education, Ph.D. and Ed.D. in Education—
    Human Sexuality Education
3700 Walnut Street
Philadelphia, PA 19104
(215) 898-5195, Fax: (215) 898-4399

University of Utah
Department of Psychology
Program: Graduate (Ph.D.) Program in Clinical Psychology
Degree: Ph.D. in Clinical Psychology
Salt Lake City, UT 84112
(801) 581-7559, Fax: (801) 581-5841

University of Washington
Department of Medicine
Program/ Degree: Postdoctoral Fellowship in Reproductive and Sexual Medicine
4225 Roosevelt Way NE, Suite 306
Seattle, WA 98105
(206) 543-3555, Fax: (206) 543-7565

University of New Brunswick
Department of Psychology
Program/Degree: M.A. or Ph.D. in Psychology
Fredericton, N.B.
Canada E3B 6E4
(506) 453-4707, Fax: (506) 453-4505

University of Guelph
Department of Family Studies
Program: Family Relations and Human Development
Degree: Msc; Ph.D.
Ontario, Canada N1G 2W1
(519) 824-4120, ext. 3582, Fax: (519) 837-1521

Charles University

Prague, Czechoslovakia

Program: Institute of Sexology, Faculty of Medicine, Postgradual Programme in Medical Sexology

Certification: Certificate for medical specialization—SEXOLOGY

Karlovo nam. 32

CS-120 00 PRAHA 2

Czechoslovakia

Phone: 02/297285

To the Owner of this Book:

We hope that you have enjoyed *Your Sexuality*. We'd like to know as much about your experiences with the book as you care to offer. Only through the comments of people who have used the book can we learn how to make it a better book for future readers.

School: _____

Your Instructor's Name: _____

1. What did you like most about *Your Sexuality*?

2. What did you like least about the book?

3. What additional inventories or exercises would you like to see included in this book?

4. In what way has this book affected your attitudes and behaviors toward sexuality (i.e., reduced, maintained, or improved)?

5. Do you plan to keep this book as a personal reference?

6. In the space below or in a separate letter, please let us know what comments you'd like to make about the book. We'd be delighted to hear from you!

Optional:

Name: _____ Date: _____

Can McGraw-Hill quote you in promotion for *Your Sexuality*?

☐ Yes   ☐ No

Sincerely,

Robert F. Valois
Sandra K. Kammermann

Fold Here

Fold Here

FIRST CLASS
PERMIT NO.
Boston, MA 02116

BUSINESS REPLY MAIL
No Postage Necessary if Mailed in United States

McGraw-Hill, Inc.
575 Boylston Street
Boston, Massachusetts 02116